Decision-Making in Conservation and Natural Resourc

Making decisions about the management and conservation of nature is necessarily complex. There are typically many competing pressures on natural systems, opportunities and benefits for different groups of people and a varying, uncertain social and ecological environment. An approach which is narrowly focused on either human development or environmental protection cannot deliver sustainable solutions.

This volume provides frameworks for improving the integration of natural resource management with conservation and supporting stronger collaboration between researchers and practitioners in developed and developing countries. Novel approaches are required when ecological and social dynamics are highly interdependent. A structured, participatory, model-based approach to decision-making for biodiversity conservation has been proven to produce real-world change. There are surprisingly few successful case studies, some of the best are presented here. Researchers and practitioners need this interdisciplinary approach, focused on quantitative tools that have been tested and applied.

NILS BUNNEFELD is an Associate Professor at the University of Stirling. His research focuses on the interaction between people and nature with an emphasis on mathematical and statistical modelling. In 2016, he was awarded a 5-year European Research Council Starting Grant (ConFooBio) on resolving conflicts between food security and biodiversity conservation.

EMILY NICHOLSON is a Senior Lecturer at Deakin University, Australia. Her research focuses on solving critical conservation problems and measuring change in biodiversity. Her work has helped to develop a new framework for assessing risks to ecosystems, the Red List of Ecosystems, adopted as the global standard by the International Union for the Conservation of Nature (IUCN).

E. J. MILNER-GULLAND is Tasso Leventis Professor of Biodiversity at the University of Oxford. In 2014 she was awarded a Pew Marine Fellowship on the use of novel approaches to addressing marine bycatch. Her ethos is to ensure that all the research she does is addressing issues identified by practitioners, and is carried out collaboratively with end-users.

Conservation Biology

This series aims to present internationally significant contributions from leading researchers in particularly active areas of conservation biology. It focuses on topics where basic theory is strong and where there are pressing problems for practical conservation. The series includes both authored and edited volumes and adopts a direct and accessible style targeted at interested undergraduates, postgraduates, researchers and university teachers.

1. *Conservation in a Changing World*, edited by Georgina Mace, Andrew Balmford and Joshua Ginsberg 0 521 63270 6 (hardcover), 0 521 63445 8 (paperback)
2. *Behaviour and Conservation*, edited by Morris Gosling and William Sutherland 0 521 66230 3 (hardcover), 0 521 66539 6 (paperback)
3. *Priorities for the Conservation of Mammalian Diversity*, edited by Abigail Entwistle and Nigel Dunstone 0 521 77279 6 (hardcover), 0 521 77536 1 (paperback)
4. *Genetics, Demography and Viability of Fragmented Populations*, edited by Andrew G. Young and Geoffrey M. Clarke 0 521 782074 (hardcover), 0 521 794218 (paperback)
5. *Carnivore Conservation*, edited by John L. Gittleman, Stephan M. Funk, David Macdonald and Robert K. Wayne 0 521 66232 X (hardcover), 0 521 66537 X (paperback)
6. *Conservation of Exploited Species*, edited by John D. Reynolds, Georgina M. Mace, Kent H. Redford and John G. Robinson 0 521 78216 3 (hardcover), 0 521 78733 5 (paperback)
7. *Conserving Bird Biodiversity*, edited by Ken Norris and Deborah J. Pain 0 521 78340 2 (hardcover), 0 521 78949 4 (paperback)
8. *Reproductive Science and Integrated Conservation*, edited by William V. Holt, Amanda R. Pickard, John C. Rodger and David E. Wildt 0 521 81215 1 (hardcover), 0 521 01110 8 (paperback)
9. *People and Wildlife, Conflict or Co-existence?*, edited by Rosie Woodroffe, Simon Thergood and Alan Rabinowitz 0 521 82505 9 (hardcover), 0 521 53203 5 (paperback)
10. *Phylogeny and Conservation*, edited by Andrew Purvis, John L. Gittleman and Thomas Brooks 0 521 82502 4 (hardcover), 0 521 53200 0 (paperback)
11. *Large Herbivore Ecology, Ecosystem Dynamics and Conservation*, edited by Kjell Danell, Roger Bergstrom, Patrick Duncan and John Pastor 0 521 83005 2 (hardcover), 0 521 53687 1 (paperback)

Decision-Making in Conservation and Natural Resource Management

Models for Interdisciplinary Approaches

Edited by

NILS BUNNEFELD
University of Stirling

EMILY NICHOLSON
Deakin University

E.J. MILNER-GULLAND
University of Oxford

CAMBRIDGE
UNIVERSITY PRESS

University Printing House, Cambridge CB2 8BS, United Kingdom

One Liberty Plaza, 20th Floor, New York, NY 10006, USA

477 Williamstown Road, Port Melbourne, VIC 3207, Australia

4843/24, 2nd Floor, Ansari Road, Daryaganj, Delhi – 110002, India

79 Anson Road, #06-04/06, Singapore 079906

Cambridge University Press is part of the University of Cambridge.

It furthers the University's mission by disseminating knowledge in the pursuit of education, learning, and research at the highest international levels of excellence.

www.cambridge.org
Information on this title: www.cambridge.org/9781107465381
DOI: 10.1017/9781316135938

First published 2017

Printed in the United Kingdom by TJ International Ltd. Padstow Cornwall
in June 2017

A catalogue record for this publication is available from the British Library.

Library of Congress Cataloging-in-Publication Data
Names: Bunnefeld, N. (Nils), editor.
Title: Decision-making in conservation and natural resource management:
models for interdisciplinary approaches / [edited by] Nils Bunnefeld, University
of Stirling, Emily Nicholson, Deakin University, Victoria, E.J. Milner-Gulland,
Department of Zoology, University of Oxford.
Description: New York, NY: Cambridge University Press, 2017. |
Series: Conservation biology | Includes bibliographical references and index.
Identifiers: LCCN 2016059490 | ISBN 9781107092365 (hard back) |
ISBN 9781107465381 (paper back)
Subjects: LCSH: Nature conservation – Decision making. |
Natural resources – Management – Decision making.
Classification: LCC QH75.D393 2017 | DDC 333.72–dc23
LC record available at https://lccn.loc.gov/2016059490

ISBN 978-1-107-09236-5 Hardback
ISBN 978-1-107-46538-1 Paperback

To the conservationists of the future

Contents

Contributors

EMILIE BEAUCHAMP Centre for Environmental Policy, Imperial College London, London UK

NILS BUNNEFELD School of Natural Sciences, University of Stirling, Stirling UK

YUNG EN CHEE School of Ecosystem and Forest Sciences, University of Melbourne, Burnley, VIC, Australia

TOM CLEMENTS Wildlife Conservation Society, Bronx, NY, USA

BEN COLLEN Centre for Biodiversity and Environment Research, University College London, London, UK

SARAH J. CONVERSE USGS Patuxent Wildlife Research Center, Laurel, MD, USA

CATHERINE M. DICHMONT CSIRO Oceans and Atmosphere, Brisbane, QLD, Australia and Cathy Dichmont Consulting, Sheldon, QLD, Australia

FIONA FIDLER School of BioSciences and School of Historical and Philosophical Studies, University of Melbourne, Parkville, VIC, Australia

ELIZABETH A. FULTON CSIRO Oceans and Atmosphere, Brisbane, QLD, Australia

GEORGIA E. GARRARD School of Global, Urban and Social Studies, RMIT University, Melbourne, VIC, Australia

KATHERINE M. HOMEWOOD Department of Anthropology, University College London, London, UK

MARIE KEATLEY Science and Management Effectiveness Branch, Parks Victoria, Melbourne, VIC, Australia

J. TERRENCE McCABE Department of Anthropology, University of Colorado at Boulder, Boulder, CO, USA

E.J. MILNER-GULLAND Department of Zoology, University of Oxford, Oxford, UK

JOSLIN L. MOORE School of Biological Sciences, Monash University, Clayton, VIC, Australia

EMILY NICHOLSON School of Life and Environmental Sciences, Deakin University, Geelong, VIC, Australia

ERLEND B. NILSEN Norwegian Institute for Nature Research, Trondheim, Norway

ANA NUNO Centre for Ecology and Conservation, University of Exeter, Cornwall, UK

CHARLIE PASCOE Parks Victoria, Bright, VIC, Australia

LIBBY RUMPFF School of BioSciences, The University of Melbourne, Melbourne, VIC, Australia

MICHAEL C. RUNGE USGS Patuxent Wildlife Research Center, Laurel, MD, USA

ELAINE THOMAS Parks Victoria, Mount Beauty, VIC, Australia

DAVID WILKIE Wildlife Conservation Society, Bronx, NY, USA

BONNIE C. WINTLE Centre for the Study of Existential Risk, University of Cambridge, Cambridge, UK

EMILY WOODHOUSE Department of Anthropology, University College London, London, UK

Acknowledgements

The idea for this book grew out of a symposium at the International Congress of the Society for Conservation Biology in 2011 in Auckland, New Zealand, where we brought together researchers who use modelling to improve decision-making in their field. This book would not have been possible without the help of many people. We thank Alan Crowden for convincing us to write this book after the symposium, and Jane Seakins and Lindsey Tate at Cambridge University Press for all their help and encouragement.

This book is a collaboration between colleagues from very different fields that all intersect at the social-ecological systems concept, including fisheries, wildlife, invasive plants as well as human well-being. We are grateful for their insightful contributions and ideas and all the effort they have put in to shape their chapters to fit into the theme of the book and connect with other contributions.

Nils Bunnefeld thanks the University of Stirling, Emily Nicholson the University of Melbourne and Deakin University, and E.J. Milner-Gulland thanks Imperial College London and the University of Oxford for their support. E.J. Milner-Gulland acknowledges the support of a Pew Marine Fellowship, and Emily Nicholson the support of a Marie Curie Fellowship from the European Commission, which brought her to Imperial College to collaborate with E.J., and a Centenary Research Fellowship from the University of Melbourne. Nils and E.J. also thank the research team of the HUNTing for Sustainability FP7 project, which launched our interest in management strategy evaluation.

We thank our families for all the support for quite some years while we worked on this book, especially Lynsey, Rowan and Martin, and Sam, Manny, Sol and Isaac.

We dedicate this book to the conservationists of the future, who face the daunting task of reconciling the increasingly difficult and urgent needs of both humanity and the environment, so that we can continue to live well with nature. We hope that this book is helpful to their efforts.

$$\textcircled{1}$$

Introduction

NILS BUNNEFELD, EMILY NICHOLSON AND
E.J. MILNER-GULLAND

1.1 THE NEED FOR THIS BOOK

Making decisions about the management and conservation of nature is complex and consequently difficult. The complexity stems from the many competing pressures on natural systems, with their opportunities and benefits for different groups of people, set within a constantly varying social and ecological environment. However, there are also opportunities for better decision-making, leading to better outcomes for all sides. This book showcases one such set of opportunities – the benefits of taking a structured, participatory, model-based approach to decision-making for biodiversity conservation.

The largely unrealised potential of using this approach to making decisions about wildlife management became very clear to N.B. and E.J.M.G. when we worked on an endangered antelope endemic to Ethiopia, the mountain nyala (*Tragelaphus buxtoni*). When we got involved in the project in 2010, the total population was estimated at just less than 4,000 individuals (Atickem et al. 2011; Bunnefeld et al. 2013). The pressures on this antelope are high because of a combination of hunting, habitat loss and poaching. The situation was complex due to high uncertainty about the population size because monitoring was limited and the impacts of habitat loss and poaching were unknown. The question to which the Ethiopian Wildlife Authority wanted an answer was how to set a sustainable quota that increases their income, while also providing benefits to local communities. The plan was to reinvest the funds into monitoring, habitat conservation and livelihood support for local people. We used a management strategy evaluation-type simulation model that incorporated the dynamics and uncertainties mentioned earlier (Bunnefeld et al. 2013) to find answers to this question. However, funding stopped before we could start the process of implementing a decision-making process, and the situation is currently unchanged, despite a pathway to better management now being available thanks to our collaborative research project. This failure to translate research into impact sparked our interest in finding examples where such a translation had taken place, and understanding the factors enabling it to happen. There are surprisingly few successful case studies; some of the best are presented in this book.

There is currently no end in sight for the present biodiversity crisis, or even a road map for slowing down current rapid biodiversity loss (Venter et al. 2016). Biodiversity loss is important for society at large because of the complex relationships between biodiversity conservation, food security and human well-being, including both synergies and trade-offs (Mace et al. 2012). Given the occurrence of environmental and climate change, and a growing human population to feed, human well-being will rely on better decisions to turn potential synergies between biodiversity conservation and human advancement into real-world opportunities for a positive change. The UN's Sustainable Development Goals (SDGs) define the way governments and businesses should set development priorities over the next thirty years (Terama et al. 2015). However, the prospects for real change are limited, if the evidence to date is anything to go by. Tittensor et al. (2014) suggest how the UN Convention on Biological Diversity's (CBD) Aichi targets are not producing the desired outcomes. What is certain is that an approach that is narrowly focussed on either human development or environmental protection cannot deliver sustainable solutions to managing the complex and uncertain social-ecological interactions and feedbacks, which constitute people's relationships with nature (Larrosa et al. 2016). With this in mind, this book brings together authors from a range of disciplines to reflect on their experiences, successful and less so, in effecting real-world change on the ground. Their experiences point to a new way to make decisions for sustainable resource management and biodiversity conservation, which may improve outcomes for both humans and nature.

1.2 A SHORT HISTORY OF QUANTITATIVE APPROACHES TO BIODIVERSITY CONSERVATION

Humans have managed and manipulated ecosystems for their own benefit for millennia, typically using conceptual models as a basis for decisions. There was an early realisation that resources are limited and that this has implications for the viability of humanity (Malthus 1798). In the 1970s, the tragedy of the commons was the prevailing theory explaining the inevitable overexploitation of natural resources (Hardin 1968), harming both the state of the natural resource and eventually people themselves through a shortage in the resource they depend upon or enjoy. The tragedy of the commons theory is based on an open access system where increased exploitation benefits a single person, whereas the costs are shared among all those using the resource (such as sheep grazing by different farmers on land over which they have no ownership). Later critiques highlighted that open access is only one of a number of potential land tenure situations; others, such as communal ownership, are more amenable to management (Ostrom 1990).

Conceptual models such as the tragedy of the commons were formalised as quantitative models to support decision-making about managing natural resources. Early examples in natural resource management (NRM) include the use of models to set sustainable fishing harvests (Gordon 1954; Beverton and Holt 1957). Such models stemmed from advances in ecology and mathematical modelling (and later economics), and predominantly found application in fisheries, forestry, agriculture and harvesting wildlife in the 1950s, based on the relationship between the rate of replenishment and growth of a resource (such as an animal or plant species) and the off-take of this resource. This was formalised into the maximum sustainable yield (MSY) – the point at which the maximum number of individuals can be taken from a population without causing a decline in numbers. Classical MSY is, however, based on strong assumptions, such as that the environment is deterministic, all individuals in a population can be represented in a single value for population size (rather than structured by e.g. age, sex or spatial location) and under the simplest formulation of density dependence (logistic growth), that density dependence operates symmetrically so that MSY is found at half of the carrying capacity (the maximum population size; Clark 1990).

In the 1990s, there was a realisation that stochastic events, such as year-on-year changes in weather and demographic variability, lead to fluctuations in population size and growth rate, increasing the chance of overexploitation and even extirpation of a local population if hunting is too heavy. Models accounting for this uncertainty led to recommended harvesting limits being related to the degree of variability in population dynamics (Lande et al. 2003). However, these models also make assumptions which are not seen in reality, such as that managers have complete understanding of the system that they manage (monitoring uncertainty) and that harvesters accurately follow agreed-upon harvest goals (implementation uncertainty); both have been relaxed in more recent models (Fryxell et al. 2010; Fulton et al. 2011b; Bunnefeld et al. 2013). These models also focus on single-species harvesting, assuming that the interactions between a given species and other components of the ecosystem are not key determinants of sustainability.

A different stream of thinking about human relationships with nature promoted the protection of natural resources and land, rather than NRM and sustainable use of wildlife. Protection of land (and later aquatic environments) from human exploitation in order to halt ongoing loss of habitat and biodiversity initiated the modern Western conceptualisation of conservation in the nineteenth century, with a strong focus on human exclusion, through the establishment of protected areas (PAs). This included the establishment of national parks in the USA – for example Yellowstone National Park in 1872 (Cross et al. 2012) – and in colonial Africa (Adams 2004). Although this conceptualisation is usually credited as originating from the USA, the theory and practice of separation of humanity from nature in order to better protect nature is widespread and ancient, manifesting itself, for example, in Indian sacred groves and Russian *zapovedniks* (Bhagwat and Rutte 2006; Degteva et al. 2015). The number of recorded PAs increased after World War II, especially in Africa and Latin America, and doubled globally during the 1970s. By 2014, around 209,000 PAs existed covering 15.4 per cent of terrestrial and inland water areas and 3.4 per cent of the oceans (Juffe-Bignoli et al. 2014). During a similar timeframe, conservation societies were founded, starting in 1903 with Fauna and Flora International, which is considered to be the first society dedicated to the conservation of wildlife through saving habitat (Adams 2004). Conservation then was focussed on preservation, PAs and small population management of species considered as valuable, mostly by foreigners for aesthetic reasons, rather than by local communities for sustainable resource use (Caughley 1994).

This type of conservation has traditionally been rather separate from the fields of applied ecology and wildlife management, because conservation in its initial conception prevents any use of natural resources. In an effort to bring the two fields together, the International Union for Conservation of Nature (IUCN) General Assembly passed the Kinshasa Resolution on the Protection of Traditional Ways of Life in 1975, asking governments not to displace people from PAs. Also, the CBD, signed at the Rio Summit in 1992, recognised local people as having rights to use their resources. Integrated conservation and development projects (ICDP) were initiated in the 1990s to create revenues from conservation (i.e. non-extractive use) and to provide incentives for local people to engage in conservation activities and comply with conservation laws. ICDPs were seen as a realistic opportunity for a win-win situation between conservation of biodiversity and development for local people (Winkler 2011). However, many ICDPs failed, for a range of reasons, many of which came down to them being implemented by conservationists who didn't understand the complexities of development as a field, and therefore made mistakes in implementation (e.g. the popularity of 'alternative livelihoods' projects; Wright et al. 2016). More recently, conservation thinking is getting closer to NRM. For example, in the oceans, we see the integration of fisheries management with marine conservation (e.g. the Convention on International Trade in Endangered Species of Wild Fauna and Flora (CITES) listing sharks at the Conference of the Parties in 2013). Similarly, the realisation that there are important non-timber forest products coming out of tropical forests (such as bushmeat, medicinal products and honey) had led to more integration of forest conservation with sustainable use, particularly where poor rural people are dependent on these resources (Laurance et al. 2012).

The exclusion of people from areas which they previously had access to as a result of the fences and fines paradigm of early conservation, and the restrictions on natural resource use required of local people under wildlife management, have often resulted in conflicts, which are widely recognised as damaging to both wildlife and human livelihoods (Redpath et al. 2015). Managing human use of an area can mean trade-offs between different ecosystem services, such as provisioning services (farming and food production) and social and cultural services (biodiversity), but also win-win situations, for instance when biodiversity underpins subsistence harvesting or provides new avenues for income generation, such as ecotourism. Understanding and working to resolve these trade-offs is key to improving socio-economic and ecological sustainability (Daw et al. 2015). Researchers have so far mainly addressed the problem by focussing on documenting the benefits of wildlife to human livelihoods and well-being. However, their research fails to address the challenge that arises when stakeholders have competing views on how natural resources should be managed, from a local (e.g. wildlife harvests) to a global scale (e.g. Aichi targets). Such conflicts are likely to increase substantially in scope and scale due to the rate of current climate change and its uncertain effects on biodiversity and food security (White and Ward 2010; Mace et al. 2012). Traditionally, the models used to represent and understand resource management issues have ignored the roots and consequences of these stakeholder conflicts (Fulton et al. 2011c), but it is clear that we need new approaches for exposing and negotiating trade-offs in order to resolve conflicts between stakeholders.

Partly as a response to these conflicts and trade-offs, conservation and wildlife management have both moved recently (in parallel mostly) towards ecosystem-based thinking and understanding interconnected-ness on the biological side. They have also both explored links between nature and human well-being (broadly defined; not just income), e.g. through the paradigm of ecosystem-based fisheries management on the NRM side (Daw et al. 2016), and ecosystem services on the conservation side (Mace et al. 2012). Both conservation and wildlife management have developed approaches for integrated management of social-ecological systems, but both are having limited success in the implementation of such frameworks. Part of the problem is the lack of communication between research and practice, which means that researchers aren't ask-ing the right questions and practitioners aren't setting themselves up to learn (Pooley et al. 2014).

1.3 FRAMEWORKS FOR CONSERVATION DECISION-MAKING

Three broad frameworks for conservation decision-making have emerged within academic circles over the last two decades, largely in parallel, but all stemming from decision science approaches from economics and with many common elements: (1) decision theor-etic approaches to conservation, including conservation planning (Shea et al. 1998; Possingham et al. 2000), which have developed recently into structured decision-making, used for example for endan-gered species management under climate change (Gregory et al. 2013); (2) adaptive management in weed control and hunting wild-life (Walters 1986); (3) management strategy evaluation in fisheries (Smith et al. 2008). Examples of all three of these approaches are found throughout this book, but the degree to which they have been used in practice to inform real-world decision-making is both variable and generally low.

1.3.1 Decision Theory and Its Application to Conservation
Decision and Planning

In the late 1980s, decision theory emerged as the basis of a new approach to conservation biology. In particular, the 1980s saw the emergence of the new discipline of systematic conservation planning (Pressey and Nicholls 1989; Pressey et al. 1993), later termed spatial conservation prioritisation (SCP), which required planners to set clear targets and objectives, identify constraints (such as costs) and then optimise land use accordingly (Chapter 9).

Spatial conservation prioritisation has had substantial success in some countries in forming the basis for conservation decision-making; for example in South Africa, it forms the scientific backbone for land use planning by the provincial government (Lötter 2014; Cockburn et al. 2016). Decision theory, in its pure sense, has been less widely translated into practice, although there have been applications in Australia and New Zealand, where it has been used by government to prioritise action for threatened species (Joseph et al. 2009; Szabo et al. 2009). Applications of decision theory increasingly deal with uncertainty, e.g. info-gap approaches that aim to make least-worst decisions in conditions of high uncertainty (Ben-Haim 2006).

Structured decision-making (SDM) is a new phrase used for many examples of decision analysis within conservation. The steps are very similar to those of decision theory, as advocated by Shea et al. (1998) for a structured approach to problem-solving (Figure 1.1): defining the decision context and objectives, possible actions, a model (be it quantitative or qualitative) to project the consequences and impacts of the possible actions on the objectives, defining trade-offs, setting up monitoring, as well as acknowledging, describing and examining uncertainty, and using similar methods for making decisions and implementation. SDM has been used, for example, in papers outlining approaches to making decisions for threatened species conservation under climate change (Gregory et al. 2013).

1.3.2 Adaptive Management

The idea of adapting actions to the fluctuations and changes in ecological systems led in the 1980s to the concept of adaptive management (AM) – a process of continual learning by doing during the process of management (Holling 1978; Walters 1986; Keith et al. 2011). Adaptive management is distinguished from trial and error management by the

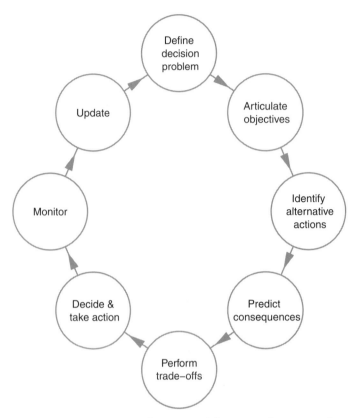

Figure 1.1 A representation of a structured decision-making approach.

prior intention to gain information while managing, in order to learn and improve, either passively through monitoring changes that transpire under management, or actively through setting management up as an experiment (Figure 1.2). Examples of passive AM include duck hunting in the USA (Nichols et al. 2007) and goose hunting in Scandinavia (Madsen and Williams 2012; Madsen et al. 2015) as well as the control of invasive plant species in Chapter 6.

While, in principle, the idea of adapting to change through monitoring and learning while carrying out management actions sounds plausible, many obstacles mean that the concept is well developed in theory by researchers but still not very much taken up by practitioners (Keith et al. 2011). One hurdle in AM is that the concept in its initial form did not include the responses of resource users to management into the equation. In fisheries, researchers recognised the importance

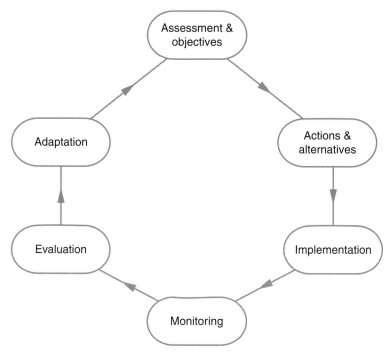

Figure 1.2 The adaptive management cycle: System assessment and setting objectives, setting up actions and possible alternatives, implementing the actions, monitoring the effects on the system, evaluating the system changes and updating knowledge and adapting objectives and actions based on these changes.

of understanding and adapting to people's responses to management in the early 2000s, but focussed their analyses on economic drivers of responses by industrial fishing fleets (Fulton et al. 2011c). Therefore, these insights are not always transferable to smaller scale operations where people are influenced by a range of social and cultural drivers beyond the profit motive (Clark 2006). Within academic conservation and NRM, there is a clear realisation that adaptive management is vital for improved decision-making, but in the real world, trial and error management, or management based on expert judgement and intuition, are still dominant, for a range of reasons set out by Keith et al. (2011).

1.3.3 Management Strategy Evaluation

Starting in the 1990s, there has been a much stronger integration of science and practice to improve management in fisheries, with the adoption of an approach called the management strategy evaluation (MSE). MSE originated from the Scientific Committee of the International Whaling Commission and was developed as a solution to the challenge of ensuring sustainable whale harvests (Punt & Donovan 2007). Eventually, the method was never used for whales, but the idea spread to fisheries management more widely and is now standard practice in many countries, including particularly Australia and South Africa (Punt et al. 2016). The strength of the MSE approach is that it takes into account three important components of wildlife management systems: (i) the ecological and social dynamics of the system itself, (ii) the observation/monitoring process with all its errors and biases and (iii) the assessment and decision-making processes of managers (Figure 1.3). MSE is especially useful when a system has quantifiable uncertainties, for example when the true population size of the resource population is not known, which is a common occurrence both in fisheries and terrestrial systems (Bunnefeld et al. 2013; Edwards et al. 2014; Punt et al. 2016). Uncertainty is too often ignored in the management of natural resources and conservation, whereas MSE puts it centre stage (Fulton et al. 2011b). Four main sources of uncertainty are addressed within the MSE framework (Bunnefeld et al. 2011):

(1) Monitoring uncertainty: managers do not directly observe the dynamics of the system, but do so only through monitoring;
(2) Structural uncertainty: there is uncertainty in how a specific system functions and responds to changes in the environment and management actions;
(3) Implementation uncertainty: management decisions are often only partially carried out by practitioners, e.g. harvest regulations are not always respected (Liberg et al. 2012) and pre-described quotas are not always filled (Knott et al. 2014);
(4) Process uncertainty: environmental stochasticity affecting natural resources makes it impossible to be sure of the correct parameters of the natural resource model.

One real world success which has been documented for MSE is the management of the Southern and Eastern Scalefish and Shark Fishery in Australia, a multi-species system comprised of many stakeholders with competing objectives, including local fishermen, environmental non-governmental organizations and governmental managers; this case study is described in Chapter 2. MSE was first implemented in

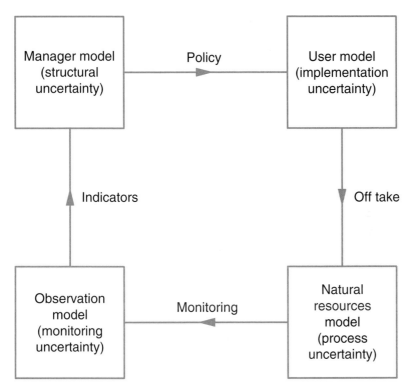

Figure 1.3 The management strategy evaluation approach: Modelling manager decisions and passing these on to the model of resource user behaviour, which then affects the natural resource through some form of action, for example harvesting. The observation model monitors the resource with uncertainty and passes indicators onto the manager model to inform management in the next time-period.

this fishery in 2005 and involved formal assessment of trade-offs, risks, uncertainties and socio-economic objectives. In the three years thereafter, the time to agreement on fishing quotas decreased from several weeks to less than two days because collaboration between stakeholders improved markedly (Smith et al. 2008).

All three of these approaches rely on clear problem definition, taking uncertainty explicitly into account. Interestingly, despite many commonalities across these approaches, there is little cross-referencing, in part because they tend to be used within different realms (marine versus terrestrial) and disciplines (fisheries sciences versus conservation versus harvesting), which are published in different journals and presented at different conferences (Figure 1.4). What these approaches

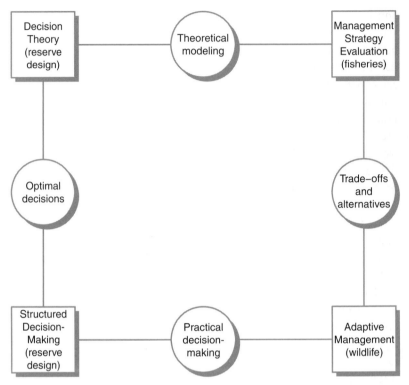

Figure 1.4 Four approaches to decision-making (in rectangles), decision theory, structured decision-making, adaptive management and management strategy evaluation with their main fields of application in brackets. Commonalities between the decision-making approaches are in circles.

all share, however, is that they are: (1) structured in their implementation; (2) based on quantitative models of how the system works; and (3) increasingly participatory, bringing stakeholders together to agree on the way forward rather than imposing management rules from above. These characteristics seem to be crucial for the success of these approaches in improving the robustness to uncertainty and to complexity (whether in conservation or sustainable use), and therefore the long-term viability of management, as highlighted throughout this book.

1.4 OVERVIEW OF THE BOOK

In this book, we look at how to make better conservation decisions, with a focus on the role of modelling. We bring together experience and knowledge from both natural resource management and conservation about how models can be used within structured, participatory decision-making processes that improve sustainability for people and nature, within complex social-ecological systems where ecological and social dynamics are highly interdependent. We shine light on the mismatch between how researchers tackle academic problems and how practitioners solve real-world management issues, by bringing together practitioners and researchers from developed and developing countries, from marine and terrestrial ecosystems, covering plants, mammals and fish; anthropologists, fisheries scientists, ecologists and modellers. The book aims to provide frameworks and approaches to improve integration of wildlife management with conservation and researchers with practitioners. The case studies are carefully selected in order to illustrate and elucidate different aspects of a common framework for linking scientific analysis with policy implementation, and to include examples at different spatial and institutional scales from local to global.

The overarching theme of the book is that management of such systems requires a structured decision-making framework, with explicit objectives for management, a predictive understanding of how management interventions will affect the system, monitoring the system to measure how the system has changed in response to management interventions, ways of analysing the monitoring data to assess success or failure of the intervention, and then feeding back the new understanding to changes in management practices. Research and management also need to encompass both the biological and human components of the system, and their multiple direct and indirect interactions, in a comprehensive way. Such an approach forms the basis of adaptive management, decision analysis and management strategy evaluation, but is yet to become well integrated into conservation science.

In Chapter 2, Cathy Dichmont and Elizabeth Fulton present their experience of carrying out management strategy evaluation (MSE) through integrated modelling. They use the Northern Prawn Fishery (NPF) and the South-East Shark and Scale Fishery (SESSF), both in Australia, as examples to show how their MSE unfolded and reflect on what drove its successes and impediments. The authors observe that participatory engagement with all user groups is fundamental for evaluating fisheries management strategies. However, this involves skills which are not normally emphasised in scientific training and career progression, such as facilitating a participatory approach, as well as the commitment of substantial amounts of time.

In Chapter 3, Georgia Garrard, Libby Rumpff, Michael Runge and Sarah Converse use rapid prototyping within an SDM framework, in order to facilitate decision-making and act relatively quickly. They use the reintroduction of whooping cranes to the Necedah National Wildlife Refuge (NNWR), Wisconsin, USA, as a case study. Rapid prototyping quickly gets you a coarse but complete picture of the decision process. This can then be refined in subsequent iterations.

In Chapter 4, Yung En Chee, Fiona Fidler and Bonnie Wintle ask why so few models are taken up and actually used; one of the reasons for this may be that it is hard to engage potential users with the process of developing models for decision-making. This chapter tests the main reasons for users engaging (or not) with model development and using the models after the initial workshops, using a sample of people who had participated in Bayesian Belief Network model-building workshops. They find that knowledge and trust positively affect willingness to adopt a model, but that external barriers are important in determining actual adoption; institutional stability and long-term investment in management processes by implementing organisations are crucial for success.

In Chapter 5, Emily Woodhouse, Katherine Homewood, Emilie Beauchamp, Tom Clements, J. Terrence McCabe, David Wilkie and E.J. Milner-Gulland take a critical view of the challenges of using human well-being as a key component of decision-making in conservation and wildlife management. Well-being is a multi-dimensional concept that can be used to understand the effects of conservation on whether affected people can live a good life, including housing, social relations and feelings of security; it includes material, relational and subjective elements. Using a range of examples, Woodhouse et al. present a framework for integrating well-being into conservation decision-making to give an improved view of the effect of conservation interventions on people's lives, livelihoods and aspirations, thus improving predictions about people's behaviour in response to interventions. The well-being concept prioritises views of those who are impacted by conservation and natural resource management, which is much needed to achieve lasting and positive outcomes.

In Chapter 6, Joslin Moore, Charlie Pascoe, Elaine Thomas and Marie Keatley use the management of an invasive willow species (*Salix cinerea*) in an Australian National Park as an example of how park managers and scientists collaborated to develop and implement a model-based management strategy together. Moore et al. used a simple metapopulation model to inform the team about knowledge gaps and to guide fieldwork to close these gaps. This model was then paired with a model trading off searching effort and control effort in order to split the time allocated to each. The models and datasets then fed into a structured decision-making framework developed and implemented by stakeholders and scientists together during workshops where management objectives were clarified and a shared understanding of the issue was built. The case study gives new and unusual insights into the challenges and opportunities for collaboration from the perspectives of the scientist and managers involved.

In Chapter 7, Ana Nuno, Nils Bunnefeld and E.J. Milner-Gulland describe their attempt to apply management strategy evaluation (MSE) to decision-making about the conservation of the Serengeti National Park, Tanzania. They used conceptual MSE models to understand the system as a whole, including the dynamics of key hunted species, the institutional structures that bound decision-making, resource user decisions and the uncertainties in monitoring the social-ecological system. They identify challenges in the development and implementation of a structured decision-making tool in the circumstances which they faced, mainly relating to the perception of scientific knowledge and data and how it should be used for management. MSE was a helpful framework for considering these issues because it helped to identify these challenges and to target research towards addressing key uncertainties, which may pave the way for a more integrated approach to management of this iconic ecosystem in the future.

In Chapter 8, Erlend Nilsen analyses the system for research into, and management of, game hunting in Norway (roe deer, moose, wolverine, lynx, willow ptarmigan). He finds that models are rarely used to make decisions even though ecosystem and population models, including harvest functions, exist for most species. Nilsen concludes that while the population and monitoring components of an MSE framework are relatively well understood for many species, the management and implementation sides of the framework are less well developed. Also, stakeholder involvement in developing objectives has not featured as a high priority when developing models in Norwegian game management.

In Chapter 9, Emily Nicholson, Elizabeth Fulton and Ben Collen investigate the usefulness of models for the development of robust indicators to measure the performance of global conservation targets and policies. They highlight the problem that monitoring of progress against globally agreed targets for conservation actions is only possible with the right indicators, which have been rigorously tested for their ability to reflect real-world change. They also argue that large amounts of resources are spent on monitoring indicators that are not fit for purpose. Modelling using an indicator-policy framework, similar to an MSE model, could play a key role in improving the outcomes of global conservation treaties.

Finally, in Chapter 10, we reflect on the key themes emerging from the chapters, synthesise the lessons that can be taken from the experiences of the authors and look ahead to the future of decision-making in natural resource management and conservation. In order to make progress, we need to face the challenges of dealing with uncertainty from, for example, climate, social, cultural and political change. We also need to find new ways of bringing together teams of researchers and practitioners willing to carry out interdisciplinary projects and to persuade governments to fund this in a way that shows commitment commensurate with the spatio-temporal scale of the challenge faced by humanity.

Part I

Approaches to Decision-Making

Fisheries Science and Participatory Management Strategy Evaluation: Eliciting Objectives, Visions and System Models

CATHERINE M. DICHMONT AND ELIZABETH A. FULTON

2.1 INTRODUCTION

Evaluating management strategies and the alternative futures for a system or resource of interest goes far beyond cranking the handle of a model. Ensuring a participatory process is very important (in our experience, perhaps *the* most important part of the approach), by working closely with all major user or interest groups in the system to elicit their understanding, objectives and options. Without the participatory angle, there is a significant risk of the work being ignored or used inappropriately. Successful and effective participatory engagement can, however, be quite challenging and involves skills and time commitments not necessarily appreciated by many scientists. Fortunately, robust methods for this kind of work do exist. In this chapter, based on experience primarily gained in fisheries and multiple-use coastal management, we will describe the good and the bad of one such approach – management strategy evaluation.

Natural resource management, such as fisheries, is inherently complex, as it involves a resource that is a national (or even global) public asset, yet (often) entrusted to a few owners (Gordon 1954; Beddington et al. 2007). This means that individual business objectives, such as maximising profits, need to be traded against the medium-term impacts of fishing on the ecosystem and inter-generational equity for a sustainable environment (Grafton et al. 2007; Costello et al. 2008). Defining objectives and trade-offs for fisheries management is, therefore, often extremely complex and politically sensitive (Gislason et al. 2000; Mardle and Pascoe 2002; Hilborn 2007). The complexity and sensitivity only increase as more cross-sectoral and cross-jurisdictional issues are tackled, such as sustainable multiple use management of coastal zones, where there is not only a broader set of interested parties and management agencies, but the system objectives held by these groups can be openly in conflict.

Current management arrangements have accrued over the past 30 years. The 1982 United Nations Convention on the Law of the Sea (UNCLOS) set the foundation for use of fish stocks, with aspects of sustainability added incrementally over the next 20 years (primarily through Food and Agricultural Organisation (FAO) guidelines), culminating in the Reykjavik Declaration on Responsible Fisheries in Marine Ecosystems in 2001, and the resolutions following the World Summit on Sustainable Development held in Johannesburg in 2002 (Rice 2014). A number of United Nations' FAO documents have been instrumental in shaping current fisheries management approaches. Chief amongst these were the FAO Code of Conduct for Responsible Fisheries (FAO 1995), the Precautionary Approach to Fisheries (FAO 1996) and the Ecosystem Approach to Fisheries (FAO 2003). These documents introduced the principles of the ecosystem-based fisheries management (EBFM) approach, and the closely related ecosystem approach (EA) and ecological sustainable development (ESD) approach. All of these approaches have an overall objective to 'sustain healthy marine ecosystems and the fisheries they support' (Pikitch et al. 2004).

The broad system perspective of EBFM means it is important to investigate the impact of fishing both at the scale of the target species' distribution and the social-ecological system (SES). The implementation of EBFM approaches involves integration of a range of data sources and disciplines – from oceanography to ecology, anthropology, sociology, psychology and economics. The breadth of tools called upon to inform such management is equally diverse, from qualitative approaches, through statistical models, to complex models involving bio-economics, ecology and biophysics (Fulton and Link 2014). One approach is management strategy evaluation (MSE), a simulation-based framework that allows evaluation of broader system-based fishery management strategies via the use of integrated models coupled with management decision rules (Smith 1994; Plaganyi et al. 2007). While MSE is a concept that can be applied more broadly, the approach was developed in support of an adaptive management process (Walters and Hilborn 1978) where objectives and performance indicators (that highlight the relative performance of decision rules against these objectives) are defined, management decisions are made and learning from these actions over time are fed back into the management system so that (hopefully) more

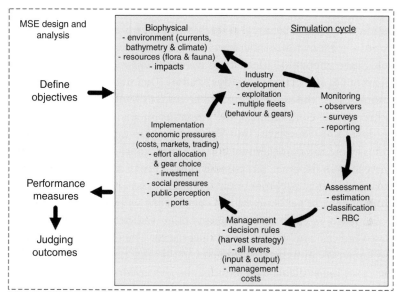

Figure 2.1 Schematic of the general structure of a management strategy evaluation (MSE) modelling framework. The components within the grey box represent the simulation model. The key (and often most difficult) parts of the MSE are those that sit outside in the white box (the definition of objectives, design of strategies to be tested and the final discussion of outcomes and uptake).

informed management decisions are made. This means that decisions are made from the start without requiring perfect information – thus conforming to the FAO code of conduct (FAO 1995) and the precautionary approach (which require the use of best available information and explicit recognition of uncertainty in all parts of the social-ecological system, with adjustments made to management actions as new information comes to light). Since an MSE simulates the entire adaptive management loop (Walters and Hilborn 1978) – i.e. the management processes, industries' activities and the biological system all together (Figure 2.1) – this 'closed-loop' simulated version of the system allows for comparison and evaluation of the relative performance of different management strategies within a consistent context (Sainsbury et al. 2000).

Internally, an MSE model consists of an operating model that can be considered as a 'virtual' representation of a resource and its users – i.e. representing the 'true' underlying dynamics of the system and the resource users. There is no set level of complexity for such a model; in some instances, it is made up of a population dynamics model of a single target species. In most EBFM cases, however, there is some further elaboration to capture the critical processes that control the dynamics of that system – e.g. environmental drivers (Punt et al. 2013), bycatch or other biological components affected by fisheries (Punt and Butterworth 1995; Dichmont et al. 2013), such as the benthos (Dichmont et al. 2008), and, in some cases, the entire associated ecosystem (Fulton et al. 2014). The anthropogenic component of the operating model can also be of varying degrees of complexity, but has to (at a bare minimum) be able to express how the management rules in play translate into realised use (harvesting in fisheries, but possibly other human activities if applied to tourism, mining, catchment management conservation, etc.). The operating model also generates all the data needed within the management model (such as catch, effort and any other indices, like size at age or survey indices) and its associated uncertainty. The management model, also known as an 'assessment model', represents how the management body uses the available data to judge the perceived state of the resource and make management decisions (such as adjusting access or allowable effort/catch levels). The details of the options available to the simulated management body – such as the types of data used, the assessment-related analysis method applied and the decision rules employed – constitute the management strategy to be tested. It is important to note that the management model remains 'ignorant' of the 'truths' included in the operating model; the management model can only access the data given to it (with all its imperfections). This reflects what would occur in real life where decisions are made only in the context of existing information. The outcome of the management strategy (e.g. the level of effort or catch, which areas and times are open to fishing) is fed back to the operating model and is used to determine the next iteration (e.g. annual step) of the dynamics of the 'true' resource being managed. The key component that links the management model and the operating model is the (model) representation of the human components (e.g. fleet movements and other human behaviour like quota trading and information sharing) that applies to the activity (e.g. effort/catch) spatially and temporally, or as required. This component is usually a complex part of the MSE since it describes the biases and variances of past human behaviour to similar management decisions while also adding stochasticity to highlight the uncertainty of predicting human actions into the modelled future. The use of an adaptive loop in the MSE means that managers learn from their decisions, but so too can the resource users adapt (within the modelled restrictions of course) to management decisions.

This implementation uncertainty can have a major impact on the effectiveness of a management strategy (Fulton et al. 2011a).

A key feature of an MSE is its ability to address uncertainty in a robust manner. Uncertainty is a pervasive feature of fisheries management problems (Walters and Hilborn 1978). This uncertainty arises both from lack of scientific knowledge on how the biological system works and the unpredictable nature of the interactions within the social-ecological system. The issue is therefore not about finding an optimal management solution but rather one that is robust to uncertainty. Uncertainty is captured in many ways within an MSE. Within an individual simulation, multiple sources of error within the adaptive management cycle are captured (Fulton et al. 2011c): stochastic variation within the resource; misreporting by industry; scientific sampling and estimation error; assessment model structural error (i.e. where assumptions in the assessment model do not match the dynamics of the 'true' resource); decision uncertainty (e.g. where political pressure can see final management decisions diverge from the assessment's recommendations); and implementation uncertainty (where the consequences of management are not fully aligned with what was intended by the management body, potentially due to a lack of regulatory control and compliance, or to other unanticipated behavioural responses and perverse incentives). Within the context of an MSE project, further uncertainty is represented by using alternative operating and assessment models to cover both parametric and structural uncertainty about how the real world works and how that is represented in the MSE framework (Dichmont et al. 2006b).

To assess the final performance of the different strategies together, their outcomes in terms of performance measures versus objectives are compared, typically via decision tables or plots. This allows for a transparent investigation of their relative robustness to the different forms of uncertainty and highlights relative trade-offs between and within the strategies.

In this chapter, two sets of MSEs are described in some detail: those used in the Northern Prawn Fishery (NPF) and the South-East Shark and Scale Fishery (SESSF), both in Australia. A further set of MSEs is briefly highlighted to show the potential of the MSE approach for information-poor fisheries, how it can be tactically (operationally) implemented for multispecies situations using minimum realistic models (MRM) and how the concept can be extended across industries and jurisdictions in support of coastal zone and integrated management.

2.2 CASE STUDIES

The examples considered in detail here are the fisheries managed by Australia's Federal Fisheries Management Authority (AFMA). Two key aspects of AFMA-managed fisheries are (i) the set of objectives under which management is undertaken and (ii) the stakeholder engagement processes used for most management decisions. It is important to highlight this context as it has facilitated the participatory aspects of the MSE approach, presenting a legitimate forum for the MSE and real-life management process to play out. Over time, resource managers and industry representatives became increasingly familiar with MSE and developed a level of confidence that the modelling approach can reflect their real-world ('on water') experience. In turn, this allowed for more time to be spent exploring alternative and potentially novel strategies, as the time needed to define objectives, elicit information and gain trust in the concept had happened previously, thus leap-frogging what can be the most time-consuming aspects of an MSE.

AFMA's objectives are to implement efficient and effective fisheries management, ensure that exploitation of fisheries resources is undertaken in a manner consistent with ESD principles, maximise economic returns to the community, ensure accountability to the fishing industry and community and achieve government targets in relation to the recovery of AFMA's costs (www.afma.gov.au/about-us/functions-and-powers/). Each fishery has to be managed under a management plan in which a key component is a harvest strategy and bycatch action plan. A harvest strategy is required for each target species in the fishery and needs to consist of explicit pre-agreed decision rules according to specific policy guidelines (www.afma.gov.au/managing-our-fisheries/harvest-strategies/). These harvest strategies are used to set the total allowable efforts (in the NPF) and total allowable catches (in the SESSF).

AFMA applies a strong co-management approach that leans heavily on two key committees – the Management Advisory Committee (MAC) that consists of eight members (an independent chair, where there is no perceived or real conflict of interest that can unduly influence a specific stakeholder, and representatives from science, management and industry) and the Resource Assessment Group consisting of fishery scientists, industry members, biologists, stock assessment scientists, fishery economists and the AFMA manager responsible for the fishery. These two groups are independent of each other and each provides advice to the AFMA executive and commissioners (Figure 2.2). The MAC provides

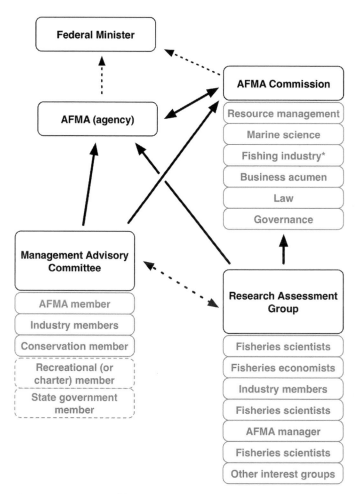

Figure 2.2 Diagram of the Australian Fisheries Management Authority's co-management structure, with the greyed boxes listing the potential membership make-up of the different parts of the organisational structure. There are caps on the industry make-up of the various parts of this structure (e.g. commissioners cannot hold a controlling interest or executive role in an entity with a Commonwealth fishing concession, nor can they hold any executive position in a fishing industry association), as well as specified terms, etc. Further details can be found on the AFMA website at www.afma.gov.au.

advice on management of the fishery, whereas the RAG is a technical committee that provides advice based on analyses such as stock status and risk assessments on the impacts of fishing on the ecosystem. The SESSF fishery consists of several sub-fisheries and is more complex

Table 2.1 *Comparison of the South-East Shark and Scale Fishery (SESSF) and Northern Prawn Fishery (NPF)*

Factor	NPF	SESSF
Method of tradeable control	Individual transferable effort units	Individual transferable quotas
Main control type	Input control	Output control
Number target species	6 species	15–30 species
Gear type	Prawn trawl	Fish trawl, Danish seine, fish longline, shark longline, gillnet
Number of sectors	Commercial	Commercial (shark, fish)[a]
Number management jurisdictions	AFMA	AFMA, with four states recognised under an OCS[b] for recreational and inshore component
Degree of autonomy	Self-managed by industry for day-to-day activities; co-management for strategic activities	Co-management for all activities
Number of RAGs	NPF RAG	SESSF RAG (head RAG), Slope RAG, GAB RAG, Shelf RAG, Shark RAG
Number of vessels (2014)	Limited entry: 51	Limited entry: 95 (45 trawlers and 50 other boats)

Note: AFMA is Australian Fisheries Management Authority. RAG is Resource Assessment Group.

[a] Recreational and charter sector (fish) and inshore state commercial catches are accounted for in the assessments and quota setting, but is not formally managed in the SESSF.

[b] Offshore Constitutional Settlement, which deals with Commonwealth and state jurisdiction and responsibilities in waters to 12 nm.

than the NPF with multiple gears and targets. It, therefore, has several RAGs and also an overarching RAG for co-ordination. In contrast, management is more delegated to the industry in the NPF (further details are discussed later). Despite these complexities, the key common element is that stakeholders in both fisheries have provided major input to the development of all stages of the MSE model and subsequent advice was taken from the MSE research. Both fisheries are limited entry with tradeable gear (NPF) or quota (SESSF) holdings. See Table 2.1 for a comparison of key elements of these two fisheries.

The NPF is a multi-species prawn (shrimp) trawl fishery consisting of several tropical prawn species (Figure 2.3). The overall fishery is made up of two parts: a banana and a tiger prawn fishery. The tiger prawn fishery

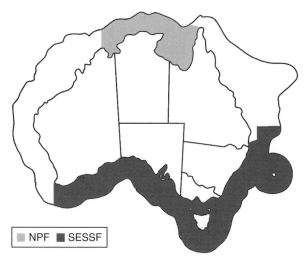

Figure 2.3 Map of the indicative location and extent of the Australian Northern Prawn Fishery and South-East Shark and Scale Fishery.

captures mainly two species of tiger prawns (*Penaeus semisulcatus* and *Penaeus esculentus*) and two species of endeavour prawns (*Metapenaeus endeavouri* and *Metapenaeus ensis*) (Venables and Dichmont 2004), while the banana prawn fishery targets the banana prawns *Penaeus merguiensis* and *Penaeus indicus* (Venables and Dichmont 2004).

The NPF is formally incorporated and most of the licence holders are members of NPF Industry Ltd. (NPFI) who have taken responsibility for tactical management of the fishery and are audited by AFMA. Voting rights within NPFI are based on the transferable gear unit holdings in the fishery. Strategic management such as the design of harvest strategies (the tactical version of management strategies) are still within the MAC, RAG and AFMA domain. The RAG still plays the major technical role in providing technical advice. The NPF has been independently and successfully green certified through the Marine Stewardship Council.

Tropical prawns are fast growing and short lived (less than two to three years). The various species have different habitat preferences and a complex, but reasonably predictable, time–space migration pattern which the fishing fleet follow. This means that each species has different susceptibility to capture within a year (see Somers, 1994; Venables and Dichmont, 2004). Fishing pressure on the stock is controlled via limiting total effort. The total allowable effort in a year dictates the amount of gear that can be employed; this is done using specific decision rules based on the status of tiger prawns. The annual allowable effort is also divided into two distinct fishing seasons so that small prawns are protected in summer and spawning prawns are not disturbed in winter/spring. Within a year, catches are first dominated by banana prawns and later by tiger (if targeting of tigers is allowed that year) and endeavour prawns, which are always caught together with tiger prawns. Co-occurrence of the tigers and endeavour prawns and the perception that tiger prawns are vulnerable to recruitment overfishing (Ye 2000) – where the adult stock can become so depleted it affects reproduction negatively – means tiger prawns were the focus of management measures for many years before multispecies MSEs were undertaken (Wang and Die 1996; Somers and Wang 1997; Dichmont et al. 2003; Punt et al. 2010,). In contrast to the situation for tiger prawns, assessments of endeavour prawns were only conducted for the first time in 2007 (Dichmont et al. 2008) using a multiple-species bio-economic model for tigers and endeavour prawns. Banana prawn recruitment is heavily affected by rainfall and other environmental factors. Although much work has been undertaken on this phenomenon (Bayliss et al. 2014, Toscas et al. 2009), the causal relationships remain obscure and hard to predict, thus making banana prawns hard to assess. For this reason, the MSEs always included the impact of banana prawn fishing on total effort, but have not been able to assess the impact on banana prawn themselves (Buckworth et al. 2014, Zhou et al. 2008). Effort, in terms of gear, season and the size of the fleet, is constrained in this fishery with the aim (and in some species this has been achieved) of reaching the spawning stock size at maximum economic yield (S_{MEY}), which is a much healthier resource than that at maximum sustainable yield (S_{MSY}) in this fishery.

Several MSEs were developed over the decade between 2002 and 2013 for the NPF, each addressing the main issues of the time. The fishery has had a long history of co-management and providing input into the assessment and various MSEs. The models, and questions addressed, are therefore the product of broad stakeholder collaborations, rather than produced by scientists and subsequently endorsed by stakeholders.

Generally, the MSEs focused on managing the tiger prawn fishery; banana prawns were included primarily to account for the impact of fishing for banana prawns on the effort available for the tiger prawn fishery, and a recent banana prawn centric MSE has also been undertaken

(Buckworth et al. 2014). The MSEs have varied in complexity, with details dependent on the specific question being addressed. These questions have arisen from policy needs and also specific industry needs. Perhaps the structurally simplest of the MSEs was developed by Dichmont et al. (2006c), who considered strategies that would support the recovery of the two target tiger prawns species. These strategies were based on reference points derived from biological and yield considerations (S_{MSY}, the spawning stock size corresponding to MSY; and E_{MSY}, the effort at which MSY is achieved). Dichmont et al. (2006a) found that management strategies based on S_{MSY} and E_{MSY} are unable to maintain both species at S_{MSY} simultaneously, primarily due to assessment bias and lack of consideration of the spatial characteristics of the resource in the NPF-wide stock assessments on which management advice has been based. From this MSE, the fishery adopted a new target reference point and recovery plan and a more structured approach to setting annual total allowable effort. This MSE addressed overfishing issues, but also industry concerns around the stock assessment model used. These new reference points and recovery plan were all developed within the RAG and MAC co-management system.

Although the work of Dichmont et al. (2006a) provided guidance on management strategies for the target species, it did not adequately address the full range of management objectives for the NPF. Endeavour prawns were not included, nor were fishing impact on the benthos and bycatch, or objectives related to the economic performance of the NPF tiger prawn fishery. The banana prawn fishery, being less predictable and therefore not easy to control, also has less benthic and bycatch impact and was therefore not included in these studies beyond what had been done before. Prawn fisheries globally are finding it extremely hard to be profitable, especially as a result of large increases in the fuel price, as fuel is a major component of the fishery's costs (Kompas et al. 2010). In addition, prawn trawling was receiving public criticism. Prawn trawls use ground chains to disturb the seabed-inhabiting prawns, causing them to move up into the path of the net. This and the small codend mesh, which can collect significant bycatch if reduction devices are not also installed in the net, has seen the practice highly criticised by those concerned about fisheries waste or potential habitat degradation. Some research on trawl disturbance and recovery has shown the impact to be large (Watling and Norse 1998), whereas those gears in use in the Great Barrier Reef and the NPF have shown much less impact (Haywood et al. 2005, Pitcher et al. 2009). Bycatch reduction devices and turtle exclusion devices have been mandatory for over a decade in Australian tropical prawn fisheries (Dichmont et al. 2007).

In response to both conservation and economic concerns, Dichmont et al. (2008) modified the MSE model of Dichmont et al. (2006c) to address the expanded list of ecosystem and economic objectives. This included the possibility of changing to an economic target: to achieve the spawning stock at maximum economic yield (S_{MEY}) by 2014, where MEY was defined as 'a sustainable catch or effort level that creates the largest difference between total revenue and the total costs of fishing for the fishery as a whole' (Kompas et al. 2010; Grafton et al. 2012). This MSE included three components: the population dynamics of the target species; the effort dynamics of the tiger prawn fishery, including the economics of the fishery; and multi-species population dynamic models designed to represent the dynamics of benthic groups (e.g. soft corals, gastropods) and investigate trawl impact and recovery. This MSE clearly showed the benefits of S_{MEY} as a target for the target species (as it is more precautionary because it reduces overall effort), for profitability (as fleets operate in areas where catch rates are high so therefore spend less fuel to catch) and for the benthic impact (as lower effort means less trawl gear and time spent on the bottom, and most of the region remains unfished).

The next MSE for the NPF was developed as AFMA was charged by its minister to manage all its fisheries using output controls through individual transferable catch quotas. In order to develop management strategies for this fishery under output controls, the MSE was modified again. In Dichmont et al. (2012), the bio-economic stock assessment model was changed to a size-based assessment (Punt et al. 2010, 2011), as this better captures the economics of the fishery and dynamics of the resource. The operating model was updated to reflect the large differences in price between small and large prawns, which was an important consideration when comparing input (total effort through gear size and season) and output (total catch) controls, and spatial species distribution and fleet dynamics, and refinements to the economically based harvest strategy to accommodate the differences between these systems, such as the distribution of effort between the banana and tiger fishery, and different cost structures. These MSEs highlighted that a slightly modified version of the present input controls outperform output controls in terms of risk and costs. Based on this scientific evidence and advice from both Northern Prawn Fishery Management Advisory Committee (NORMAC) and AFMA, the harvest strategy was updated to include these changes and the minister agreed to this exception given the direction always included that the move to output controls needed to be economically better than the present system. The fishery also obtained MSC accreditation based on this input control system, which was also likely to have been influential.

The final MSE for the NPF to be discussed was undertaken between 2010 and 2013, and considered the ecosystem-scale questions, for example whether prawn trawling distorts the ecosystem structure and function, especially spatially. It was undertaken when Australia was developing a set of marine spatial closures throughout its exclusive economic zone (EEZ), which affected the NPF because some of the potential closures fell within the actively fished zone. Moreover, these new closures would be on top of a complex set of spatial closures implemented by the fishery as part of its management plan. These closures are aimed at avoiding key habitats such as seagrass and fishing in areas known to contain juvenile prawn. In order to look more closely at different forms of spatial management and how these impact not only the target species but also the ecosystem in general, and the benthos and key species (such as turtles and seasnakes) in particular, a new MSE was developed in Dichmont et al. (2012). The biggest technical challenge for this MSE was in creating the operating model by joining several models together into a single framework: the previous fleet dynamics, habitat and target species formulations were adopted from Dichmont et al. (2008), and these were coupled with a spatial food web model implemented using Ecospace (Pauly et al. 2000). To make the simulations more tractable, now that there was full ecosystem coverage, the operating model was narrowed to the Gulf of Carpentaria (within the NPF). This meant the various components of the operating model could be run at the appropriate spatial and temporal steps: the benthic impact model at a 6-minute grid and annual time step; the Ecospace model, also at an annual time scale, but on a 3.75×3.76 minute spatial grid; prawns at the stock scale with a weekly time step (given the complex spatio-temporal dynamics of these short-lived species); and the fleet movement model at a weekly time scale mapped to both the stock and grid level. This MSE further demonstrated the small (<10 per cent) impact of the fishery on the overall ecosystem and benthic habitats. It also demonstrated that the MSE-tested spatial closures to protect sharks, seasnakes, the benthos and ecosystem structure, together with the existing fishery specific closure regimes, adequately address conservation objectives for most components of the system.

Together, this series of MSEs has helped shape the form of the tactical management applied in one of Australia's most lucrative fisheries and has helped the fishery to be recognised at an international scale as a benchmark-setting example of sound ecosystem-based fisheries management (Gillett 2008). However, it cannot be stressed strongly enough the key role that co-management and stakeholder participation had in the process. The Commonwealth Scientific and Industrial Research Organisation (CSIRO) discovered this resource, which meant that managers, scientists and industry have worked together from the start of the fishery (Dichmont et al. 2007). Conservation members were instrumental in highlighting the pending threats to the fisheries' existence unless clear action was taken to reduce bycatch and turtle interactions and reduce potential benthic impacts. Stakeholders were involved in the whole process, from highlighting research priorities, undertaking the research and providing management advice. This meant that uptake of management legislation and policy and the level of scientifically based management decision-making is high. Furthermore, the articulation of strategic visions to tactical measures, such as harvest strategies, have helped the fishery move from a co-management model to a self-management system, where the active management of the fishery is undertaken by the fishery, and AFMA and NORMAC audit the process. The key to this success was: (a) the committee structures that AFMA maintained (Figure 2.2), which kept dialogue open even when the divide between stakeholders (including scientists) was very wide and acrimonious due to, initially, disagreements on stock status and, later, disagreements on the degree of caution to be applied and (b) thought leaders in all the key sectors who have driven collaboration towards ultimate ideals such as green certification, more industry autonomy and long-term profitability.

2.2.1 South-East Shark and Scale Fishery

This fishery covers 3.7 million km² of the waters across all Australia's south-eastern EEZ (Figure 2.3). It spans many community and subsystem types, from shallow bays out across the continental shelf and slope, to seamounts, submerged canyons and the open ocean. The fishery is quite diverse, with at least 148 species harvested commercially in the region, including finfish and chondrichthyans; high-value invertebrates (e.g. abalone and rock lobster) are also harvested in the area, separately to the SESSF. Environmentally the region includes tropical, subtropical, temperate and subpolar regions; geologically, there are patches of all types from fine silts to rocky reefs and exposed limestone bedrock; oceanographically, it is shaped by the Leeuwin, Zeehan and East Australian currents – the latter in particular is rapidly extending poleward under climate change (Hobday and Pecl 2013). In addition, more than 77 per cent of Australia's population (>18 million people) live within 50 km of the coastline in this southeast region (Australian Bureau of Statistics 2011). Historically, this has seen the area experience some of Australia's most substantial cumulative pressure due to fisheries activities (commercial and recreational), industrial and agricultural contaminant release, pest and invasive species and habitat modification due to urban and other coastal development. Fishing has been one of the largest of these pressures, as the inshore areas have been commercially exploited for over 160 years. The more offshore waters, which are the focus of the SESSF, were first fished in the early 1900s.

The fishery is run under a cost-recovery scheme, with licence fees paying for management, research and development. The fishery was under input controls (i.e. limits on total effort) up to the mid-1980s, after which time a quota management system on the main target species became the main management lever, with individual transferable quotas (ITQs) implemented in 1992. Nevertheless, by the late 1990s/early 2000s, the SESSF had a number of overfished species and suffered a poor economic performance. By 2004 there was general agreement across all stakeholder groups that the management measures were failing to address the legislated ecological and economic goals, nor was it meeting social needs and expectations. By agreement of all parties, an ecosystem-level MSE was developed in 2005–2009 and helped determine possible strategic management directions.

Given the complexity of performing an ecosystem-level MSE, it was important that stakeholders had a long history of exposure to MSEs, using them to consider single-species management questions for the fishery (e.g., Little et al. 2011). The benefits of the approach had been clearly demonstrated, with a series of single-species MSEs being used to help define many aspects of the management system; most recently, a tiered system of harvest strategies attempted to address the catch–cost–risk trade-off (Dowling et al. 2013, Smith et al. 2013). Against this background, it was a natural extension to take the concept to the ecosystem scale.

The specification of management objectives, performance measures and management strategies was done by a group of stakeholders

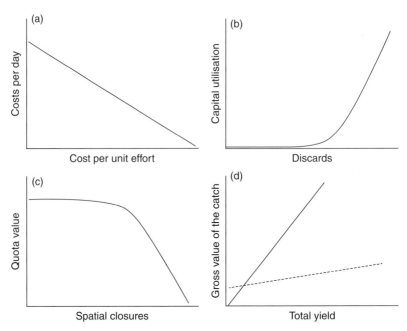

Figure 2.4 Example of qualitative relationships between key system properties and economic indicators drawn up by expert participants in the SESSF qualitative MSE (Smith et al. 2007a). This was a means of codifying their knowledge of system function so that their thinking about the potential evolution of the SESSF under different management options was transparent and reproducible. Multiple relationships were possible, as shown in (d). Redrawn from Smith et al. (2007a).

with diverse backgrounds, including managers, industry, economists, scientists and environmentally focused non-government organisations (eNGOs), who had a long history of involvement in the fishery. An even broader group participated in the definition of subsequent rounds of management strategy elaboration (e.g. fisherman posted in quite detailed alternatives to be trialled). The MSE then used a two-phase approach to evaluating these strategies. The first phase (Smith et al. 2004) used expert knowledge to predict system evolution under the alternative strategies. This knowledge was not expressed in the typical Delphic style, where expert information is provided purely in a narrative form. Instead, for reproducibility and transparency, the knowledge was formalised in a conceptual, qualitative model of system connections, defined via simple sketches of the relationship between system components, such as biomass, catch, prices, etc. (Figure 2.4). The second phase of the project featured a quantitative evaluation, using the end–to-end (whole of ecosystem) modelling framework, Atlantis, to represent the ecosystem and its users (Fulton et al. 2014). Atlantis is a deterministic, coarsely spatially resolved model that tracks key biophysical components of the physical environment and (age-resolved) food webs in the region on a diurnal time step. It also tracks the activity and take of the main fleets, whose effort allocation is dictated by social, psychological and economic drivers.

Both phases of this work highlighted that there are no simple solutions to ecosystem-based management in a fishery as multi-sector and multi-species as the SESSF. Instead a balanced and integrated set of management measures, which represent a combination of a variety of input, output and technical management measures, is required to achieve alignment of management intent and outcome across social, cultural and economic drivers. Each of the management strategies explored had strengths and weaknesses, with no single strategy dominating on all aspects of performance. Despite individual transferable quotas receiving a lot of positive attention in the literature (e.g. Grafton et al. 2006; Costello et al. 2008), their simulated performance was undermined when ecological interactions and incentive structures formed across species and markets led to behaviour (e.g. high grading, over-catch and shifts in targeting to less regulatory constrained species) that reduced the efficacy of the management approach. Similar outcomes, where unanticipated behaviours undermined the performance of ITQs, have been observed in some real-world fisheries (Chu 2009).

Likewise, spatial management has been a popular literature topic in the scientific literature (e.g. Gell and Roberts 2003; Crowder and Norse 2008), but was not a complete solution by itself in this MSE analysis. While spatial management was found to be an indispensable component of a successful management portfolio, it was not sufficient by itself. This is because it is not universally effective across species types (e.g. prey species do not benefit to the same extent as predators) and has the potential to result in economic collapse of fisheries in systems with extensive closures (Fulton et al. 2014). Overall, the integrated management strategy (which explores taking a balanced approach across all management options – quotas, spatial management, gear controls, input controls, surveys and observers etc. – tailoring their implementation to what will best address each of the fishery objectives) had the fewest shortcomings, consistently performing well against objectives and avoiding pitfalls that undermined the performance of the other management strategies.

When the project first began in 2005, integrated management was so far removed from the management practices of the time that it was nicknamed the 'blue sky' strategy in the stakeholder discussions. By the time the project finished in 2009, the fishery's management had shifted substantially, incorporating many features of integrated management strategy as the new 'business as usual' – a direct result of information and inspiration coming from the MSE. An Australian Ministerial Direction of 2005 (available at www.daff.gov.au/fisheries/domestic/fishingfuture) was informed by the SESSF experience and has taken the integrated management to a national policy scale.

Along with the work in the NPF, the SESSF MSE clearly demonstrate that workable solutions to EBFM addressing a multitude of objectives can be found. These experiences also show that successful system-level management options can be jointly uncovered by bringing together ideas from all groups interested in the fishery – industry, conservation, community, managers and scientists. Importantly, MSE can generate truly new learning and can benefit from 'shared knowledge acquisition' and it can be done without automatically requiring a quantitative model (so long as the experts involved have a very good understanding of the specific system). By allowing open and transparent discussion of pressing management questions, it allows for a quick transition from strategic to the tactical with directly implemented management policy, systems and harvest strategies. This was demonstrated in both case studies, often repeatedly. For example, without the MSE as a common touch point, it is doubtful if the widely divergent preferences of the different SESSF stakeholder groups (some of whom were wedded to existing structures, others to an expansion of standard regulatory quota measures, and another group to the wide-scale application of fisheries closures) would have reached a mutually agreeable outcome as quickly – taking the proposal to ministerial authorities in under two years of the project's beginning – or one that was so radically different to what was in place.

2.3 DATA-POOR AND MINIMUM REALISTIC MSES

MSEs were initially applied to data-rich fisheries and this often formed the basis of criticism of MSE (Rochet and Rice 2009). However, as demonstrated above for the SESSF, it can be successfully applied using simpler or non-quantitative methods and MSE is increasingly being applied successfully in data-poor fisheries. This has been important to

Australian fisheries management. The 2007 directive that Australia's Harvest Strategy Policy (DAFF 2007) had to be applied to all AFMA-managed fisheries within a short timeframe meant that harvest strategies for many data-poor fisheries were implemented before any MSEs were developed. Harvest strategies were initially developed without testing, based only on stakeholder engagement (Dowling et al. 2008). Testing these harvest strategies therefore occurred once they had already been applied for several years. The post hoc MSEs showed that the harvest strategy of many of the data-poor fisheries was reasonable in its untested form, but that key modifications were required (Haddon 2012). This exercise highlighted that MSEs can be successfully applied to data-poor fisheries and that their development is justified, as they can identify oversights not captured by other methods.

The Queensland spanner crab fishery provides an early example of an MSE applied to a data-poor fishery in Australia. The fishery was one of the first in Australia to adopt harvest strategies, even though the fishery did not have an assessment (Dichmont and Brown 2010), as the only available data was a short time series of catch and effort data. In this period, it also used independent economic advice to move to an output control (total allowable catches (TAC) and ITQs). The MSE was built entirely with collaboration of fishers and managers (Dichmont and Brown 2010) and was iteratively updated with industry input as more information about the resource became known. For example, initially the trend of the five-year catch rate was used to set the TAC. There was a simple half up or full down set of rules depending on the scale of the catch rate change. The TAC was only increased by half as much as the increase in catch rate, as there was concern that the new system may be over-ridden using political influence and therefore more precaution was needed. Two major factors were considered over time. The harvest strategy was not being over-ridden so the precaution was removed, and there was signs as the length of the data improved that there was an underlying environmentally driven cyclicity to recruitment. The latter meant larger changes in TACs than was useful to manage the fishery. The MSE toolbox was created in Microsoft Excel, as this was a package that industry partners were able to use on their own to test their ideas. In several of the iterations, the final management strategy used in the daily management of the fishery was developed by industry using the Excel MSE tool. Furthermore, assumptions about the possible hyper-stability in the catch rate data, and the uncertainty about the cyclicity being an environmental signal only, meant that the fishery started funding an independent survey, which was included in the harvest strategy.

2.4 MULTI-INDUSTRY, MULTI-JURISDICTION MSES

A challenge with all tools is their appropriate application. Can a tool developed in one context be usefully applied in another – to bring a new perspective – or will the new context be incompatible? Experience to date in taking the MSE approach to new arenas, such as conservation and multiple use management more broadly, has reinforced both strengths and weaknesses of the approach. The MSE approach (or closely related variants) has previously been applied to a range of resource use topics beyond fisheries, for example, forestry and watershed management (Ghebremichael et al. 2013). Over the last decade in Australia, it has been taken to the system level along the north-west Western Australian coast to help find ways to equitably manage environmental assets and industrial activities. This coast is noted for its exceptional beauty, but it is also experiencing a significant increase in the level of natural resource extraction and export (Australian Bureau of Statistics 2012). In addition to long-standing industries such as fishing and agriculture, there are expanding tourism, shipping, mining, oil and gas extraction ventures. Associated with this is pressure for expansion of urban infrastructure, services and amenities in what has historically been a remote and sparsely populated region.

Single-sector MSE has been used in the region to look at the management of recreational fishing (Thebaud et al. 2014), but system-level operating models have now also been developed for consideration of strategic cross-industry and cross-jurisdictional management strategies. This work has had two major outcomes. First, it has shown that such an undertaking is possible, though exceptionally challenging at a technical level. Ensemble approaches pulling together hybrid models (combining agent-based, differential and statistical models) were required (Fulton et al. 2011b), with the data collection methods used to supply the models just as diverse (Gray et al. 2013).

The second lesson was that engagement and uptake was a lot more difficult and achieved only mixed success. Locally there has been uptake, with model outputs used to inform some management and development decisions (e.g. around the level of infrastructure and tourism development allowed at specific points along the northwest coast of Australia). More broadly, however, the degree of uptake is not as great as for fisheries. This also occurs even when the MSE is actually developed as an engagement tool so stakeholders can 'play' with the scenario part of the model (Dutra et al. 2014). There are three main reasons for this development that have a bearing on any future attempts to take the approach to other large-scale problems:

1. Clear ownership and jurisdictional mandates are important. Within the Australian coastal zone, there is no clear reporting body charged with management of the system as a whole and this significantly complicates the engagement and reporting process (and makes enactment of any outcomes more difficult even if supported by all participants) (Dutra et al. 2015).

2. History matters. The long familiarity with the approach in Australia's federal fisheries and the trust built over time with the participatory process has made the application of the approach much simpler than for those industries where the use of simulation models may be considered with some suspicion and where familiarity with adaptive management concepts is in its infancy. This includes scepticism about the method by scientists in other fields who have tended to approach management issues through risk and vulnerability assessment approaches. Moreover, the successes reported here came on the back of over a decade of engagement among scientists, industries and managers. The early MSEs may have been viewed with some scepticism but by the 2000s these were a trusted approach. It is also possible that the adoption of MSEs in fisheries may have been more natural given the use of stock assessment modelling (a component of the MSE) prior to MSE uptake and therefore did not need such a major shift in thinking. The same dependence on simulation models for tactical management decisions is not yet true of other sectors, such as conservation.

3. Stakeholder complexity can be a significant barrier to uptake. The participatory approaches crucial to the success of the approach (for elicitation of otherwise unavailable information, co-production of knowledge around management strategies and dissemination of outcomes) break down with large bodies of people representing different and many stakeholders. While fisheries can be large, and consist of diverse groups of people, the co-management system used in Australia's federal fisheries means there are already clear representatives who speak with authority on behalf of the different sectors. The same is not true for other industries and especially for the

general community. Boundary organisations (institutions that facilitate knowledge transfer between science and policy makers) represent one engagement route, but experience in many forms of natural resource management has shown even that may not be sufficient if dealing with large populations or geographic regions, as it can be hard to reach the sufficient number of people and the sheer size of the exercise means there can be little regulatory flexibility of action (Dutra et al. 2015, Pomeroya et al. 2001).

Thus while we argue that the MSE principles remain pertinent to a broad range of topics and technical (computing) aspects and are equally adaptable, the hardest part of any MSE happens outside the computer. Any potential user of the MSE approach must recognise the potential engagement barriers. They must ensure sufficient resources and time are put into the exercise and to think carefully about how they will identify, engage and communicate with the important actors in their system of interest. Both the NPF and SESSF cases are characterised by their long and continued engagement with the MSE approach and has accepted its iterative approach. As more case studies come to the fore and experiences from them become shared, the adoption of MSE outside the fisheries domain will allow for shared learning.

2.5 WHAT HAS BEEN LEARNT

Two diametrically opposed schools of thought exist regarding the use of models to manage complex systems. The first is that, because fisheries management is a wicked problem (Rittel and Webber 1973), the use of models to aid management of complex marine ecosystems and fisheries is bound to fail. Among the reasons for this anticipated failure are that there is no clear definition of objectives, no optimal solution and no objective answers and solutions. The opposite school of thought holds that, although fisheries management is a wicked problem, some form of management is needed, and, even though an optimal solution may not be possible, a model-based adaptive management framework would allow management to move forward even under uncertainty (Walters 2007). The adaptive management loop explicitly involves iterative decision-making, evaluating the outcomes from the previous decisions and adjusting subsequent actions on the basis of this evaluation. From the social sciences, there is evidence that the complexities of management can be addressed only through direct involvement of stakeholders in the management process (Dietz et al. 2003, Ludwig 2001) and is greatly enhanced in environments fostering the co-production of knowledge (Hadorn et al. 2008).

This requirement for participatory processes, however, does not preclude the use of models to determine management strategies. Van Vugt (2009) identifies four essential components for achieving effective environmental management: information, identity, institutions and incentives. Stakeholders need to be informed about current understanding of the environment and the limits to this understanding, and need to identify strongly with a core social group to seek the best outcomes for the group (Sen and Neilsen 1996). Strong institutional arrangements, or at least well-recognised boundaries, are needed to enable stakeholders to influence management, and the management system must create the right incentives to achieve the stakeholders' objectives (Pomeroya et al. 2001).

The NPF is a good example of what Van Vugt (2009) describes. The industry has a strong identity in the form of an incorporated company and was actively involved in determining which assumptions were to be applied in the modelling analyses, ensuring information was as accurate as possible, discussing results and making final recommendations to the AFMA Commission. The industry was aware of the limitations of the model and accepted it as the best available science despite these limitations. The institutional arrangements for stakeholder involvement have been described as world's best practice (Gillett 2008). The fishery is green certified by the Marine Stewardship Council (MSC, www.msc .org/), and a rights-based management is in place in the fishery to provide the appropriate incentives to achieve the management objective. These factors are fundamentally important in ensuring that management objectives will be achieved.

The SESSF, by its very nature, is not as cohesive a community as the NPF. It is not incorporated and is still made up of a variety of operations (from small family businesses to large corporations) using different gears, targeting different species and fishing from multiple ports dotted along south-eastern Australia. Nevertheless they too conform to Van Vugt's (2009) essential components. By using RAGs and MACs defined at the sub-fishery level, there is a clear identity and a relatively open flow of information between scientists, managers and fishery representatives. Fishery members are engaged with the modelling process. Despite fears initially held by the scientists that the complexity of an ecosystem model would be daunting or rejected by the fishers, the reverse was true, with the fishers recognising in the model the key system features they knew to be important to their day-to-day experiences. Inspiration drawn from the MSE process led to a complete overhaul of the fisheries management arrangements. The complex nature of the fishery means challenges remain, but the fishery is in a significantly better state than it was a decade ago, with some operators now MSC certified.

MSE lessons have also been learned by scientists, management and industry bodies. MSE models are often complex to develop and code. Even incremental change in thinking around fisheries management options and operational objectives (as was the case in the NPF) typically leads to significant changes being required of the MSE code. For example, changing from an S_{MSY} to S_{MEY} target meant adding an economic component to each of the steps in the MSE. Similarly, adding ecosystem components required a completely new operating model. Although this is in some way unavoidable, as models tailored to one question must be reshaped for new contexts (or abandoned and better targeted models developed a new), it can be hard for non-modellers and funding bodies to appreciate the time investment required given 'a model already exists'. While retrofitting past MSE models may seem an attractive means of reducing costs when faced with new questions, we would caution that careful thought needs to be given to each case as trying to adapt past assumptions and modelling decisions can be as costly (even more costly) than starting afresh. Using objectified code structure can allow for easier code refinement, additions and expansion, but assisting non-modellers to understand the modelling process and the need for the use of the correct tool for the new problem remain a requirement of the engagement process.

MSEs can move from providing strategic advice to tactical advice very quickly. In most of the MSEs discussed here, one of the suite of management strategies tested became the basic form of the management used for the fishery. In nearly all cases, this management option was co-developed by the participants rather than being proposed fully formed by one group or another. This co-production of knowledge and the resulting rapid uptake of the outcomes is beneficial in one form, but in translating from strategic visions to operational implementation, care is needed to ensure that appropriate assumptions about the meaning of the results are made as adoption is often quicker than initially considered.

Testing the models using past data to articulate the degree of 'implementation uncertainty' highlighted and supported the view that, even in a well-managed fishery, representing the human dimension is an essential component of the MSE. For example, in the NPF, internationally recognised for the standard of its management, uncertainty around the implementation of a management action remained in the form of a combination of scientific uncertainty (predominantly in estimating the degree to which fishers were adapting their vessels to changing management and economic situations) and the ability of fishers to legally minimise the effect of a management measure.

The greatest lessons learned by the fisheries scientists developing MSEs, however, were in terms of how strongly the value of the MSE as a decision support tool depended upon the success of the participatory aspects of the MSE approach. Successfully implementing an MSE requires good resourcing, particularly for the participatory components. This is amongst the most underappreciated aspects of using MSE, especially for those without long experience in its application. Looking across the examples outlined here, but also at more than 40 years combined accumulated experience in MSE projects and more broadly again at successful instances of adaptive management, it is clear that stakeholder engagement, and how well that works, is key. Without engagement from the start of the process, the models would languish in a back room through lack of credibility and being seen as a 'black box'. To be successful, it cannot be a token effort where experts come in at the beginning have a workshop to gather views on the topic, disappear 'to do the real work' and re-emerge at the end of the process to impart distilled wisdom (or worse still only do the imparting of wisdom) on the assumption that the audience will 'adapt and adopt' (Daniell 2008). The perception of token consultation could be worse than no consultation at all. Instead, true collaborative, iterative participation in the modelling and management strategy design and evaluation process is necessary. This will require compromise and discussion of shared as well as competing views. It will also require flexibility amongst the modelling team which will need to deal with shifting understanding and evolving concepts of desirable strategies and be clear on what can and can't be incorporated as the project unfolds (a blanket refusal to budge is unhelpful but pragmatism around drawing a line under model development steps is also required). In reality, this inclusiveness of alternative ideas can improve cohesion as people's views are not excluded at the start, but rather the final strategy is developed from a suite of ideas based on clear (and pre-agreed) scientific output.

One of the concepts that can be difficult to communicate but must be conveyed to any group working on the MSE is that the process is not about producing the 'right and optimal outcomes'. In social-ecological systems with multiple objectives, finding a single best solution is incredibly unlikely, if not impossible, perhaps costly and often a divisive exercise. It is, however, what modern society and language often conditions people to expect. In addition, people intuitively think in an immediate and linear way (Kahneman 2011). Consequently, time needs to be spent supporting people's learning around complex systems, better equipping them to use all available information for decision-making. The MSE can be a useful training tool in this role.

The make-up of those involved in the participatory exercises is also important. It is important to be as inclusive as is practicable. It is important to have some representation of those who will live under the management decision as it is only through understanding their responses that clarity can be brought to the question of implementation uncertainty. Previous understandings around the value and intent of MSEs have mistaken it for a process that simply focuses on playing out specific management levers with perfect knowledge and no human responses beyond complete compliance; this could not be further from the case. Not only is the final product stronger for including that source of uncertainty, but it also improves co-learning as everyone involves gets a greater appreciation of the contribution of actions at different scales and how processes can interact. This co-learning can go a long way to more effective outcomes, creating a sense of ownership and commitment around the outcomes. Successful implementation of the outcomes is far more likely however, if the MSE is undertaken within a forum with jurisdictional legitimacy. That is participants must include, or at least be recognised by, people with the jurisdictional authority to respond. This can be a formal role (such as a regulatory manager) or a social role (e.g. local champion), but without their participation and support, the uptake (and potentially even the contributions of participating stakeholders) is likely to be minimal. Given the role of MSE as a decision support tool, it is perhaps not surprising that many of the same lessons hold for adaptive and co-management more broadly (Pomeroya et al. 2001; Greig et al. 2013; Beratan 2014).

2.6 CONCLUSIONS

MSE is an immensely powerful and flexible tool. Beyond capturing the closed loop nature of decision-making, there is no specific form to an MSE – it can be as simple or as complicated as the problem requires. The participatory aspects of MSE mean it is not necessarily a cheap option. Nevertheless, when done well, MSEs can move from providing strategic advice to tactical advice very quickly. By providing a common talking point for discussion and learning, an MSE can help to remove barriers to understanding or thinking and act as a catalyst for rapid change in management.

There is a duality to MSE. At face value, it is a simple concept, representing each step involved in adaptive decision-making and how those steps interact. Appreciating and capturing the nuances of the interactions, the feedback and the many sources of uncertainty can be far more difficult. For some, even recognising the existence of the uncertainties and feedback can take considerable time. Nevertheless, the approach can be a valuable tool. It marries the adaptive, flexible, evidence-based and iterative nature of adaptive management with the transparency, inclusiveness and consultation of co-management. When MSE fails, it is because it has fallen foul of the same issues of resourcing, scale and legitimacy that can bedevil adaptive and co-management systems. At its best, however, it benefits from the strengths of adaptive and co-management approaches and can highlight unanticipated consequences, trade-offs and reach acceptable solutions that seemed beyond the capacity of the status quo conditions.

Rapid Prototyping for Decision Structuring: An Efficient Approach to Conservation Decision Analysis

GEORGIA E. GARRARD, LIBBY RUMPFF,
MICHAEL C. RUNGE AND SARAH J. CONVERSE

3.1 INTRODUCTION

Conservation decisions are hard. They possess many of the features that characterise difficult decisions (see Clemen 1991), including multiple stakeholders with different perspectives, multiple objectives and uncertainty about how the system in question will respond to potential management actions. In addition, difficult trade-offs may be required to address competing objectives. However, decision problems are not necessarily as complex as they initially appear (Keeney 1994).

Decades of research in decision science have indicated that it is possible to improve the effectiveness of decision-making through the implementation of a rigorous protocol that involves breaking decisions into a series of manageable components and analysing the components to deal with the challenges of and impediments to decision-making. The components common to all decisions have been invariably identified as (1) defining the decision to be made, (2) specifying objectives, (3) identifying actions, (4) estimating the extent to which actions will achieve objectives (including uncertainty) and, finally, (5) identifying the optimal decision (Hammond et al. 1999; Possingham et al. 2001; Gregory et al. 2012; Conroy and Peterson 2013). Decision analysis (also known as structured decision-making, particularly in the conservation settings; Gregory et al. 2012) is both the process of deconstructing decisions, and using a broad set of tools – developed in the fields of decision science, risk analysis, modelling, statistics, psychology and others – for analysing decision components and constructing frameworks for making decisions more effectively.

The rapid uptake of structured decision-making (SDM) in conservation science over the last 15 years is evidence of the challenge of solving complex conservation decisions, as well as the benefits resulting from applying decision theory to solve them (Possingham et al. 2001; Williams et al. 2002; Runge 2011; Gregory et al. 2012; Converse et al. 2013a). SDM has been adopted as a standard of practice in natural resource management agencies in Canada and the USA and is also increasingly practiced in Australia, New Zealand and other parts of the world (Gregory et al. 2012). Structured decision-making has been applied to an array of conservation problems, including environmental monitoring (Neckles et al. 2014), endangered species management (Gregory and Long 2009; Martin et al. 2011), invasive species management (Blomquist et al. 2010; Moore et al., Chapter 6), species reintroductions (Converse et al. 2013b), forest and fisheries management (Bain 1987; Marcot et al. 2012), identification of ecological thresholds (Addison et al. 2015), allocation of conservation resources (Converse et al. 2011) and adaption to climate change (Mills et al. 2014).

Rapid prototyping is a technique commonly used to develop an SDM framework. With roots in engineering and modelling, rapid prototyping as applied to SDM aims to quickly produce a representation of a decision that captures all the essential elements of the decision in a simplified form (a decision 'prototype') (Naumann and Jenkins 1982; Nicolson et al. 2002). The early focus on development of a coarse but complete representation of a decision problem enables decision-makers to quickly identify the components of their decision and recognise the central aspects of the decision problem that are worth investment of their time and resources. Since 2007, the US Geological Survey, in cooperation with the US Fish and Wildlife Service's National Conservation Training Center, has been training agency employees in the use of rapid prototyping to implement SDM for a range of conservation and environmental management problems.

In this chapter, we explore how SDM and rapid prototyping can be applied to assist conservation decision-making. We begin by describing SDM in greater detail. We then describe the process of rapid prototyping and illustrate, using case studies from our own experiences, its potential for improving conservation decisions.

3.2 STRUCTURED DECISION-MAKING

Structured decision-making (SDM) is a framework for facilitating transparent, logical and consistent decision-making that draws upon elements of decision theory, risk assessment and a variety of other fields

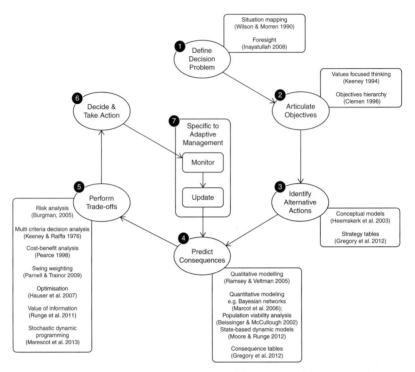

Figure 3.1 A diagrammatic representation of the structured decision-making process showing the six components of the decision (ellipses). The process of SDM can be supported by a wide range of qualitative and quantitative decision-analysis tools (boxes, with examples). The tools chosen should be fit for purpose, and the needs and capabilities of those involved (Addison et al. 2013). Figure adapted from Converse et al. 2013a and Addison et al. 2013.

(Martin et al. 2009; Runge 2011). The framework guides users through a systematic process whereby a problem is broken down into a common set of decision components, each of which can be explored with a range of qualitative and quantitative decision-analysis tools (Figure 3.1).

The basic premise of SDM is that decision-making should be driven by the values (Keeney 1994) of decision-makers and stakeholders (Runge 2011). After a clear articulation of the decision context (Step 1, Figure 3.1), these values are codified in the process as objectives (Step 2), which then provide the focus for the ensuing decision-making process. Next, the objectives are used as a basis for developing alternative management actions or strategies (Step 3), and then scientific data and judgements are utilised in the process to examine the (potential) outcomes of those alternatives in relation to the objectives (Step 4). It may be that, at this point, participants are able to simplify the problem such that a reasonable course of action is evident (Step 6, bypassing Step 5). For example, it may transpire that one of the alternative actions being considered is outperformed by another action when measured against each objective (a so-called dominated alternative, see Gregory et al. 2012), and the removal of this alternative makes the decision clear. Or, the problem may not involve multiple objectives but instead require identifying the optimal action conditional on a single objective (or a single objective and some number of decision constraints, e.g. staying within budget). However, when the decision is not clear after assessing the consequences of alternative actions, it may be necessary to conduct a trade-offs analysis (Step 5), in which anticipated change in the state of one objective (in relation to the estimated consequences) is weighted against that of others.

In the event that uncertainty affects the choice of management alternatives, it may be reasonable to take extra steps within the SDM framework to resolve the uncertainty (Step 7). That is, monitoring data can be used to iteratively update knowledge and help improve management decisions to best achieve the relevant objectives. This is referred to as adaptive management, which is a form of SDM, applicable when decisions are recurrent and hampered by critical uncertainty (Williams et al. 2007; Runge 2011). Thus, the adaptive management framework extends the SDM framework by incorporating extra steps to provide a plan for motivating, designing and interpreting the results of monitoring.

The prescriptive approach of SDM has several key benefits. First, decomposing a complex problem allows people to analyse each part in more detail and can facilitate a shared understanding of the complexities and intricacies of the problem. Second, a more detailed exploration of the problem can encourage creative thinking about potential alternative solutions, and help identify key knowledge gaps. Last, by encouraging participants to consider evidence-based components of a decision (i.e. estimation of consequences) separately from the values-based components (such as setting objectives and making trade-offs), this structured process can help to mitigate against inadvertent personal biases which may occur in an unstructured approach to decision-making (Maguire 2004).

Decisions can be difficult for a number of reasons, and challenges may arise at all stages of the SDM process (Figure 3.1). First, development of a decision-making framework may be complicated by linguistic uncertainties, deeply held values and challenges associated with defining the scope of the decision. For example, even determining the spatial scale at which decisions about management should be assessed can be challenging (Blomquist et al. 2010). Second, most people struggle to articulate the objectives for a decision. Even experienced decision-makers find this difficult (Bond et al. 2008). Third, a common challenge is failing to distinguish appropriately between means and fundamental objectives: for example, a decision-maker may be focused, in the context of an endangered species management decision, on providing habitat. However, in this context, habitat is a means to an end, whereas the status of the endangered species itself is the fundamental objective. Focusing on means rather than fundamental objectives can lead to an overly limited set of alternatives and potentially poor decision outcomes (Keeney 2007). Fourth, when identifying a set of alternatives, participants may struggle to think outside the bounds of existing management actions (i.e. anchoring; see Burgman et al. 2011b), or find it difficult to identify a manageable set of alternatives from an overwhelming number of possible actions. Fifth, assessing the consequences of alternative actions often involves both quantitative and qualitative measures, which may require complex empirical and conceptual models. Sixth, trade-offs and optimisation can present technical challenges that require specific knowledge and expertise. In all of these cases and others, decision analysis provides a way to frame and recognise the challenge, as well as tools to overcome the impediments (Figure 3.1).

It is worth noting that the process of working through the steps of SDM does not guarantee a decision per se. However, though participants may not agree on a course of action, they can probe non-intuitive results by re-visiting each step of the SDM process. For instance, participants can attempt to diagnose elements they may have missed when formulating the problem (e.g. objectives, alternatives), and/or further examine the impact of uncertainty and value judgements on the 'preferred' outcome.

3.3 RAPID PROTOTYPING FOR STRUCTURED DECISION-MAKING

When an automobile company designs a brand new car model, it does not produce a full version of the car at the first attempt. Instead, it likely begins with a sketch of the exterior shape and a rough engineering design. This first conceptual prototype might evolve into a small physical prototype, which might undergo testing in a wind tunnel, along with a more detailed engineering analysis. This process is likely to be repeated with increasingly sophisticated prototypes being tested, redesigned and enhanced, taking into account a larger array of considerations, including fuel efficiency, performance, marketing, production costs, safety and reliability. This process of rapid, iterative prototyping is common practice in all fields of engineering. Why shouldn't conservation decision-making (conservation engineering, if you will) proceed in the same way?

3.3.1 What Is Rapid Prototyping?

Rapid prototyping is an approach for developing an SDM framework. Rapid prototyping promotes an iterative decision-structuring approach, by emphasising rapid progression through the development of the decision framework, from objective setting to estimating outcomes from various decisions and even 'solving' the problem (*sensu* 'decision sketching': Gregory et al. 2012). With each iteration, the formulation of the decision is revised and improved, and an updated prototype emerges. Early iterations should be especially rapid, with a focus on quickly sketching the broad outlines of the decision framework. In some cases, one or two iterations may suffice for a decision, but often more detailed work is necessary to adequately address the challenges associated with the decision.

Rapid prototyping has a number of benefits when used to develop decision-making frameworks. First, it is an efficient way to outline the overall framework and identify the structure of the decision. The rapid progression through the decision-making framework allows users to build the basic decision structure without getting stuck on individual components. In some cases, this will paint a picture clear enough that the decision can be made without further analysis. Second, it allows decision-makers to identify any impediments to the decision and what additional tools, expertise and other resources are required to solve them. Last, rapid prototyping can help to avoid investing in unnecessary detail because decision prototypes are developed only to the point needed for the decision-maker to make the decision. This might mean that only the first or second prototype is needed.

A key feature of rapid prototyping is that it can be undertaken using the skills and resources available. Typically, rapid prototyping is accomplished in a workshop setting (perhaps over multiple workshops) led by an experienced facilitator. Experienced facilitators will almost certainly be required for complex multi-stakeholder, multi-objective decisions but, with proper attention to decision structuring and necessary decision elements, the rapid prototyping approach to SDM can be effectively utilised by anyone wishing to make a decision. Because rapid prototyping encourages decision-makers or their support staff to work through the decision problem iteratively, key obstacles are identified along the way and skill and data limitations will be exposed during the process (see Blomquist et al. 2010), thereby identifying the resources that should be gathered for further development of the decision.

Because it can be undertaken with the skills and tools at hand, and is based around the well-described SDM process, rapid prototyping can, in theory, be undertaken by anyone wishing to make a decision. However, it should be noted that there are situations in which a rapid prototyping approach will not be helpful. These are primarily situations in which SDM itself is not appropriate. SDM will not work when applied to a problem that is not a decision problem (for example, when a decision about the best course of action has already been determined by other means, or when the problem is one of finding the right technical solution for a challenging question), nor when conflicts prevent stakeholders engaging in the process (in which case successful conflict resolution is needed before a decision-analytic framework can be developed). In other situations, time and resource constraints may preclude the use of decision analysis, which requires, at the very least, buy-in and commitment from the decision-maker(s) and major stakeholders. Decision-makers may not be willing to invest time and resources if the problem is not of sufficient interest to them, or if they are more comfortable and familiar with an unstructured, implicit approach to decision-making. While we believe that SDM and rapid prototyping are generally applicable to conservation decision problems if the will exists to do so, in practice, some problems are simply too complex to deal with meaningfully, given the time and resources allotted. Having said this, rapid prototyping can invite quick insights and fast development while avoiding over-investment in unnecessary analysis, making it an efficient approach to decision structuring when resources are limited.

In essence, rapid prototyping is an approach for stepping through the SDM framework (as shown in Figure 3.1) and fleshing out each element of the decision over a series of iterations. In this section, we draw on our own experiences in structured approaches to conservation decision problems to describe the process of rapid prototyping.

3.3.2 The Diagnostic Phase – Developing the Decision Structure

In our experience, the development of the first prototype usually begins before any workshop is convened. The first prototype begins to take shape during an informal diagnostic phase, when the decision-maker specifies a (perhaps vague) problem statement. This may occur within the decision-maker's work group or during a conversation with an experienced decision analyst. The purpose of this initial diagnostic phase is to determine whether the problem specified by the decision-maker is appropriate for an SDM framework. This involves clearly identifying that there is a decision to be made and obtaining a commitment from the decision-maker and stakeholders that they are willing to engage in the process. At this time, the decision-maker will need to think about what information or expertise is required to make the decision, who should be involved (e.g. stakeholders) and a timeframe for making the decision. This process may reveal that further development of decision prototypes is unnecessary, either because there is sufficient information structured in such a way that the decision is clear, or because the problem identified is not appropriate for an SDM approach (e.g. it is not really a decision problem, or conflicts must be resolved before the stakeholders are willing to engage in the process).

At this diagnostic stage, the structure of the decision is likely taking shape in the decision analyst's mind: the number and nature of the objectives, the types of actions, the work that will need to be done to predict consequences and the sorts of analytical tools that might be needed to identify a preferred alternative. This need only be a vague sketch at this point, but it helps to frame the processes for further development.

3.3.3 Refining the Prototype

After initial diagnosis, attention is focused on developing and refining the decision prototype. Depending on the nature of the problem, this may occur in a workshop or series of workshops and may involve a broader range of participants, including the decision-maker, stakeholders and experts. In order to develop the decision prototype, participants work through the structured decision-making steps, beginning with the decision context and objective setting, and ending with the analysis of trade-offs/optimisation and the decision itself. The aim of the process is to develop the full prototype; that is, to work through each of the SDM steps at least once, but only seeking to roughly sketch each of the elements.

Participants should proceed through the steps until a major impediment to the decision is identified. In other words, until the group identifies one aspect of the decision that makes it difficult to decide on a course of action. Perhaps the objectives are unclear or disputed amongst stakeholders, perhaps it is difficult to determine what alternatives are available or there might be major uncertainty reducing the precision of predictions made about the impacts of different actions on the objectives: all of these are examples of impediments. Once identified, it is worth spending some time trying to resolve that impediment, and then continuing through the steps to see what impediments remain. There are no generalisable rules governing the amount of time that should be allocated to resolving impediments; this must be considered on a project-by-project basis and is influenced by a number of factors, including the perceived benefit of resolving the impediment and the time available to complete the prototype. This process of progressing through the decision-making steps and resolving impediments is repeated until all steps have been addressed and either no impediments remain (and the decision can be made) or it is clear that the impediments will not be resolved without further expertise or data.

This sounds simple, but can be surprisingly challenging. Getting all the way through the decision structure reasonably quickly is important, but some impediments will be impossible to fully resolve in the first iteration. This can be frustrating and challenging for participants who wish to make each step perfect before moving on to the next. But there are benefits to developing the first prototype at a coarse level. Perhaps the greatest benefit is simply to get a clearer picture of what the decision problem actually is; without the first prototype, participants may have very different visions of the decision, but those differences may not be apparent to them, which can lead to poor communication and even conflict (Redpath et al. 2015). Having a common vision of the structure of the decision invites clearer discussion of the component elements. Another benefit of the first prototype is it can often identify the most challenging impediments to making the decision, allowing focused discussion and development in subsequent prototypes.

3.3.4 Identifying Participants

A critical step is determining who will participate in the rapid prototyping process and at which point(s) they will be involved. It may be that the only participant is the decision-maker. The decision-maker may also choose to include individuals or representatives with an interest or stake in the decision outcome and experts with subject matter expertise relevant to specific decision elements. As a general rule, the rapid prototyping process focuses on the desired objectives and values of the decision-maker, and so it is critical that the decision-maker (or proxy) is present for the process of defining the decision problem, objective setting and the trade-offs (in the case of multi-objective problems) and decision phases. In addition, the decision-maker may be required during the process of identifying alternative actions to determine what actions are feasible and acceptable. Key stakeholders should be present during objective setting to ensure that all relevant values are taken into account and may therefore also be critical to the decision framing and trade-offs stages. Technical and specialist expertise is often required when developing alternatives, predicting the consequences of alternative decisions on objectives and conducting the optimisation.

3.3.5 Subsequent Prototypes and the Stopping Point

A key feature of rapid prototyping is that it is iterative. Once one decision prototype has been developed, participants have the option (and are encouraged) to go back to the start of the SDM process and cycle through it again. In this way, rapid prototyping produces multiple prototypes, each one building on earlier prototypes to foster continual improvement. So, in theory, the rapid prototyping process is never-ending; there is no well-defined stopping point because it is always possible to continually improve elements of the decision analysis. In reality, the rapid prototyping process ends when the decision-maker is able or prepared to make a decision. But it is not possible to describe a generally applicable stopping point. The point at which a decision-maker is prepared to make a decision is highly variable and can only be determined on a case-by-case basis. Among other things, a decision-maker's stopping point will be influenced by his or her level of comfort and satisfaction with the status of the decision sketching and risk tolerance, the importance of the decision, the type of decision (i.e. one-off vs. repeat decisions), the degree to which the decision satisfies any statutory requirements and the level of commitment from individual and organisational participants.

Sometimes, the decision-maker will be ready to make a decision within the timeframe of a typical workshop (for example, three to five days). However, for many decision problems, the rapid prototyping process will extend beyond the period of a single workshop. It is common that, at the conclusion of a rapid prototyping workshop, participants will have developed a thorough understanding and sketch of the decision problem, but will have also identified a task or number of tasks to be completed in order to make the decision. These tasks may include additional modelling, data collection and/or consultation and engagement with a broader group of stakeholders. In the next section, we discuss some typical outcomes from rapid prototyping SDM workshops, and illustrate these with conservation decision case studies. It is important to note, however, that this is not an exhaustive typology; any number of outcomes may arise from different combinations of data, stakeholder and technical needs.

3.4 A TYPOLOGY OF OUTCOMES FROM RAPID PROTOTYPING FOR SDM

The potential outcomes of rapid prototyping are varied and depend on the decision context, available data and expertise, and the nature of the uncertainty surrounding the decision. Here, we demonstrate the role of rapid prototyping for (1) resolving the decision without models or additional technical expertise; (2) identifying the need for specific subject matter expertise (e.g. expert elicitation); (3) identifying information gaps that require new research; and (4) identifying the need for adaptive management to resolve critical uncertainties. In so doing, we have drawn from our own experiences: however, we do not claim that this typology is complete. Additional outcomes are possible. For example, a rapid prototyping exercise may reveal that the decision problem was incorrectly specified, in which case the decision might need to be reframed for a subsequent prototyping exercise, or the existence of impediments that cannot be overcome by resolving scientific uncertainty, such as values-based conflicts. In the latter case, other frameworks and tools may be necessary, such as those pertaining to conflict resolution.

3.4.1 Resolving the Decision Challenge

In the simplest case, the rapid prototyping approach to SDM may produce a decision sketch that is sufficient to make a decision. This happens in two ways: when the major impediment to the decision is simply being able to see the core structure of the problem amidst a host of complexities; or when the major impediment lies in one particular element of the decision and is easily removed. The decision process around impoundment management at Necedah National Wildlife Refuge provides a good example of how rapid prototyping can help to clarify a decision problem such that a decision can be made.

From 2001 to 2012, Necedah National Wildlife Refuge (NNWR), in central Wisconsin, USA, was the site for reintroduction of whooping cranes (*Grus americana*) using a soft-release method that involved training birds for migration using an ultralight-led technique (Urbanek et al. 2005; Mueller et al. 2013). Birds were shipped from the captive breeding centre in the late summer of their first year and housed in communal pens on NNWR through the fall, until they departed on southward migration behind ultralight aircraft. These pens were, critically, sited within wetlands so that birds could roost in water, which had previously been shown to improve post-release survival (Gee et al. 2001). In 2007, there were three of these ultralight training sites located around NNWR. All of the sites were needed to accommodate annual release cohorts.

NNWR had historically used drawdowns to manage the impounded wetlands where the training sites were located. Wetland drawdowns were typically initiated in mid-summer, and wetlands were reflooded in fall. The vegetative growth achieved provided food sources for migrating birds upon reflooding. Thus, a conflict had arisen between providing training sites for whooping cranes (because water roosting sites would be eliminated if wetlands were drawn down) and providing productive wetlands to meet other NNWR management goals, such as management for black terns (*Chlidonias niger*) and ducks and reduction of invasive exotic species. In addition, whooping cranes released in previous years were using wetlands for nesting, and drawdowns were expected to result in nest failure for these birds. Other objectives included providing public viewing opportunities at training pens, reducing disease risk at pens, minimising the disturbance associated with training activities and minimising costs.

These conflicts were challenging to negotiate for members (including NNWR) of the Whooping Crane Eastern Partnership (WCEP), which managed the reintroduction, resulting in discord and gridlock. In 2008, an SDM process was undertaken to help NNWR chart a course for simultaneous management of its wetlands and the crane reintroduction programme. In the process of prototyping, the first useful simplification of the problem came about when it was realised that, but for the need to provide training sites, the drawdown issue would be relatively easy to accommodate: drawdowns could be initiated as usual, except where nesting whooping cranes were present. In those cases, the drawdown could be delayed until the nesting birds either failed or until the chick(s) were old enough to fly and could leave for nearby wetlands. It was further realised that two of the training sites (#2 and #3) could be modified relatively easily so that they would be usable in a drawdown year and would also provide for public viewing. Thus, with these realisations, the decision became substantially simpler: how to provide a replacement for site #1 in a drawdown year. A set of actions was identified including establishing an entirely new training site, various modifications of site #1 or expanding site #2 or #3. The workshop team engaged in an expert elicitation process to score each of the alternatives against a simplified set of objectives, and facilitators used swing weighting (Goodwin and Wright 2004) and the simple multi-attribute rating technique (Edwards, 1977; Goodwin and Wright, 2004) to evaluate the alternatives. After one prototype of that process, the decision-maker declared that he was ready to make the decision and chose construction of an additional site. An additional site was constructed and was used the following year. Also during the following year, a wetland drawdown was carried out on one of the largest ponds on NNWR, with no negative impacts on the ultralight training programme.

Decisions often appear relatively easy in retrospect, even though they might seem intractable at the start. Before the simplifications and accommodations were developed during the workshop, the WCEP members were stuck. In the end, with an investment of only a few days of work, the group developed a solution that met the needs of all parties. As an added benefit, this experience also provided useful training in SDM for the participants. This was the first exposure that WCEP had to SDM, but it has since been used multiple times by the group (e.g. Runge et al. 2011b; Servanty et al. 2014).

3.4.2 Identifying the Need for Specific Subject Matter Expertise or Information

Another typical outcome from an initial rapid prototyping exercise is the identification of further expertise, analyses or information necessary to make a decision. Because rapid prototyping encourages participants to work through the entire decision structure quickly, it allows decision-makers to identify where the real impediments to the decision lie, without investing too much energy in resolving issues that have little or no bearing on the final decision. Sometimes, once the problem is correctly framed, it becomes clear that the key to solving the problem is identifying particular information or expertise that is absent. Once this is obtained, the decision-maker has all the information necessary to make the decision. The rapid prototyping process may also identify the need for additional information or analyses that go beyond what can be accomplished in the development of a prototype, including predictive modelling, sensitivity analyses or simulations. The decision process to determine how staff at the US Fish and Wildlife Service's Washington Fish and Wildlife Office should allocate effort to consultations about a threatened fish species under Section 7 of the Endangered Species Act is a good example of a rapid prototyping exercise that revealed the need for further information and expertise.

During a workshop in July 2007, a team including staff from the Washington Fish and Wildlife Office (WFWO) of the US Fish and Wildlife Service (USFWS) prototyped a decision problem involving workload allocation under Section 7 of the US Endangered Species Act (ESA). Section 7 of the ESA requires federal agencies to consult with the USFWS when any action they plan to take may have an influence on a USFWS-managed species listed under ESA. During Section 7 consultations, USFWS staff have the opportunity to recommend changes and improvements to projects so that they do not threaten listed species. In some cases, consultation can provide a net positive for the species (e.g. through mitigation actions).

The WFWO was most concerned with one species: the threatened bull trout (*Salvelinus confluentus*). Decreasing staffing at the WFWO, along with an increasing consultation workload for bull trout, had resulted in a situation where regulatory deadlines were often exceeded and opportunities to improve projects were missed. Therefore, the team wanted to develop an approach for better allocating staff time to consultations (Converse et al. 2011). During the prototyping process, it was recognised that workload allocation should focus on how to allocate work so that the staff could best 'move the needle' – that is, allocate their time to actions where their involvement could lead to the greatest expected improvements for bull trout.

During the workshop, the team articulated the management objective as: 'Maximize the conservation effectiveness of bull trout consultation, while completing work within regulatory time frames' and decided that both formal consultations (those where expected effects are significant) and informal consultations (those where expected effects are beneficial or insignificant) would each be allocated to two bins: one bin where a minimum amount of work would be done to complete the regulatory requirements of consultation (short bin), and one bin where time would be invested to improve the project from the standpoint of bull trout conservation (long bin). From there, it was necessary to determine how different projects would be allocated to these bins, and the amount of time to spend on projects in the various bins.

At the end of the first workshop, the basic decision framework had been developed, but more work was needed; in order to complete the decision framework, specific expertise was needed to develop a model that could be used to estimate the potential value of each consultation project for bull trout conservation. After the workshop, the team initiated work with an expert panel to develop the tools necessary to allow completion of the framework. From this panel, information was elicited, which allowed for statistical development of a 'potential value model'. The model was designed to allow quick assessment of incoming projects and score them on the total conservation value that staff could be expected to extract through the consultation process. The information elicited included the experts' own assessment of potential value, and the variables that they used to assess the potential value. A statistical fitting procedure was then used to convert this information into a quantitative model.

Information was also elicited from the panel to develop a function relating time spent on a consultation to the proportion of the potential value realised, and the amount of time necessary to complete the minimal work needed for projects assigned to the 'short bin'. These two pieces of information allowed for the optimal decision to be found through a simulation-based search. The search resulted in a decision rule, which assigned informal and formal consultations to a bin based on their assessed potential value scores and prescribed the optimal time to be invested in consultations in the various bins.

This decision tool was put into use in the WFWO, beginning approximately two years after the initial workshop. The prototyping team also emphasised the importance of ongoing monitoring for improving the tool. Decisions are often based on data that are, while the best available, perhaps not entirely adequate. Ongoing monitoring is critical for improving decision tools that are used iteratively over time; the theory and practice of adaptive management is relevant to the collection and application of post-decision monitoring data to improve decision tools for subsequent decision-making.

3.4.3 Identifying Information Gaps that Require New Research

Rapid prototyping can lead to the identification of an information gap that must be resolved in order to proceed with the decision. In this instance, new knowledge is necessary (as opposed to just sourcing additional information, as was the case in Section 3.4.2, above). In this way, rapid prototyping workshops may precipitate a research project, aimed particularly at filling identified research gaps. Here, we illustrate this outcome using an example of the management of white-nose syndrome in threatened bats in Indiana.

White nose syndrome is a fungal disease affecting cave-hibernating bat species in east and central North America. It spreads rapidly and since its first documentation in eastern New York in 2006, white nose syndrome has spread to at least 19 US states and four Canadian provinces, killing millions of bats (Thogmartin et al. 2013). In 2009, concerned about the rate of spread and lethal nature of the disease, the USFWS, in conjunction with the US Geological Survey, National Park Service and various state wildlife agencies, participated in a rapid prototyping SDM workshop to determine what management action should be taken to minimise the effects of white nose syndrome on native bat populations (Szymanski et al. 2009). During the rapid prototyping exercise, managers refined the problem to apply only to areas that were close to, but not yet affected by the disease, and identified six fundamental objectives and 23 management alternatives. Assessment of the consequences of each management alternative on each objective – estimated via expert elicitation – revealed no clear best management strategy. A weighted trade-off analysis led to a preliminary recommendation focused on restricted human access to caves.

The workshop revealed that varying value judgements between different decision-makers about the relative importance of competing objectives would lead to different decisions (Szymanski et al. 2009). However, almost all decision-makers agreed that preventing the spread of white nose syndrome was the most important objective. This objective had proven to be the most difficult to quantify during the workshop and, as such, one of the key outcomes of the rapid prototyping exercise was the recognition of the need for the development of quantitative, predictive models of disease dynamics based on empirical evidence, as well as additional research investigating the impact of white nose syndrome and potential management strategies on other obligate cave biota (Szymanski et al. 2009). Subsequently, a number of research projects have provided further evidence about the spread, management and impact of this disease on native bat species (Foley et al. 2011; Maher et al. 2012; Thogmartin et al. 2013).

3.4.4 Identifying the Need for Adaptive Management to Resolve Critical Uncertainties

All conservation decisions are made in the face of uncertainty, but not all uncertainty is critical to be resolved before making a decision. Sometimes, during the development of a decision prototype, the decision-maker and analyst will realise that a source of uncertainty is irrelevant to the decision (e.g. because it is associated with an irrelevant objective or dominated alternative, or because any value over the range of uncertainty would lead to the same decision). Other times, uncertainty about the ultimate decision may be resolved by sourcing the right expertise or information, or using more sophisticated techniques to improve the precision of estimated consequences. However, not all uncertainty can be resolved in this way. In some cases, the value of information is high, that is, the expected outcomes can be improved by resolving uncertainty before committing to a long-term decision (Runge et al. 2011b). In such cases, the decision-maker may pursue either research in advance of making the decision, or else adaptive implementation to allow incremental learning as management proceeds. Managing the reintroduction of whooping cranes in Wisconsin provides an excellent example of how rapid prototyping can identify critical uncertainties that are impeding a decision, and inform the development of adaptive management strategies to resolve them.

As noted earlier, the reintroduction of a migratory population of whooping cranes in Wisconsin has been an important recovery strategy for this endangered species. The initial reintroduction was successful, in that chicks released to the wild learned their migratory paths behind ultralight aircraft and were subsequently able to undertake the return migration on their own. As they matured, the birds exhibited appropriate breeding behaviour, finding mates, establishing territories, building nests and laying eggs. But very few of the nests were successful; in many cases, the pairs abandoned the nests before the eggs had hatched. In 2009, a workshop was convened to consider the possible causes of reproductive failure and the possible solutions (Runge et al. 2011b). Eight hypotheses were identified, with corresponding likelihoods based on the weight of available evidence assigned to them. Seven potential strategies for enhancing reproductive performance of the whooping

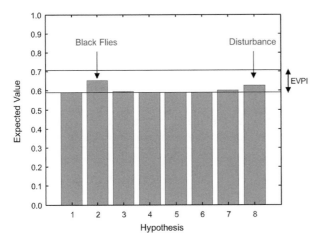

Figure 3.2 Partial expected value of perfect information (EVPI) regarding eight hypotheses for the reproductive failure of whooping cranes in the Eastern Migratory Population (Runge et al. 2011b). Of the eight hypotheses, resolution of the black fly hypothesis alone was expected to recover nearly half of the total value of perfect information. This insight motivated targeted research and adaptive implementation of management actions.

crane pairs were proposed and their potential for success was evaluated relative to which of the underlying hypotheses might be true. In the face of uncertainty, that is, without resolving uncertainty about the cause of reproductive failure, the best management action (meadow restoration) had an expected fledging rate of 0.185. A value of information analysis (Runge et al. 2011b) revealed that, if the underlying cause of reproductive failure could be resolved, then the recommended action depended on the underlying cause, and the expected fledging rate increased to 0.232 (a 26 per cent increase). Analysis of the partial value of information indicated that if only one hypothesis could be investigated and either confirmed or refuted, then the best hypothesis to test was the one that implicated black flies as cause of nest abandonment; resolution of this one hypothesis alone recovered 54 per cent of the total value of information (Figure 3.2). This prototype analysis was undertaken in a short period of time through expert elicitation and identified a critical set of uncertainties that impeded a management decision. From this prototype, a strategy was designed and implemented, with experimental reduction of black fly density in the treatment area (Converse et al. 2013c); it appears that this resulted in higher nesting success in the population, but did not fully resolve the problem of poor reproductive success. The science and management team is now engaged in a process of revising the competing hypotheses and developing new management actions in the spirit of two-phase, or double-loop, learning that is central to adaptive management (Williams et al., 2007).

3.5 CONCLUSIONS

We have drawn on our combined experience in facilitating rapid prototyping exercises to highlight the benefits of this approach for structuring environmental decisions. Development of a complete decision-analytic framework can seem daunting, especially in conservation problems that may be challenging due to multiple objectives, risk, inadequate information, ineffective governance, complex system dynamics and the complexity of available management alternatives. Sorting through such a problem, and committing to a thorough analysis of all elements, can make the use of formal methods of SDM seem overwhelming to a decision-maker. But the use of these tools can be made more approachable through iterative prototyping – development of increasingly detailed versions of a decision analysis with frequent feedback from the decision-maker. Just as a car manufacturer does not build a new model in its full detail at the first try, so, too, a decision framework can be built in phases, with elements refined and details added as needed, until the analysis provides the insight needed to make the decision.

Understanding Uptake of Decision-Support Models in Conservation and Natural Resource Management

YUNG EN CHEE, FIONA FIDLER AND BONNIE C. WINTLE

4.1 INTRODUCTION

Computer-based decision-support models are designed to aid complex decision-making, but are often underused (McIntosh et al. 2008, 2011). Many claim that stakeholder participation in model development will promote acceptance of these models, particularly in situations where stakes are high, values are contested, knowledge is uncertain and decisions are urgent (Voinov and Bousquet 2010; Carmona et al. 2011). Stakeholders are a 'peer community' that extends beyond technical experts, to include people affected by the decision, people who can influence the decision, people with specific local knowledge and people charged with responsibility for making the decision. When stakeholders participate in the modelling process, they get the opportunity to clarify the problem, learn about their system and its dynamics under different conditions and explore and compare the consequences of different management options (Prell et al. 2007; McIntosh et al. 2008; Henriksen et al. 2012; see also Dichmont and Fulton, Chapter 2). It is generally thought that engaging stakeholders in participatory modelling fosters understanding and trust, which in turn promotes actual model use. While these beliefs are intuitive and plausible, there is surprisingly little empirical evidence behind these assumptions (Henriksen and Barlebo 2008; Wassen et al. 2011). This chapter presents our first efforts at investigating these claims.

This chapter explores two main concepts – knowledge and trust – and the relationship each has with model adoption, or at least, willingness to adopt the model. We begin with an overview of our methods and measurements. The rest of the chapter presents our initial thoughts

Authors are listed alphabetically by last name; all authors contributed equally to this work.

(our prior beliefs) regarding the role of each concept, followed by lessons learned from our data and analysis. We end the chapter with an examination of external factors – independent of any individual's intentions – that may present barriers to model use.

4.2 METHODS AND MEASUREMENTS

4.2.1 Recruitment and Participants

We took a purposive approach to sampling as we specifically wanted to interview people who have participated in model-building workshops that used Bayesian networks (BNs, see Box 4.1) as the main modelling tool. We concentrated on BNs because these graphical models, implemented in user-friendly, interactive software, have been a popular modelling tool in the natural resource management (NRM) community here

---

Box 4.1 A Brief Introduction to Bayesian Networks

Bayesian Networks (BNs; Pearl 1991; Korb and Nicholson 2010) are used to model systems that involve uncertainty. This may be due to natural variation, imperfect understanding of the system, incomplete data or some combination of these. In BNs, a set of nodes represents the salient variables in the system of interest. For example, the BN in Figure 4.1 depicts regional-scale conditions (e.g. habitat density, large log density trend, human population density and predicted road densities) that affect the population density of American martens (*Martes americana*). For each variable, all relevant and discernible states are defined (e.g. zero, low and high habitat density). Arrows indicate where conditional dependencies exist between 'parent' and 'child' nodes. The network of nodes and arrows expresses the chain of logic or causal argument that links events to outcomes. Underlying each child node is a *conditional* probability table (CPT) that quantifies the probabilistic effects that parent nodes have on it (parent nodes contain a *marginal* probability table).

The graphical structure of BNs allows compact (and easily reconfigurable) representations of interacting variables in potentially complex systems. When the graphical structure is fully specified, and the CPTs parameterised, the BN model can be used for predictive and diagnostic reasoning about uncertain systems. BNs can also be extended to explicitly aid decision-making by including decision nodes to represent specific choices and utility nodes to measure the cost of particular choices as well as the value of predicted outcomes. In the example BN, the grey boxes denote decision nodes relating to timber management and road development, and the hexagons are utility nodes that tell us about the cost of different management choices or the social value associated with different states of marten population density.

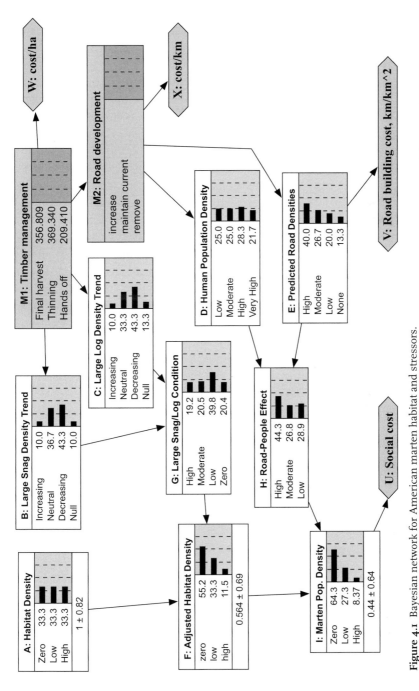

Figure 4.1 Bayesian network for American marten habitat and stressors.
(*Source:* https://web.archive.org/web/20170222003620/http://www.plexuseco.com/BNApplications/bnmodelnewapps.htm).

in Australia and overseas (Aguilera et al. 2011; Barton et al. 2012). We used the snowball sampling method to recruit interviewees. We first identified individuals who met the criteria for inclusion through our contacts in the NRM and environmental modelling community and then sought their recommendations for other potential interviewees.

We interviewed 31 people (6 women, 25 men) in total. Respondents came from 19 separate workshops that had been conducted in urban and regional centres across southeastern Australia. They self-identified as environmental scientists (13), environmental/NRM managers (9), policymakers and/or planners (5), horticulturalists (2), a nurse and a farmer. Some respondents also had more than one 'role' – almost half (48%, 15 of 31) were project managers; 6 were modelling facilitators and 25 were workshop participants.

The hour-long interviews were done face-to-face. Respondents filled out structured survey items that we developed from relevant literature and answered open-ended questions. Interviews were recorded, with consent from the interviewee, and transcribed. A coding manual was created to categorise the themes that emerged in the open-ended interviews. All interview items were coded using this manual. The third author (B.W.) coded all interviews, and the second author (F.F.) double coded 20% (6 of 31) of the interviews. Percentage agreement of accuracy of the original coding was 93% and the inter-rater reliability measured by Cohen's kappa was 0.79. This suggests robust coding categories, producing a good deal of consistency between the independent coders.

Although we interviewed 31 people, the sample size often varied between items (from $n=26$ to $n=31$). This reflects the nature of surveys and interviews; some participants chose not to answer some questions, or simply did not have an opinion about some items we asked about. For a number of questions, the summed percentage across different response categories exceeds 100%. This is because, in many cases, participants offered more than one, non-mutually exclusive response to the question asked (for example, there might be more than one reason why someone participated in the workshop: e.g. for their scientific expertise and their local knowledge).

4.2.2 Measuring Intentions versus Behaviour

Despite the title of our chapter, our empirical research did not include a final measure of 'model uptake'. In many cases, our respondents' projects were still in progress at the time of our interview, and it was too early to tell whether, or to what extent, the model would be adopted. Our

Table 4.1 *Categories of Responses to the Interview Question, 'Would You/Do You Use the Model?'*

Responses		% of Respondents	n/N
Yes	Using model	13	4/31
	Use static output	29	9/31
	I would use it	55	17/31
No	No faith in model	6	2/31
	System too complex/uncertain to trust the model	13	4/31
	Impractical to implement (e.g. due to social or political barriers)	10	3/31

discussion and our correlational analyses therefore rely on a proxy measure for actual adoption: their intention to use the model, hereafter called 'willingness to adopt'.

We measured 'willingness to adopt' with a direct interview question: 'Would you or do you use the model?' We then coded responses to this question into several categories, shown in Table 4.1, and then further collapsed those categories to 'yes' or 'no' for the purpose of calculating Spearman's correlation (*r*) values to assess relationships with other items, for instance, specific scale items about trust and knowledge.

An important caveat is that there are limits to what an expression of intention can tell us about actual implementation. According the theory of planned behaviour (Ajzen 1991), intentions (in this case, adopting BN models for decision support) are formed by attitudes (e.g. how favourably we regard the model), subjective norms (e.g. perceived social pressure to use, or not use, a decision support model) and perceived behaviour control (e.g. whether we think we can run the BN model ourselves, or what obstacles we perceive to their use). Under some conditions, intentions will be a good predictor of behaviour, but not always; perceived behavioural control can disrupt the intention–behaviour link, as can external obstacles, or 'actual behavioural control'. We discuss logistical barriers and external factors that may stop even the best of intentions from being translated into actual behaviour at the end of this chapter.

4.3 RESULTS AND DISCUSSION

4.3.1 Knowledge

Before we go further, we need to clarify the term 'knowledge'. We did not test knowledge directly, that is, we did not give our participants a

BN 'test' or formally examine their understanding. Instead, our survey items (Table 4.2) ask about statistical training, self-ratings of knowledge, interest and experience, familiarity with BNs and opinions about their relative difficulty compared to other models.

4.3.1.1 Our Prior Beliefs

We began this project wondering whether limited statistical knowledge might threaten model acceptance and the chance of uptake. At the same time, we knew there were also reasons to *not* expect a relationship between statistical knowledge and acceptance of BNs. For decades, sociologists of science have admonished a 'deficit model of science', in which reluctance to accept new technologies (e.g. genetically modified food, nuclear power, nanotechnology) is attributed to a deficit in relevant scientific knowledge, or lack of scientific literacy more generally (Wynne 1992). At the risk of being accused of subscribing to this outdated theory, we nonetheless decided to investigate the relationship between knowledge and willingness to adopt.

4.3.1.2 What We Have Learned

Our sample was statistically literate, but had little prior knowledge of BNs. Together, the participants' responses to questions about statistical training and their self-knowledge items paint a picture of a statistically literate group of respondents. All but 3 of our 31 respondents had knowledge of some tertiary level statistics. For many (39%, 12 of 31), this was simply an introductory applied statistics course, but for most (52%, 16 of 31) it was more. Most had some hands-on experience in using statistical methods, and largely neutral attitudes towards or no opinions about Bayesian methods. The majority (61%, 19 of 31) reported they rarely read statistics or methodology articles, but almost two-thirds (65%, 20 of 31) rated their statistical knowledge as above average; another 23% (7 of 31) rated themselves as about average. Just over a third (35%, 11 of 31) said their work involved a lot of statistics, and a further 16% (5 of 31) said it involved a moderate amount.

Despite high levels of statistical literacy, our respondents rated their familiarity with BNs as low. When we asked them to recollect how they felt about BNs *before* the workshop, familiarity ratings were very low: over 90% (29 of 31) of responses clustered between the scale markers 'never heard of them' and 'heard of them, but unsure how they work' (the lowest 3 points of our 13-point response scale). Familiarity ratings for how they feel *now* increased by an average of 3.4 points on

Table 4.2 *The Full Set of Structured Response Survey Questions about Statistical Knowledge, Presented with Their Corresponding Scale*

All scales were 13-point scales (0–12). For reporting purposes, responses were collapsed into three categories using breakpoints at 5 and 7.

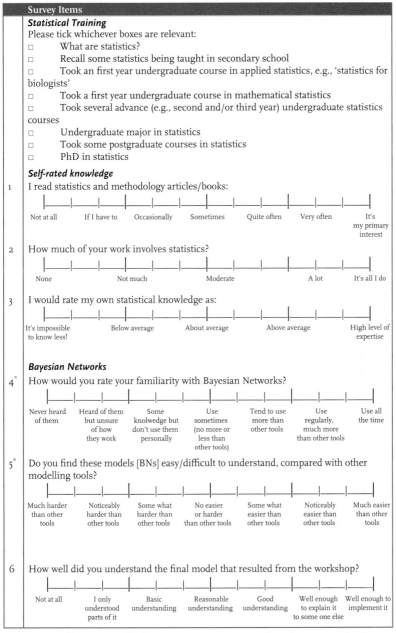

Survey Items

Statistical Training

Please tick whichever boxes are relevant:

☐   What are statistics?

☐   Recall some statistics being taught in secondary school

☐   Took an first year undergraduate course in applied statistics, e.g., 'statistics for biologists'

☐   Took a first year undergraduate course in mathematical statistics

☐   Took several advance (e.g., second and/or third year) undergraduate statistics courses

☐   Undergraduate major in statistics

☐   Took some postgraduate courses in statistics

☐   PhD in statistics

Self-rated knowledge

1   I read statistics and methodology articles/books:

Not at all   If I have to   Occasionally   Sometimes   Quite often   Very often   It's my primary interest

2   How much of your work involves statistics?

None   Not much   Moderate   A lot   It's all I do

3   I would rate my own statistical knowledge as:

It's impossible to know less!   Below average   About average   Above average   High level of expertise

Bayesian Networks

4[*]   How would you rate your familiarity with Bayesian Networks?

Never heard of them   Heard of them but unsure of how they work   Some knowledge but don't use them personally   Use sometimes (no more or less than other tools)   Tend to use more than other tools   Use regularly, much more than other tools   Use all the time

5[*]   Do you find these models [BNs] easy/difficult to understand, compared with other modelling tools?

Much harder than other tools   Noticeably harder than other tools   Some what harder than other tools   No easier or harder than other tools   Some what easier than other tools   Noticeably easier than other tools   Much easier than other tools

6   How well did you understand the final model that resulted from the workshop?

Not at all   I only understood parts of it   Basic understanding   Reasonable understanding   Good understanding   Well enough to explain it to some one else   Well enough to implement it

[a]   Respondents were asked to answer questions 4 and 5 twice: once reflecting on their familiarity with and the relative ease/difficult of BNs before participating in their relevant model building workshop, and a second time reflecting feelings now.

the 13-point scale. But responses were still predominantly (75%) clustered at the low end of the scale, around the marker 'some knowledge but don't use them personally' (i.e. between points 4 and 6 of the 13-point scale). Nevertheless, a shift of 3.4 points is over a quarter of the full response scale. Clearly, the workshop instruction and explanation made an impact on this item.

We also asked respondents to rate how easy BNs were to understand (relative to other methods), again, recollecting how they felt *before* the workshop and subsequently, how they feel *now*. *Before*, the majority (56%, 13 of 23) were neutral about whether BN models were easier to understand than other modelling tools. When considering how they felt *now*, their ratings increased by an average of 2 points on our 13-point scale (15% of the scale). Figure 4.2 shows the *before* and *now* responses to the familiarity with BNs, and ease of understanding items. We additionally asked respondents to rate their understanding of the final model produced in the workshop. Just over three quarters (22 of 29) rated their understanding 'good' (Figure 4.2). In response to an interview question, over three-quarters (77%, 24 of 31) said that they would be willing to adopt the model.

A little bit of (BN) knowledge goes a long way. Our results suggest that even a rather vague sense of familiarity with the method is sufficient to carry the positive attitude towards adoption. This claim is based on a detected relationship between our scale item 'familiarity' (see Table 4.2) and our interview question about 'willingness to adopt' (i.e. 'would you/do you use the model?'). The correlation between responses on these two items is high (Spearman's r=0.62) – but only for the *now* familiarity rating, not the *before* rating (Figure 4.3). We find this relationship especially interesting, for two reasons. First, nearly three-quarters (74%, 23 of 31) of the responses to the familiarity *now* question clustered around the scale marker 'some knowledge [of BNs] but don't use them personally'. The other quarter of responses were evenly distributed either side of this cluster (13% were less familiar, i.e. 'heard of them but unsure how they work'; 13% were more familiar, i.e., used them 'more than other tools' or 'regularly', data not shown). This relationship stands out amongst other potential correlates of willingness to adopt (e.g., UnderstandFinalModel r=0.39; EasyToUnderstandNow r=0.42; Figure 4.3). Second, the correlation between familiarity *before* and willingness to adopt is weak (r=0.11). Earlier, we described the average shift in responses from *before* to *now* as a quarter of the response scale, or 3.4 points. It is therefore the growing of familiarity with BNs through the workshop process that brings the

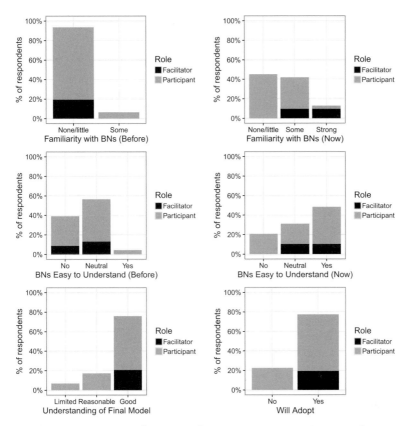

Figure 4.2 Summary of responses from questions on Bayesian networks (see Table 4.2). For all questions, n ranged from 29 to 31. The exception was the question on whether BNs were easy/difficult to understand compared with other modelling tools before participating in the workshop. Of the respondents, 26% (8 of 31) did not give an answer. In retrospect, we should have provided a 'don't know' option for this question.

association with positive attitudes towards model adoption, rather than previous exposure or experience before the workshop.

We find the relationship between nascent feelings of familiarity and willingness to adopt encouraging, as it suggests that an individual's positive attitude towards model adoption does not depend on them having a high degree of BN skill and expertise. This alleviates the potential burden facilitators may feel to offer extensive statistical instruction in BNs; our results suggest that such an investment may not be necessary. Here we have provided evidence that even a reasonably new and vague familiarity with BNs is associated with a positive intention to adopt the

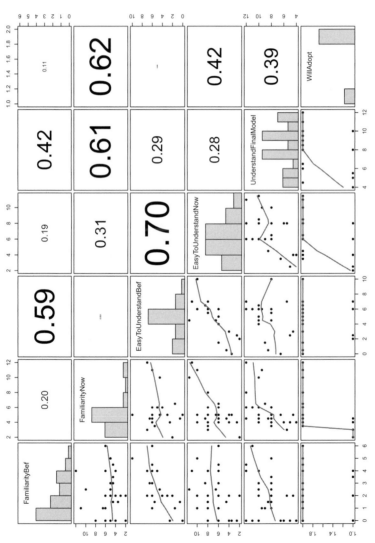

Figure 4.3 Scatter plot matrices, histograms and Spearman's correlations for knowledge factors and willingness to adopt. On the diagonal are histograms for each factor. Below the diagonal are pairwise scatterplots with a loess smoother. Above the diagonal, pairwise Spearman's correlations are shown with font size scaled by the absolute value of the correlation.

Figure 4.3 *(continued)*

FamiliarityBef = How would you rate your familiarity with BNs before the workshop?
FamiliarityNow = How would you rate your familiarity with BNs now?
EasyToUnderstandBef = Do you find BNs easy to understand (compared with other modelling tools) before the workshop?
EasyToUnderstandNow = Do you find BNs easy to understand now?
UnderstandFinalModel = How well did you understand the final model that resulted from the workshop?
WillAdopt = Willingness to Adopt (Yes/No).

model. However, we caution against over-interpretation: this is evidence pertaining to a knowledge (familiarity)–intention relationship, not an understanding–behaviour relationship. While we cannot make claims about uptake behaviour based on our data, it does suggest that a vague familiarity with – rather than an extensive knowledge of – BNs may be sufficient to encourage uptake.

4.3.2 Trust

Trust is a basic necessity for virtually all forms of exchange (Arrow 1974). Knowledge sharing for collaborative learning is no exception (Usoro et al. 2007). This is well-recognised and numerous papers have emphasised the importance of communication and trust-building as a foundation for effective engagement and collaboration among actors in science, policy and management (e.g. Gutrich et al. 2005; Reed 2008; Webb et al. 2010). In situations that involve a scarce resource, competing interests, incompatible objectives and potential for conflict, the task of building trust amongst diverse actors is challenging and there has been little in-depth treatment of just *how* to accomplish this.

Although ubiquitous and superficially obvious, trust is a complex construct. There are many ways to define it. In line with Mayer et al. (1995, p. 712), we regard it as a 'willingness of a party to be vulnerable to the actions of another party based on the expectation that the other will perform a particular action important to the trustor, irrespective of the ability to monitor or control that party'. Different authors from psychology, management and organisational theory (e.g. Kramer 1999) have identified a multitude of factors that influence the formation of trust belief (e.g. Butler 1991 identified 11). However, we follow Mayer et al. (1995) and Dietz and Den Hartog (2006) in collapsing the range of factors in the literature into a parsimonious set of five factors: propensity to trust, and perceived ability, integrity, reliability and benevolence. The definitions and shades of meaning of these factors are given in Table 4.3.

In Table 4.3, we map example items from our trust surveys on to the five factors identified above. We do this for two aspects: *interpersonal trust* (e.g. trust in modelling facilitators) and *trust in models*. As the five factors were primarily developed to measure interpersonal trust, generalising to trust in models is controversial. Trust in models has clear parallels with the literature on trust in automation – that is, trust in technology that 'actively selects data, transforms information, makes decisions, or controls processes' (Lee and See 2004, p. 50). While the mainstream trust literature provides an appropriate theoretical base for understanding trust in automation, we should be cautious when generalising from one to the other. Particularly because automation lacks independent intentionality, such as the intention to behave with benevolence and integrity, and there is no process of social exchange in interactions with automation, as there is with interpersonal trust (Lee and See 2004). We nevertheless align our trust in model items with the five factors in Table 4.3, and suggest it be interpreted as a guide to loosely equivalent factors, rather than a claim to rigorous conceptual validity.

Table 4.4 shows the full list of trust survey items, with response scales. We consider two elements of *interpersonal trust*: trust in the modelling facilitator and trust in the way the broader participatory process was managed (Items 14–18 in Table 4.4). There will naturally be interactions between interpersonal trust in the facilitator and perceptions of the participatory process, and these may be difficult to separate. Nevertheless, we make this distinction because the modelling facilitator of a workshop may not be the same person managing the participatory processes of recruitment, liaison, follow up and so on. This distinction between facilitator and process becomes important, and complex, in some of the cases discussed in our interviews. This is especially true when the job of facilitating particular workshops is subcontracted to a third party (i.e. neither the primary modeller nor project manager).

Whilst there are no standard methods or measures for evaluating the quality or effectiveness of a participatory process, Rowe and Frewer (2000) have proposed a set of desirable features, such as independence (unbiasedness), clarity of task definition, availability of resources to fulfil the brief and genuine ability to influence decisions. We addressed these in our interview questions on trust in facilitators and the management of the participatory process.

Table 4.3 *Definitions and Meanings of Factors that Influence the Formation of Trust Belief*

Factors	Definition in the Context of Assessing Trustworthiness	Example Questions from Our Survey: Modelling Facilitators	Example Questions from Our Survey: Models
Propensity to trust	An inherent *level of willingness to trust others*	Is well-regarded by people whose judgement I trust I was in a good mood on the day of the workshop	BNs have been highly recommended to me When I think of the whole model building experience, I have a good feeling about it
Ability	Trust in the knowledge, skills and capability of another	Knowledgeable about BNs	Risk of inappropriate decision based on this model is high/low
Integrity	Trust in the adherence to a set of acceptable principles by another	Integrity	BNs more transparent
Reliability (predictability)	Trust in consistency and dependability of another	Incorporated contributions from participants appropriately into the model	Gut feelings are more reliable for making decisions than models
Benevolence	Trust in the goodwill and motives of another	Really wanted to help clarify what was important to us and work towards a solution	Reliance on the model will save the agency time and resources

Source: After Mayer et al. 1995; McFall 1987; Dietz and Den Hartog 2006.

Table 4.4 *Structured Response Trust Survey Questions Presented with Their Corresponding Scale*

All scales were 13-point scales (numbered 0–12). For reporting purposes, responses were collapsed into three categories using breakpoints at 5 and 7.

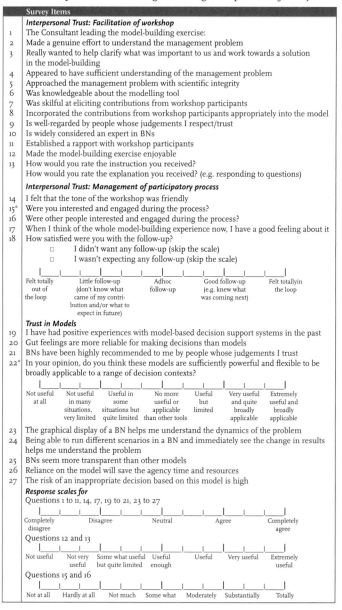

	Survey Items
	Interpersonal Trust: Facilitation of workshop
1	The Consultant leading the model-building exercise:
2	Made a genuine effort to understand the management problem
3	Really wanted to help clarify what was important to us and work towards a solution in the model-building
4	Appeared to have sufficient understanding of the management problem
5	Approached the management problem with scientific integrity
6	Was knowledgeable about the modelling tool
7	Was skilful at eliciting contributions from workshop participants
8	Incorporated the contributions from workshop participants appropriately into the model
9	Is well-regarded by people whose judgements I respect/trust
10	Is widely considered an expert in BNs
11	Established a rapport with workshop participants
12	Made the model-building exercise enjoyable
13	How would you rate the instruction you received? How would you rate the explanation you received? (e.g. responding to questions)
	Interpersonal Trust: Management of participatory process
14	I felt that the tone of the workshop was friendly
15*	Were you interested and engaged during the process?
16	Were other people interested and engaged during the process?
17	When I think of the whole model-building experience now, I have a good feeling about it
18	How satisfied were you with the follow-up?

☐ I didn't want any follow-up (skip the scale)
☐ I wasn't expecting any follow-up (skip the scale)

| Felt totally out of the loop | Little follow-up (don't know what came of my contribution and/or what to expect in future) | Adhoc follow-up | Good follow-up (e.g. knew what was coming next) | Felt totallyin the loop |

	Trust in Models
19	I have had positive experiences with model-based decision support systems in the past
20	Gut feelings are more reliable for making decisions than models
21	BNs have been highly recommended to me by people whose judgements I trust
22*	In your opinion, do you think these models are sufficiently powerful and flexible to be broadly applicable to a range of decision contexts?

| Not useful at all | Not useful in many situations, very limited | Useful in some situations but quite limited | No more useful or applicable than other tools | Useful but limited | Very useful and quite broadly applicable | Extremely useful and broadly applicable |

23	The graphical display of a BN helps me understand the dynamics of the problem
24	Being able to run different scenarios in a BN and immediately see the change in results helps me understand the problem
25	BNs seem more transparent than other models
26	Reliance on the model will save the agency time and resources
27	The risk of an inappropriate decision based on this model is high

Response scales for
Questions 1 to 11, 14, 17, 19 to 21, 23 to 27

| Completely disagree | Disagree | Neutral | Agree | Completely agree |

Questions 12 and 13

| Not useful | Not very useful | Some what useful but quite limited | Useful enough | Useful | Very useful | Extremely useful |

Questions 15 and 16

| Not at all | Hardly at all | Not much | Some what | Moderately | Substantially | Totally |

a This question was not asked of respondents who were facilitators.

b Respondents were asked to answer this question twice: once reflecting on whether they thought BNs were sufficiently powerful and flexible to be broadly applicable to a variety of decision contexts *before* participating in their relevant model building workshop, and a second time reflecting on those ratings *now*.

4.3.2.1 *Our Prior Beliefs*

When people participate in a well-facilitated and meaningful model-building process, where they are afforded the opportunity to contribute substantively to defining the problem, developing objectives, sharing knowledge, questioning assumptions and jointly constructing the knowledge base for the model, participants will develop trust in the resulting models and uptake will follow naturally.

4.3.2.2 *What We Have Learned: Interpersonal Trust*

Modelling facilitation is a complex job and yet we found it was done surprisingly well. It was interesting and unexpected that evaluations of the facilitators were so overwhelmingly positive. For example, all 31 respondents agreed that their modelling facilitator made a genuine effort to understand the management problem, really wanted to help clarify what was important to them and work towards a solution in the *model building* and appeared to have sufficient understanding of the management problem. Nearly all respondents agreed that their modelling facilitator approached the management problem with scientific integrity (97%, 30 of 31), was knowledgeable about the modelling tool (94%, 29 of 31), was skilful at eliciting inputs from workshop participants (87%, 26 of 30) and incorporated the contributions from workshop participants appropriately into the model (90%, 27 of 30).

Respondents were also positive about the reputation of the facilitators: 86% (19 of 22) agreed that the modelling facilitator was well-regarded by people whose judgements they respected or trusted, and 62% (18 of 29) agreed that the facilitator was widely considered to be an expert in BNs. Nearly all the respondents (93%, 28 of 30) reported that the modelling facilitator established a rapport with workshop participants and made the model-building exercise enjoyable for most of them (70%, 21 of 30). With respect to technical matters in the workshop, 97% (28 of 29) found the instructions received to be very or sufficiently useful, and 79% (23 of 29) found the explanations provided very useful.

In the interview, we provided opportunities for respondents to elaborate on the performance of the modelling facilitators. The coded interview responses are summarised in Table 4.5. Respondents overwhelming felt that their facilitator was independent with respect to the management problem, and had sufficient understanding of the problem (90% and 93% respectively). The majority (73%) also agreed that the facilitator appreciated the constraints they were subject to. When asked about things in particular that the facilitator did really well or poorly,

Table 4.5 *Interview Responses about Interpersonal Trust in Modelling Facilitators*

Interview Question	Responses	% of Respondents	n/N
Were facilitators neutral / independent?	Neutral/independent	90	27/30
	Biased (management problem)	10	3/30
	Biased (BNs)	7	2/30
Did they have sufficient understanding of the problem?	Yes	93	26/28
	No	4	1/28
	Don't know	4	1/28
Did they appreciate the constraints you're working under?	Yes	73	19/26
	No	27	7/26
	Not applicable[a]	13	4/30

Interview Question	Responses	Count of Positive Responses	Count of Negative Responses
Was there anything in particular that the facilitators did really well (positive) or poorly (negative)?	Managing personalities	3	0
	Engaging stakeholders	3	3
	Made an effort	9	0
	Explaining BNs	6	0
	Technical competence	5	1
	Facilitation	4	1
	Structuring models	2	0
	Eliciting information	2	2
	Managing time / info	2	6
	Collating data	4	0
	General comment	11	0
	Subtotal	51	13

[a] Some respondents who did not have a management-related role with respect to the problem declined to provide a response to this question.

there were four times as many positive comments as negative comments (Table 4.5). These interview results reinforce the positive findings from the trust survey data.

Our highly positive evaluations of facilitators perhaps require explanation. They may, of course, be the result of a biased sample, where only those with positive feelings about their experience replied to our request to be interviewed. Whilst we do not dismiss this possibility, a more typical bias pattern would be a bimodal distribution, that is, a disproportionate number of both positive and negative responses because people with extreme experiences self-select. Although social norms might sometimes inhibit negative personal statements in recorded interviews, our respondents also had the opportunity to express any neutral or negative sentiments on our survey scales that they filled in themselves. They took no such opportunity. An alternative explanation for the consistently positive ratings may reflect the fact that almost all (94%) of our respondents had been involved in more than one workshop, and some 40% had been involved in more than five workshops. They therefore had the opportunity to build rapport and genuine trust over multiple encounters. If respondents ever did have misgivings about facilitators, they had been resolved through repeated interaction.

Experiences of the broader participatory process were also very positive. The majority (71%, 20 of 28) felt that their participation in the workshop would make a difference (Table 4.6). There was strong agreement that people were clear about what was expected of them in the workshops (86%, 24 of 28), and 40% of respondents (12 of 30) believed that relevant people were included in the workshops. However, two-thirds of the respondents (20 of 30) suggested that some people were missing, either from the scientific (7%), technical (17%) or broader community (17%), but many of them (35%, 7 of the 20) believed that these absences were not a serious problem. Only one person thought it was a problem, and 17% of respondents (5 of 30) thought there were excess people in the workshop (Table 4.6).

Over 90% felt that the tone of the workshop process was friendly (27 of 29). All participant respondents reported being personally interested and engaged, and 93% of respondents (28 of 30) believed that others in the workshop were highly interested and engaged. On the whole, after the experience, more than half (55%, 17 of 31) had a 'good feeling' about it, whilst 42% (13 of 31) were neutral and only one reported a negative feeling. Respondents were mostly satisfied with the level of follow up (71%, 17 of 24), but a quarter (6 of 24) felt 'left out of the loop'.

Table 4.6 *Interview Responses about Management of the Participatory Process*

Interview Question	Responses	% of Respondents	n/N
Was it clear what was expected of you?	Yes	86	24/28
	Somewhat	14	4/28
	No	0	0/28
Did participant believe their participation would make a difference?	Yes	71	20/28
	Some	21	6/28
	No	7	2/28
Were the relevant people there?	Yes	40	12/30
	Some missing but OK	23	7/30
	Broader missing	17	5/30
	Scientific missing	7	2/30
	Technical missing	17	5/30
	Some missing not OK	3	1/30
	Excess people	17	5/30
Did you have access to resources? (e.g. background information, data, maps, experts, decision analysts, etc.)	Yes	46	13/28
	No, but didn't need	29	8/28
	No, and needed	18	5/28
	Data doesn't exist	21	6/28
Was the workshop well planned and executed?	Yes	71	20/28
	Somewhat	11	3/28
	No clear agenda	7	2/28
	Facilitator inexperience	7	2/28
	Time poorly managed	18	5/28
Did you look at the problem from many different perspectives?	Yes, formal	53	16/30
	Yes, informal	13	4/30
	No, should have	3	1/30
	No	0	0/30
	Not relevant	30	9/30
Were group dynamics managed effectively?	Yes	89	24/27
	Somewhat	7	2/27
	No	4	1/27
Did you have direct interaction with the model?	Yes	31	9/29
	No	69	20/29

Three-quarters of respondents (21 of 28) said that they either had access to the necessary resources, or did not need them. But about 20% reported that they did not have the necessary resources and/or the relevant data did not exist (Table 4.6). Though some respondents were critical of aspects of workshop process such as the lack of a clear agenda (7%, 2 of 28) or poor time management (18%, 5 of 28), most respondents

(71%, 20 of 28) agreed that the workshops were well-planned and well run, with adequate time for discussion and deliberation.

About half the respondents (53%, 16 of 30) reported formally examining the problem from different perspectives, and a further 13% reported doing so informally. To explore issues of conflict, we asked if group dynamics were managed effectively in the workshop, and prompted respondents to consider how potential conflict was managed and whether people had equal opportunities to contribute. A massive 89% (24 of 27) of the participants believed that group dynamics were well managed, with another 7% stating that they were somewhat well managed (including someone who thought contributions were unequal between participants, but not to the detriment of the process). Managing a group well – particularly one that contains vocal and/or domineering individuals – is not easy but can be worthwhile. For example, one interviewee – self-described as 'cantankerous' – revealed that he had been deliberately placed in a sub-group with a well-respected and neutral academic, after an initial workshop revealed that conflicts of interest and personalities within the broader group would be detrimental to the whole exercise. He clearly thought this was a good idea:

> R9: Well, you're in a workshop, in a group situation and you have opposition companies there who will utilise your information for their financial gain and you can do vice versa. But what happens, is people close up and you don't say anything... or you give misinformation to mislead your opposition companies. So I don't think [the facilitators] got a great deal [from the first, large workshop]. That's why they went to the [smaller] workshop situation, where there were about two, three people with non-conflicting interest... it was a strategy to get the confidence of the interviewees, to express their techniques [knowledge].
> I: So you thought that your skills or knowledge would be...
> R9: Used by the competition against me, virtually giving my bank account details to them... you've got to realise that within the academic community there's this perceived sharing of knowledge. But in the commercial world, no, you've got to maintain a cutting edge above everyone else. [...] So that's why they went those [smaller] workshops.
> I: Right OK.
> R9: So I was there with Dr XXX, so there was no conflict of interest, which I guess made me comfortable and made him comfortable, and of course, he's a knowledge sharer, I'm a knowledge user. So [the facilitator] wanted that knowledge to come out of me and to be

questioned by Dr XXX in the same process, and that was a comfortable way of doing it, for sure.

Over two-thirds of the respondents (20 of 29) did not get to interact directly with the model (Table 4.6). In most cases, this was because the purpose of the workshop was to jointly develop and parameterise the model, and there was no operational model as such for hands-on interactive use. Nevertheless, some respondents reported that they would have liked the opportunity to interact with the model.

One issue that emerged from a few interviews was a preference for a facilitator who had some connection to the local community:

> R24: The way it worked was the [principal contractors...] engaged a consultant to run the meetings and the local level workshops, and that consultant was from...you know, outside the local area. I just thought it would be better run if there was more direct involvement by someone at a local level. For me, it was the local issues, and the consultants tend to sort of fly in for the afternoon and then tend to disappear.

This sentiment was echoed by another respondent:

> R29: Yeah there's always a bit of...what would you call it, a healthy scepticism, I suppose, of people sitting in [the capital city] coming to the coast to tell us how it all works and what's going on, but that was certainly balanced out by incorporating local consultants trained in that system to be able to prepare the plans or to do the work with the model.

4.3.2.3 What We Have Learned: Trust in Models

Trust in models is conceptually complicated, but was not a barrier for most respondents. It is clear that participants felt a high degree of interpersonal trust in both the people and process. But did they feel the same level of regard for the models themselves? Our trust survey questions asked about a respondent's general trust in models, trust in BN models in particular and trust in the BN model that resulted from the participatory model-building process (Table 4.4).

Our sample included respondents with a mix of modelling experience, ranging from no experience at all, to some experience, to skilled modellers. Over half of the respondents (55%, 16 of 29) had had positive experiences with model-based decision support systems in the past, and the same percentage (17 of 31) agreed that gut feelings are less reliable for making decisions than models. For both questions, most of the remaining respondents were neutral. About two-thirds of respondents (66%, 19 of 29) reported that BNs had been highly recommended to them by people whose judgement they respect or trust.

To canvass respondents' views on the capabilities of BNs, we asked for their opinion on whether BNs are sufficiently powerful and flexible to be broadly applicable to a range of decision contexts – an attribute we call 'versatility'. Thinking about their opinion *before* the workshop, 50% (10 of 20) felt BNs were highly versatile, while 25% thought they were moderately versatile and 13% considered them limited. Over a third of the respondents (11 of 31) felt unable to answer the question, and in retrospect we should have offered a 'don't know' option. Giving their opinion *now*, the non-response rate to the question fell to 3%, and the percentage who considered BNs to be highly versatile rose to 80% (24 of 30).

Anecdotally, common reasons that have been used for advocating the use of BNs include: (a) that the graphical structure maps and communicates relationships explicitly; (b) that this makes BNs more transparent; and (c) that the ability to explore the outcomes of different scenarios aids problem understanding (Reckhow 1999; Cain 2001; Bromley et al. 2005; Henriksen et al. 2012). In our empirical data, most respondents (80%, 24 of 30) agreed that the graphical nature of BNs helped them understand the dynamics of the problem and a similar percentage (83%, 25 of 30) concurred that observing the changes from running different scenarios was helpful to understanding.

Almost two-thirds (63%, 19 of 30) agreed that BNs seem more transparent than other models, while 23% (7 of 30) were neutral on this point and 13% (4 of 30) disagreed. Probing further on issues of transparency, our interview questions (Table 4.7) focused on the extent to which boundary conditions (i.e. spatial and temporal context), choices and assumptions were explicitly addressed in the BN development.

Among the respondents, 79% of them indicated that the spatial extent of the problem was defined before the workshop (e.g. 'the BN only applies to this particular catchment'), and where it was not, it was discussed and resolved during the workshop (Table 4.7). Unfortunately, temporal extent was less clear. Only 38% of respondents recalled a time horizon being specified beforehand (e.g. 'the BN applies for the next 5 years'). In other cases, it was discussed (34%), but not always resolved (17%).

Table 4.7 *Interview Responses about Transparency and Clarity in the BN Model Development Process*

Interview Question	Responses		% of Respondents	n/N
Did you discuss the spatial extent of the problem?	Defined beforehand		79	23/29
	Can't recall		0	0/29
	Discussed	Yes	21	6/29
		No	0	0/29
	Resolved	Yes	21	6/29
		Partial	0	0/29
		No	0	0/29
Did you discuss the temporal extent of the problem?	Defined beforehand		38	11/29
	Can't recall		7	2/29
	Discussed	Yes	34	10/29
		No	21	6/29
	Resolved	Yes	17	5/29
		Partial	21	6/29
		No	17	5/29
Were other assumptions explicitly acknowledged?	Defined beforehand		38	10/26
	Can't recall		23	6/26
	Discussed	Yes	38	10/26
		No	8	2/26
	Resolved	Yes	12	3/26
		Partial	23	6/26
		No	8	2/26
Were you satisfied with the trade-offs that were made?	Yes	Generally	87	26/30
	Somewhat	Difficult to do	13	4/30
		Discussed	17	5/30
	No	Not handled well	3	1/30
		Model overly simple	3	1/30
		Model overly complex	3	1/30

For some, this was problematic. For example, when asked whether the temporal extent was discussed and agreed on, one commented: '*No, no. It's an interesting point. I remember during the development [wondering] if we were going to do seasonal probabilities as an input. [For example], algal blooms... if you average them over a year they look unusually bad in winter and unusually good in summer.*'

The majority of respondents (77%, 20 of 26) recalled at least acknowledging, if not always fully discussing, other assumptions in the model-building process (Table 4.7). And finally, despite the difficulty of negotiating necessary trade-offs in model development, 87% (26 of 30) were satisfied with the trade-offs made, with regard to matters such as simplicity versus detail and complexity of model structure (Table 4.7).

Many people appreciated the features of a BN that are associated with transparency. One commented: '*The [BN]...certainly beats the Multi Criteria Analysis in being able to graphically illustrate. [...] being able to click this and show the relationship change [...] people love that.*' But not everyone is comfortable with it. Some participants spoke of concerns that greater transparency exposes decisions to external scrutiny, which is not always welcome. For example, when asked if there was any resistance to using BNs as a modelling tool within their organisation, R11 remarked: '*Yeah, I think there's a resistance to structured decision-making generally. BNs are just another one. [...] I think there's also resistance to transparency generally. Because Ministers and the people subordinate to them like to make decisions without being [scrutinised]... You know... it's a command and control thing.*'

Table 4.8 gives a snapshot of people's perceived strengths and weaknesses of BNs generally, as identified in the interviews. The most oft-cited strengths included flexibility (to incorporate information from diverse sources), good conceptual overview and the ability to support scenario and probabilistic analysis. A respondent with quantitative modelling experience and a sophisticated understanding of uncertainty articulated the rationale for moving away from deterministic models in favour of a tool like BNs:

> R4: *I've got a new project coming up and I'm considering using those ahead of some deterministic models. [...] Because I know the flexibility in them and well, first you get that explicit probability distribution carried through the entire model, and you can show that. I think with a lot of environmental data and especially with the type of projects I work on, they're only one-year projects and so the data isn't very good, [BNs] focus on the uncertainty rather than anything else and I think that's really important. A lot of the models being developed here now are very complex deterministic models with many, many variables and people don't know how to handle the uncertainty in the data, so [...] maybe you can do a [sensitivity analysis], you know, with one of the parameters, how are you going to do it for multiple and I think that's why a Bayesian Network is strong in that sense, yeah.*

The interview findings on perceived strengths of BNs are consistent with the survey results and provide corroborating evidence for the reasons to use BNs that are cited in the literature. The two most commonly raised weaknesses of BNs were that they can be subjective and difficult to understand. However, all in all, there were roughly twice as

Table 4.8 *Interview Responses about Perceived strengths and Weaknesses of BN Models*

Responses	% of Respondents	n/N
Strengths		
Easy	21	6/28
Graphical	18	5/28
Conceptual overview	46	13/28
Structured thinking	11	3/28
Causal relationships	21	6/28
Drill-down	11	3/28
Identify gaps	14	4/28
Communication	18	5/28
Flexible (incorporate information from diverse sources)	50	14/28
Updatable	21	6/28
Probabilities good	29	8/28
Transparent	25	7/28
Scenario analysis	29	8/28
Total positive comments = 88		
Weaknesses		
Hard to understand	21	6/28
Complexity	14	4/28
Scale	14	4/28
Continuous variables are often discretised	11	3/28
Clunky	11	3/28
Not dynamic	14	4/28
Subjective	25	7/28
Hard to weight opinions	7	2/28
Errors compound	11	3/28
Not informative	21	6/28
Total negative comments = 42		

many positive comments made throughout the interviews than negative comments (Table 4.8).

With respect to the BN model that resulted from the participatory model-building process, no one in our sample definitively identified other types of models that they felt would be more appropriate for the job – 85% felt that there probably weren't other types of models that would be more appropriate (Table 4.9). Some of those respondents (9 of 22) explicitly referred to other existing (numerical) models that were relevant to particular aspects of the management problem, but ultimately, none felt these other models to be more appropriate than BNs for the problem they were addressing. Despite this, a sizeable percentage

Table 4.9 *Interview Responses about Trust in Models*

Interview Question	Responses	% of Respondents	n/N
Other types of models more appropriate for the job?	Yes	0	0/26
	No	85	22/26
	Don't know	15	4/26
Resistance to using BNs within your organisation?	Yes	39	11/28
	No	57	16/28
	N/A	4	1/28
Did the final model address the right question and objectives?	Yes	77	23/30
	No	10	3/30
	Don't know / No final model	13	4/30
Did the final model reflect your conceptual view?	Yes	77	23/30
	No	0	0/30
	Don't know / No final model	23	7/30

Table 4.10 *Interview Responses about the Benefits of Using the BN Model*

Responses	% of Respondents	n/N
Scientific	24	7/29
Accountable	28	8/29
Updatable	7	2/29
Structured approach	24	7/29
Good overview	14	4/29
Brings info together	7	2/29
Better than before	7	2/29
Reflects uncertainty	7	2/29

(39%, 11 of 28) reported resistance to using BNs within their organisation (Table 4.9). We explore some of the possible reasons for this later, in our discussion on external barriers to model uptake. The majority of the respondents felt that the final model from the workshop process addressed the right question and objectives and reflected their conceptual view (77% and 77% respectively, Table 4.9).

When asked the question 'What do you believe are the benefits of using the current model?', respondents highlighted accountability and a structured, scientific approach as the key benefits (Table 4.10).

To gauge how respondents felt the resultant BN model would perform in practice, we asked if they thought (i) relying on the BN model would save their organisation time and resources and whether (ii) the risk of an inappropriate decision based on the model would be high or low (items 26 and 27, Table 4.4). Most respondents (59%, 17 of 29) agreed that reliance on the BN model would save resources, but about a third (31%, 9 of 29) were sceptical, and 10% (3 of 29) disagreed outright. With regards to the risk of an inappropriate decision based on the model, 64% (18 of 28) agreed that such a risk was low, while 21% (6 of 28) were neutral and 14% (4 of 28) disagreed.

There appears to be broad, high-level endorsement of the resultant BN models. Collectively, the results for interpersonal trust and trust in models paint a picture of conditions that are conducive to model uptake. So how do they relate to a willingness to adopt?

In summary, interpersonal trust matters most. In our sample at least, it seems interpersonal trust factors have the greatest influence on respondents' willingness to adopt the final BN decision support model. The correlation between willingness to adopt is much higher for the set of facilitator-related factors than for the set of trust in model responses. For the former, Spearman's r ranged from 0.44 to 0.52, indicating a moderately strong positive relationship between favourable perceptions of facilitator ability, integrity, reliability and benevolence and willingness to adopt (Figure 4.4). There was much greater variation in the absolute correlation values between willingness to adopt and trust in model responses, with r ranging from a low of 0.097 ('GutFeelLessReliable') to 0.43 ('RiskInappropDecLow', see Figure 4.4).

Respondents in our sample had very high levels of interpersonal trust in their workshop facilitators. And this trust does indeed appear to be strongly related to their willingness to adopt the models produced in their workshops. Respondents' general trust in models was generally positive, but also ambivalent, and the correlation between these items and willingness to adopt were less clear. These findings are consistent with what has been found in the literature on environmental information systems – namely that non-technical factors are often better predictors of model implementation at an individual level than technical attributes of the modelling technology (Diez and McIntosh 2009).

An anecdotal observation made during our interviews was that people's predispositions towards uncertainty and subjectivity may play an important role in forming their trust in models and the modelling process. Those who were more resistant to the process were often those who were uncomfortable with models for decisions in highly uncertain contexts. (In cases where there is a lack of data, it is true that models are more reliant on subjective judgements.) 'System too complex/

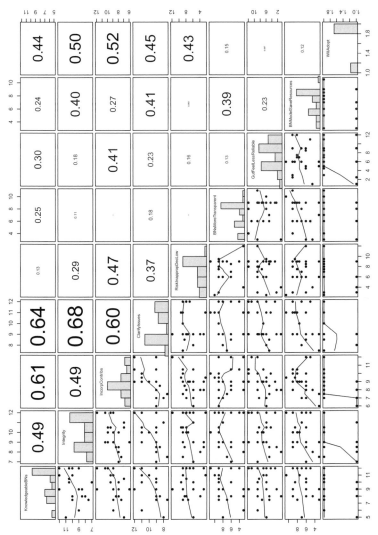

Figure 4.4 Scatter plot matrices, histograms and Spearman's correlations for eight trust factors and willingness to adopt. The first four factors relate to interpersonal trust in the modelling facilitator and the next four to trust in models. On the diagonal are histograms for each factor. Below the diagonal are pairwise scatterplots with a loess smoother. Above the diagonal, pairwise Spearman's correlations are shown with font size scaled by the absolute value of the correlation.

Figure 4.4 *(continued)*

KnowledgeableBNs = facilitator was knowledgeable about the BN modelling tool;
Integrity = facilitator approached the management problem with scientific integrity;
IncorpContribs = facilitator incorporated participant contributions appropriately into the model;
ClarifyIssues = facilitator really wanted to clarify what was important to workshop participants and work towards a solution in the model building;
RiskInappropDecLow = the risk of an inappropriate decision based on this model is low;
BNsMoreTransparent = BNs seem more transparent than other models;
GutFeelLessReliable = gut feelings are less reliable for making decisions than models;
BNModelSaveResources = reliance on the model will save the agency time and resources;
WillAdopt = willingness to adopt

uncertain to trust the model' was the most common explanation given by the respondents who were not willing to use the model (4 out of $n=7$, Table 4.1).

Understanding the different dimensions of trust can be empowering. It means you can identify the dimensions you can influence (e.g. how people feel about the facilitator) and those you can't (e.g. an individual's predisposition towards using models versus gut feelings for decision-making). The good news from our research is that those you can change – interpersonal trust issues – may matter more in creating positive intentions towards model use than the ones you can't change.

4.3.3 When Good Intentions Fail to Translate into Behaviour: Managing Change and External Barriers to Model Uptake

4.3.3.1 *Our Prior Beliefs*
We initially thought that, with the factors of knowledge and trust in hand, all that was left to consider was how people felt about the current management of the problem – whether (or not) there was a perception that the old ways of doing things were no longer effective. This, we thought, would tell us if there was any appetite for change.

4.3.3.2 *What We Have Learned*
Failure to move from model development to implementation may not always be the fault of an individual's readiness for change, or their

levels of knowledge or feelings of trust. The fault may not lie with factors internal to any individual at all, but rather in external, real-world barriers.

There may be organisational-level barriers such as political changes that result in different priorities or pressure to undertake particular activities or report on activities in a particular way (Diez and McIntosh 2009). Other organisational barriers include lack of top management support and insufficient funds to resource ongoing model use. At a more mundane level, barriers might arise from project disruptions, inadequate model documentation, user support material and technical trouble-shooting support. All, or any of these, can impact on whether the model is successfully implemented.

We asked our interview respondents a number of questions about the previous management of their issue, whether change, and in particular a change to this kind of structured decision model, was necessary. Their answers to these questions are summarised in Table 4.11. We also asked them a series of questions about project continuity, model documentation and training resources for model use.

When asked if the previous management of their issue worked well, not a single one of our respondents answered 'yes' unequivocally; 54% (14 of 26) said 'kind of' and the remainder gave an clear 'no' (Table 4.11). While 57% felt that the need for change was obvious, 32% were more tentative in their assessment and only 11% did not consider that management had to change (Table 4.11). Over three-quarters (78%, 21 of 27) said that this type of change was required or at least 'a good first step', while the remainder had no opinion, were hesitant or simply disagreed (Table 4.11). A similar percentage (76%) reported feeling no personal resistance to the process, though some 57% thought they sensed resistance in others (Table 4.11). An encouraging 86% of respondents said they thought using the model would be less effortful, no more or less effortful or more effortful, but worthwhile (Table 4.11).

While these views are positive for orienting management towards structured decision support, a number of our respondents indicated they had experienced previous fads and enthusiasms for various tools and methods touted to be the solution to their management problems. They are understandably frustrated, weary and sceptical of claims of this nature, and possibly resistant to investing time and energy into learning and adopting a new approach.

In our sample, most respondents (70%, 21 of 30) had not yet experienced any disruptions to their project. The remaining 30% had already

Table 4.11 *Interview Responses about the Process of Change Management*

Interview Question	Responses		% of Respondents	n/N
How structured was the management before?	None		7	2/29
	Ad hoc response		38	11/29
	Some planning		48	14/29
	Full planning		7	2/29
Did previous management work well?	No		42	11/26
	Kind of		54	14/26
	Yes		0	0/26
Was the need for management change obvious?	Yes		57	16/28
	Kind of		32	9/28
	No		11	3/28
Was this the sort of change that was required?	Yes		63	17/27
	Good first step		15	4/27
	Hesitation		7	2/27
	No		4	1/27
	No opinion		11	3/27
Did you personally feel resistance to the process?	Yes	Models inaccurate	10	3/29
		Waste of time	7	2/29
		Model tells us nothing new	10	3/29
	Somewhat		14	4/29
	No		76	22/29
Did you sense resistance from others?	Yes	Models inaccurate	20	6/30
		Waste of time	0	0/30
		Model tells us nothing new	20	6/30
	Somewhat		27	8/30
	No		43	13/30
Amount of effort involved in using the model?	Less effortful		32	9/28
	No more or less		4	1/28
	More and worthwhile		50	14/28
	More not worthwhile		14	4/28

experienced disruptions to personnel, funding and/or the timeline of the project. Three-quarters of respondents (18 of 24) found some form of model documentation (e.g. report, user manual, tutorial, etc.); one failed to find any and five respondents did not look. The vast majority (94%) of those who found documentation thought it was 'good/fine'. We were surprised by these figures, having expected that poor documentation or unclear reports might be one of the biggest barriers.

It seems that the big obstacles may be elsewhere, such as political changes and bureaucratic impediments, or funding availability.

R29: ...we get restructured you know on a fairly regular basis where there's new masters and new systems [...] computer systems or approaches that were OK in the previous department, you move into a new regime and... oops... it's all gone and there's heaps of checks and controls and security worries, so that any sort of special software needs all sorts of special authorisations and as soon as you have to do authorisations it means paperwork [...] if you're not highly motivated it doesn't end up on your system...

R21: Implementing it? Well, that's always been our worry... I mean if they were able to get the model up to a very functional standard that we could do more prediction with it and we could encourage other people to use it, we didn't have the resources...There was no way local government can fund that sort of thing unless you're one of their huge cities [...] people in that business don't understand the real constraints of the finances of local government [...] most of them around here are bankrupt, we're just holding our head above water [...] That's where we stand in trying to implement anything; it can't be done unless we get government grants.

4.3.4 Where Does That Leave Us?

In the methods section, we mentioned the theory of planned behaviour. According to this theory, intentions are formed by attitudes, social norms and perceived behavioural control. The translation of intentions can be disrupted by perceived behavioural control (e.g. the model is too hard to use; I'm not going to be able to implement it) and 'actual' behavioural control (e.g. the sort of barriers we mentioned here). The gap between intention and implementation will be determined by how many of those actual factors are obvious to potential users ahead of time, that is, how many of them feed into their intentions via perceived behavioural control. If they are aware of future problems that will result in poor user support for example, their intentions will be adjusted. If they are not aware of such things, their intentions will remain positive, but there will be low correspondence with actual implementation. How much this varies from context to context will depend, in part, on the predictability of the political climate and the transparency of management and process in the given agency or organisation.

4.4 CONCLUSIONS

Throughout this chapter, we have explored several potential drivers of successful model implementation. We started with discussions of knowledge and trust. Our interview and survey research with 31 participants in model building workshops afforded us a data set for exploring the correlations between those factors and an individual's intentions towards model adoption.

We found substantial correlations between interpersonal trust items related to the modelling facilitators and the willingness to adopt the final model. We also found an interesting and potentially important relationship between knowledge of BNs and willingness to adopt the final model. This knowledge need not be extensive – the workshop process need not aim to develop high levels of technical expertise. A vague sense of familiarity with BNs carries the relationship with willingness to adopt.

Finally, we raised the issue of what factors are likely to disrupt the transition from intentions to use model-based decision-making to their real-world implementation. We discussed various external barriers that sit well outside the realm of individual attitudes or abilities – for example, the predictability of the political climate and the funding availability for implementation resources. How well or often implementation follows from intention will depend on how accurately these sorts of barriers can be forecasted. We conclude by suggesting that forecasting of potential external barriers should be a critical part of model implementation project management; without it, no amount of investment in improving trust, knowledge or other individual attitudes will amount to success.

ACKNOWLEDGEMENTS

This research was funded by The University of Melbourne's Interdisciplinary Seed Funding Scheme 2012. Y.E.C. was supported by ARC Linkage Project LP110100304. Y.E.C. and B.C.W. were also supported by the Australian Research Council (ARC) Centre of Excellence for Biosecurity Risk Analysis and the ARC Centre of Excellence for Environmental Decisions.

Understanding Human Well-being for Conservation: A Locally Driven, Mixed Methods Approach

EMILY WOODHOUSE, KATHERINE M. HOMEWOOD,
EMILIE BEAUCHAMP, TOM CLEMENTS, J. TERRENCE
McCABE, DAVID WILKIE AND E.J. MILNER-GULLAND

5.1 INTRODUCTION

Over the last decade or so, well-being has become a buzzword in sectors as diverse as health, self-help and economics and has entered the mainstream as a national policy target in several countries, including the UK (Abdallah et al. 2012). In international development, the concept has emerged in response to the inadequacy of uni-dimensional measures of poverty such as income or consumption (Ravallion 2003). For policymakers, a focus on human well-being holds the promise of a new perspective on development and social change – a positive measure of success that takes into consideration the multifaceted components of a good life from housing to social relations to feelings of security. For natural resource managers and conservationists, it points to links between the natural and social dimensions of systems, the importance of ecosystem services for well-being (Millennium Ecosystem Assessment 2005) and the complexity of people's lives, incentives and aspirations, which are both shaped by and shape their natural environment. But can this wide-ranging and multi-dimensional concept be of practical use for decision-making in natural resource management, and how can conservationists go about understanding and measuring it on the ground?

There are both ethical and pragmatic reasons for incorporating human well-being into conservation decision-making processes. First, understanding well-being can elucidate incentives and help to explain behaviour and responses to interventions, as improving one's own well-being is a primary driver of an individual's decision-making (Deci and Ryan 2000). Conservation tends to focus on practical benefits and economic incentives, but well-being is more complex than this; people do not act as rational automatons driven by single motives, but by a range of incentives, norms and aspirations. Interventions that support local well-being, when broadly conceived, can increase environmentally desirable outcomes, by creating positive local perceptions and engagement, improving the legitimacy of the intervention and ultimately its success (Coulthard et al. 2011). Second, focusing on well-being provides a way to integrate social goals into conservation decision-making. Conservation has the potential to deliver ecosystem services to benefit people, but policies that limit resource use, such as protected areas, may present significant costs (West et al. 2006). Natural resource management is not only technical but a social and political process of engagement with people, with a substantial ethical component. Attention to ethical components is perhaps most critical in materially poor areas of the Global South, where conservation interventions may exacerbate poverty and inequality in already vulnerable communities reliant on natural resources.

A well-being perspective, therefore, can provide comprehensive insights into local priorities, elucidate the multifaceted incentives of resource users, the social impacts of conservation and support understanding of local people's responses to interventions, hence ultimately improving the design and implementation of management interventions. The challenge lies in accounting for the complexities and diversity of human well-being. The strength of the concept lies in its breadth, but this has also tended to result in vague conceptualisations and superficial engagement. There is, however, increasing convergence on a conception of well-being in international policy as a positive physical, social and mental state (Stiglitz et al. 2009; Summers et al. 2012). We present a human well-being framework in line with this three-dimensional conception, which provides a structured yet flexible means of analysing well-being for use in conservation decision-making. We discuss approaches for applying the framework to collect locally relevant but broadly comparable social data, and for incorporating well-being into natural resource management, including in defining objectives, designing strategies and monitoring and evaluation. Insights from a range of previous research are provided, including four case studies. We lastly examine the challenges and potential directions for conservation researchers, practitioners and policymakers in engaging with and applying a human well-being framework.

5.2 WHAT IS HUMAN WELL-BEING?

There are five key ways in which human well-being stands apart from standard measures of poverty and social development, such as income, mortality rates or health indicators. First, well-being is multi-dimensional and holistic, taking into account the dimensions of people's lives which they have reason to value, from material goods to social solidarity.

Second, it focuses on what is good and positive in people's lives, counteracting development discourse which has historically been dominated by terms like poverty and deprivation. Well-being counteracts the stigma of being labelled poor, and instead offers what White (2010) terms 'inclusive aspiration'. The third aspect of well-being is that it has both objective and subjective dimensions. It is intuitive that well-being has something to do with 'feeling good' or 'happy', which is a subjective state that can only be judged by the individual. There are some objectively verifiable indicators of well-being, some of which can be agreed as basic human rights such as enough food and shelter. Other objective indicators include material assets such as wealth and possessions, the subjective significance of which will vary across cultures and contexts. Fourth, well-being has a social dimension, because people experience well-being as part of society, rather than as isolated individuals. Finally, well-being prioritises the views and perspectives of those people whom interventions and development changes will impact, because in order to operationalise the concept, their particular circumstances and conceptualisations need to be understood. A common framework must therefore have enough flexibility to accommodate diverse and local understandings.

One framework which encapsulates and balances these aspects of well-being has been developed by a group of social scientists through a project called Wellbeing in Developing Countries (WeD), which involved the empirical study of development in four countries in the Global South – Bangladesh, Ethiopia, Peru and Thailand. It was developed for the study of situations where poverty is prevalent and is particularly appropriate to communities heavily dependent on natural resources (McGregor and Sumner 2010), but it is applicable to any context. WeD defines well-being as 'a state of being with others, which arises where human needs are met, where one can act meaningfully to pursue one's goals, and where one can enjoy a satisfactory quality of life' (University of Bath 2002). Well-being is conceptualised in three interacting dimensions: the objective, material circumstances of people and the extent to which their needs are met; a relational dimension focusing on how people engage with others to meet needs and achieve goals; and their subjective evaluation of their lives and the meanings they ascribe to achieving their goals. This provides a space for self-evaluation, where people can describe experiences, how satisfied they are with what they have and what they can do and be. Objective indicators – which are externally observable and verifiable – are incorporated too, as expressions of satisfaction may not reflect material impoverishment. Aspirations can be limited by the circumstances in which people find themselves; for example, if people have never had access to piped water, they may not register it as a need.

The WeD framework draws on the work of Amartya Sen, a pioneer of development economics, who put forward the idea that poverty is not just about what you have, but what you can claim (entitlements) and what you can do (capabilities). He viewed development as centring on having the freedom to live the life which you have reason to value (Sen 1999). The WeD framework, however, is unique in incorporating a social perspective to these ideas. This recognises that despite an emphasis on individualism in modern capitalist societies, behaviour and decisions are not always made with individual gains in mind, but for the fulfilment of social obligations and social good, in accordance with cultural conventions which are often not consciously considered. The objective and subjective dimensions of well-being are socially and culturally constructed through relationships in particular societal contexts (McGregor 2007). Culture and values shape social relations and perceptions of what constitutes material success. Material goods have cultural and social dimensions; for example rice in Bangladesh is considered a basic need and sharing it indicates shared identity (White 2010). The relational dimension also acknowledges that people have social (as well as material and psychological) needs including family, communities and social networks. In a well-being assessment in Zambia, for example, people emphasised the ability to take care of others as a priority after meeting their own material needs, showing that well-being for them united material, relational and moral dimensions (White and Jha 2013). Through this three-dimensional conceptualisation, the WeD framework avoids a reductionist view of well-being in favour of a necessarily complex perspective.

Our framework (Figure 5.1), based on the WeD research, can guide the scope of well-being analyses, and suggests the different types of data that need to be collected (e.g. objective livelihood data combined

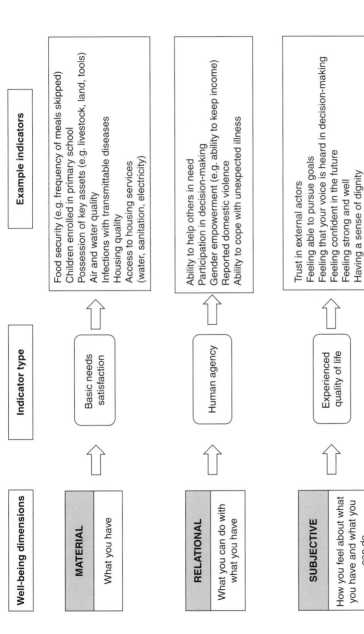

Figure 5.1 Framework for researching human well-being based upon Britton and Coulthard (2013) and McGregor and Sumner (2010), and drawing upon the 'Voices of the Poor' research (Narayan et al. 2000).

with subjective evaluations). Example indicators provided are based upon empirical research of the World Bank's 'Voices of the Poor' project, which found components that were commonly considered to constitute well-being among individuals across twenty-three countries (Narayan et al. 2000). These indicators are for illustrative purposes, and locally specific indicators will need to be developed that are most relevant to the local context and the intended or implemented management strategy (see the discussion that follows). Indicators should span the three dimensions. For example, in considering which aspects of well-being may relate to a payment for ecosystem services (PES) programme, the obvious choice would be to look to the material domain. Commonly, indicators of material well-being would be restricted to objective indicators, for example the economic costs and benefits of participating in a PES scheme (Jack et al. 2008). Taking WeD's three-dimensional conceptualisation, however, suggests the need for attention to be paid to relational aspects – the structures affecting the distribution and access of income or benefits, what different groups will be able to do with income and distribution within households. The subjective dimension suggests the importance of indicators about feelings of fairness, and values that shape satisfaction and meanings about material well-being. All of these have been found to be important determinants of the success of PES interventions (e.g. Clements et al. 2010; Muradian et al. 2010; Narloch et al. 2013).

5.3 THE SIGNIFICANCE OF NON-MATERIAL WELL-BEING TO CONSERVATION

Given the emphasis on material dimensions of well-being in conservation, and in social development discourse more generally, it is worth highlighting how attention to non-material aspects (subjective and relational) can be significant to management, particularly with respect to local legitimacy and participation. For example, understanding that fishing holds powerful social meaning, going beyond a job to being a 'way of life' explains fierce resistance to alternative livelihood policies (Pollnac and Poggie 2008). Results of well-being analyses show that people do not think in narrow economic terms about their lives. During research on well-being in Bangladesh, for instance, people revealed that the ideal society is one with both material goods and respect (including good treatment and honour; White 2010). Research also shows the importance of moral and religious dimensions of well-being. For Tibetan Buddhists, being happy is connected to being virtuous, and ensuring good relations with local gods embodied in the landscape through non-extractive behaviour is considered vital for a healthy community. However, these requirements are negotiated and moderated by everyday needs for fuel wood, for example (Woodhouse et al. 2015a).

Institutions – the formal and informal 'rules of the game' within societies and cultures – constrain or enable people in their pursuit of well-being, structuring their relationships with other people and their natural environments. The institutions that conservation interventions construct or work through may impact people's lives and well-being. For example, a traditional system of taboos on consumption of wild species in Madagascar called 'fady' offers protection for certain threatened species but has been weakened by the imposition of external conservation rules (Jones et al. 2008).

Subjective well-being depends on previous experiences, and both fears and aspirations about the future. This highlights the importance of security – predictability and feeling confident in the future – as a component of well-being. Perceived future well-being can impact current well-being and therefore can also have an impact on decision-making regarding natural resource use. In northern Tanzania, perceived risk to future access to land and resources was greatest in households near to Tarangire National Park and was factored into decisions to convert land from pasture to agriculture in order to secure this land against potential future limits to use, for example through extension of the National Park (Baird et al. 2009). This land conversion led to a reduction in the conservation value of the land. Uncertainty can result from the change brought with interventions, but improved governance and local control of resources through management programmes may conversely allay concerns about the future, improve subjective well-being, and reduce environmentally damaging preemptive actions.

5.4 RESEARCHING WELL-BEING FOR CONSERVATION: APPLYING THE FRAMEWORK

Meeting the challenge of applying such a multi-dimensional concept in practice requires the translation of the universal framework into concrete terms relevant to the local context (McGregor 2004). To achieve this, the analytical constructs of this framework (the three dimensions) are externally defined to provide a structure for comparisons but local indicators and the methods and tools used vary between settings. The

WeD framework provides the space to use quantitative, qualitative and participatory methods, in a complementary way tailored to the context and the needs of the study. Researchers need to consider who the end-users for the research are, and its primary purpose. Research with the primary aim of supporting conservation managers and communities in decision-making may take a very different approach to that directed at providing evidence of social impacts for donors, for instance. We next outline approaches to using the well-being framework to capture the different dimensions – material, subjective and relational – emphasising the need for mixed methods and a flexible approach.

5.4.1 Developing Indicators Based on Locally Driven Qualitative Understanding

The dimensions and domains of the framework (Figure 5.1) provide structure to the research questions and analysis of data. Qualitative research – using semi-structured, informal interviews and participant observation – which is flexible, open to unexpected findings and may take a participatory approach, can provide the details on local definitions and language for well-being and the priorities and aspirations that people have. For example, Abunge et al. (2013) used focus group discussions with different stakeholder groups (e.g. women fish vendors and beach seine captains) connected to a Kenyan coastal fishery to understand how well-being is understood by different types of people, how it is linked to coastal ecosystem services, how and why it has changed and the hopes people have for the future of the fishery. Open-ended questions, such as 'How would you describe in general a person who is doing well in this community?', encouraged people to open up and discuss what constituted a good life in this particular context. These types of discussions – held individually or in focus groups, and centred on goals, types of resources and components as outlined in the framework, changes experienced and aspirations – can identify locally important well-being components, issues and specific indicators of change.

Qualitative research is also valuable at the start of research to understand the historical, political and cultural issues which can shape people's perceptions and the role of institutions. This research is vital in developing locally relevant questions for any planned structured and standardised questionnaires. Although spending time in the 'field' provides important firsthand knowledge, field research should be augmented

with reviews of the social science, historical and anthropological literature. Interviews with local experts such as project managers and local
leaders who have lived and worked in the area for some time can provide
an understanding of culture and history, although researchers need to be
aware of how an individual's particular perspectives and agendas shapes
this information. More in-depth interviews with these key informants
who have particular knowledge and expertise can point towards aspects
of well-being for further investigation with community members, and
the larger sets of ideas and beliefs of which they are a part. The structural
differences in age, race, sex and class are important predictors in differences of conceptions of well-being, aspirations and opportunity as well
as well-being achievement (Daw et al. 2011). Qualitative understanding about these social structures can ensure these different groups are
targeted for research and represented in decision-making. A conscious
intention may be required to create a separate space to enable marginalised voices (for example the landless or migrants) to be heard, rather
than having data collection dominated by community leaders and those
proclaimed as spokespersons.

The development of specific indicators for different aspects of
well-being allows the development of quantifiable well-being targets, baselines for monitoring, relationships between variables to be
defined and the magnitude of changes attributable to interventions
to be measured. Of course, as a multi-dimensional concept, there
can be no single measure and aggregating measures into overall
scores inevitably leads to a loss in the nuances of change in different
dimensions. Standardised indicators designed for universal application may be irrelevant to the particular local context, and instead, a
specific set of indicators, representing each of the three dimensions,
well-grounded in local understandings of well-being, can work best
for practical application as a simple monitoring tool. For example, in
evaluating well-being outcomes of Farmer Field Schools (extension
programmes for agricultural development) in East Africa, statements
about well-being collected through qualitative interviews were transformed into well-being indicators, which included land and livestock
ownership, food security, diet quality and education (Friis-Hansen
and Duveskog 2012). Inclusion of subjective and non-observable well-
being such as security or social dynamics would involve making decisions about how amenable the component is to quantification, scaling
or yes/no answers. In-depth understanding based on qualitative data

can complement and enhance the quantitative indicators, and avoid reductionism for the sake of quantifiable results.

5.4.2 Understanding and Measuring Subjective Well-being

Well-being is at least, in part, concerned with how people feel about their lives. Material needs and wants such as money, housing, livestock or consumer goods are relatively straightforward to either observe, or for people to describe and quantify in interviews. Non-material, social and cultural aspects may not be as readily expressed as they can be taken for granted, or be more sensitive to discuss: for example, the importance of having a good relationship with one's spouse, or concerns about changes occurring to cultural practices. The broad domains (Figure 5.1) can be used as prompts in qualitative research processes. The sensitivity of certain issues, for example the significance of cultural practices, highlights the importance of field teams who have local knowledge, language skills and are independent of management interventions (Camfield et al. 2009).

It is possible to develop quantitative measures of subjective aspects of well-being. The WeD group developed a quality of life survey based on a definition of subjective well-being as personal satisfaction with the respondent's achievement of life goals. Through an exploratory phase of research on goals and resources, a standardised survey adaptable to each country was developed for comparative purposes. The survey asked respondents to rate on a three- or five-point scale, how satisfied they were with each item (e.g. health, community peace, education of children). The need to understand values and context to interpret results of questionnaires such as these was highlighted by the fact that in Bangladesh, people seemed reluctant to say that they were dissatisfied because this could be seen as showing a lack of respect to Allah (Copestake and Camfield 2009). Similarly, the Wellbeing & Poverty Pathways project (University of Bath 2011) has developed a psycho-social model for measuring 'inner well-being' comprising seven domains, using quantitative measures grounded in qualitative insights to explore people's movement in and out of poverty. Answers to questions such as 'do you feel you have the power to change decisions that affect you?' on a five-point scale showed the insecurity and lack of agency people felt in Chiawa, Zambia, where, despite and in part because of investments in tourism, conservation and agriculture, people's lives were largely becoming more precarious and marginalised (White and Jha 2013). The subjective is often approached through this type of quantitative approach, e.g. Likert scales, but this must be complemented with contextual and qualitative understanding, as in the WeD research, to avoid concealing meanings and nuances.

Following criticism of conventional top-down technocratic interventions, the concept of participation has emerged since the 1990s as an essential element of people-centred development, which aims to put the poorest first, and in control of the process. In conservation and natural resource management, in particular, participatory approaches have become popular due to cost-effectiveness and perceived efficiency at accessing local understanding. Both quantitative and qualitative methods for integrating well-being can be more or less participatory, with researcher attitudes being the crucial factor in better listening and learning from people who are targeted for interventions during their design and evaluation. The Voices of the Poor research programme used a participatory approach, involving over 60,000 men and women, to gain perspectives of poverty and well-being from the poor. There is a selection of participatory tools which have been designed to aid this process – such as focus group discussions, village histories and resource mapping – in which outputs are constructed in a group of local people. In Kenyan coastal communities, Abunge et al. (2013) paid attention to social relations and differences in power by interviewing crew and captains separately and were able to draw out differences and agreement through discussion, and potential conflicts between groups in their pursuit of well-being. For formal evaluation purposes, scoring and ranking of outcomes in community groups can be used as a participatory method of evaluating interventions (Catley et al. 2013). For example, the ranked outcomes method (Howe and Milner-Gulland 2012) is an inclusive evaluation tool which could be applied to well-being evaluations. Box 5.1 describes a rapid participatory social evaluation of livelihood projects in Tanzania using this method. The benefit of a participatory approach is that it can lead to collective action, but there is a tendency that a collective focus emphasises shared public goods over private, or the goals of a dominant group (Copestake and Camfield 2009). It perhaps works best when complemented by individual and structured questionnaires, and informed by qualitative understandings of politics and nuances of expression in the local language.

Box 5.1 The Ranked Outcomes Approach to Evaluating Social Impacts of Conservation Interventions: A Case Study in Tanzania

The ranked outcomes approach is a tool for post-hoc evaluation of interventions involving stakeholders, with a low tech, relatively simple but robust method. The method involves developing a list of desirable outcomes for a project portfolio, which can be identified and agreed by project staff, independent reviews and local people, potentially in a participatory way. These are categorised into topics, e.g. education, livelihoods, legacy, and conservation goals such as species protection. Outcomes are ranked within each category by different stakeholders according to their priorities, and then whether or not they have been met is evaluated separately, for example as a binary assessment based on a review of project documents, interviews with staff or local people, and direct observations to assess whether the outcome has been met. The priority score is multiplied by the outcome score to reach a category score.

Sainsbury et al. (2015) tested the method for a portfolio of small-scale income generating projects such as beekeeping, tree planting and fuel-efficient stoves, in communities adjacent to a nature reserve in the Tanzanian Eastern Arc Mountains (Figure 5.2). Outcomes were developed and prioritised with project staff and independently evaluated. Outcomes were also prioritised in village focus groups, and individuals were surveyed regarding

Figure 5.2 Tree planting performed best in the ranked outcomes assessment, as evaluated by both villagers and the independent assessor, while fuel-efficient stoves performed poorly, due to poor design and implementation. Photos: Neil Burgess.

whether the outcomes were met and then scored on a binary scale. Outcomes included, for example, 'jobs created directly in the project' and 'improved capacity of people involved'. Although there was broad agreement on the performance of particular projects (e.g. tree planting was agreed to be the best-performing by both villagers and the independent assessment), there were some differences between perceptions of implementers and beneficiaries on the most important outcomes and on which projects had delivered most. There were also differences between individual assessors and between villages, highlighting the importance of understanding heterogeneity in perceptions. The method converts qualitative statements on planned and realised outcomes into a quantitative score weighted according to priorities, allowing comparison between projects and sites. It provides useful insights, especially in data poor situations where there are no baselines available, and where there is poorly defined or shifting priorities. As an inclusive process, it can feed into adaptive management, highlighting where aspects of the project are not working for people. The method could be applied to well-being evaluations to first prioritise aspects of well-being which an intervention could target, and then to assess fulfilment of the outcomes – including both observable and subjective aspects.

5.4.3 Understanding the Relational Dimension of Well-being

Research into well-being involves understanding multi-scalar power structures, which can span local social and cultural norms, national policy and global information networks, and be impacted by external interventions. Autonomy and freedom of choice within institutional structures are key elements of relational well-being (Figure 5.1), and may be affected by restrictions on access to land or the imposition of new governance frameworks. Institutional profiling in which local people are asked about the key institutions and relationships in their communities, using visual methods, can support understanding of the influences at different scales on local lives and how they have changed in response to interventions (Messer and Tomsley 2003). Indicators related to the relational dimension such as empowerment can be developed, for example perceived influence in community affairs or control over relevant natural resources (Gurney et al. 2014).

5.5 THE IMPORTANCE OF MIXED METHODS

Mixed methods are critical in understanding well-being. Standardised questionnaires with closed-ended questions, often used in conservation science, produce quantitative data with external validity; the results are representative of the population and generalisable. Qualitative approaches such as semi-structured or informal interviews, and participant observation, on the other hand, can be used to ensure the study investigates what it claims to (Drury et al. 2010). Qualitative approaches, on the whole, do not seek large sample sizes but in-depth understanding of processes, values and relationships and are particularly useful in a cross-cultural context where a researcher's assumptions and categorisations are unlikely to capture local complexities. They also allow time and space for better rapport building, to understand sensitive or unexpected issues related to gender or belief systems for instance, which may impact on ideas about well-being and use of natural resources.

Quantitative methods are particularly useful for investigating the more observable and material aspects of well-being and can also be used with sensitivity and in combination with qualitative methods to research subjective and relational dimensions. Some aspects of well-being such as changes in social dynamics may not be quantifiable at all, or be unexpected, in which case qualitative data can stand alone. For example, qualitative interviews provided subjective perspectives on wealth, collective action, access to natural resources and psychological stress, suggesting that a community-based natural resource management project was successful in the Peruvian Amazon (Gockel and Gray 2009). Despite their potential for providing powerful insights, qualitative methods are often deemed 'unscientific', and either ignored, added on, or remain unacknowledged rather than fully integrated as a means of providing contextual understanding and explanatory power. The WeD group itself has developed a toolbox of methods (University of Bath 2002) which blend qualitative and quantitative methods, and used together give insights on the different dimensions of well-being. These have been applied, not only in a range of countries in the Global South, but in research into differentiated well-being processes and outcomes, and the policy implications for fishing communities in Northern Ireland (Box 5.2).

Overall, a mixed methods approach will enrich understanding of well-being, by examining different facets and discovering fresh perspectives. To take an example from the development literature, an evaluation of conditional cash transfer (CCT) schemes in Nicaragua (providing payments on condition of participation in education and health programmes), quantitative questionnaires measured school enrolment and attendance, types of food consumed and household demographics and economy to establish the average effect of the programme. Results from this quantitative survey showed that the programme was well-targeted at the poorest. But qualitative findings showed that targeting was poorly understood and people did not know why they were included or excluded, causing stress and tension that shaped public attitudes towards the programme (Adato 2008). Having this kind of information is vital for designing or adapting interventions which avoid these tensions, for example ensuring good communication, that targeting chimes

---

Box 5.2 Understanding Well-being in Northern Ireland's Fishing Society and Implications for Management

Both the reduction in fish stocks and increasing policy restrictions may place heavy burdens on fishers and their families, who have an important role to play in effective and sustainable co-management of fisheries. Using a well-being framework, Britton and Coulthard (2013) were able to examine how costs were distributed in communities, and the broader social, political and ethical considerations for fisheries policy in Northern Ireland. They applied the WeD framework of material, social and subjective dimensions and used components of the WeD toolkit adapted for the context, combining quantitative and qualitative approaches. The framework was applied to five coastal areas representing the diversity of fisheries in the region from small-scale inshore fisheries to large-scale offshore vessels. The following tools were used (Figure 5.3):

(i) *Community profiling*: combining secondary data and key informant interviews to understand the local and regional context, including for example the economic recession, fisheries policy, e.g. EU quota systems, and changes in fishing;

(ii) *Resource profiling*, a questionnaire covering material, natural, human and social aspects of well-being, highlighting for example the lack of education in the community, but its importance for accessing alternative livelihood sources;

(iii) *Governance relationship assessment* of relationships (local, national and global) important for influencing fishers' behaviour and shaping well-being outcomes. Fishers were asked to rank local, national and global relationships in the order of importance and score and explain their satisfaction with each. Of greatest importance were national and EU fisheries governance structures in which fishers felt they had no voice. The decline in fisheries was felt to have impacted relations of reciprocity in previously tight knit communities;

(iv) *Global Person Generated Index (GPGI)*, a questionnaire which aims to understand subjective well-being. Respondents are asked to nominate aspects of their life which contribute to well-being and rate their satisfaction with these.

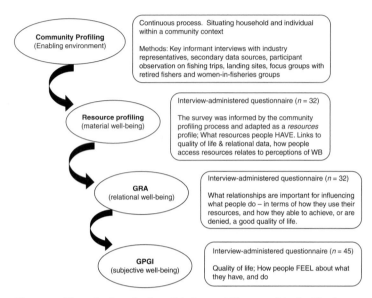

Figure 5.3 The mixed methods well-being tool kit as used in the Northern Ireland fisheries context (from Britton and Coulthard 2013).

By disaggregating data by gender, the analysis showed the gendered nature of well-being. Men rarely cited money as important but prioritised job satisfaction as the thing which they most wanted to change. Financial issues and community spirit were more often raised by women, who often run the business side of fishing enterprises, and are left when men are away at sea. A sense of freedom, self-worth and independence were also important for both groups, and had lower satisfaction levels for men. Overall, the methods provided a way to capture the changing shape of complex, socially grounded well-being outcomes in fishing communities, and the subjective meanings and values associated with fishing livelihoods.

Several insights important for policy came out of the study. First, the dissatisfaction with relationships with the state and the EU, indicating a need for greater participation in decision-making such as fisher forums. Dissatisfaction with material security indicated a need for additional income-generating activities for times when fishers are not at sea. The economic recession and subsequent decline in jobs in construction meant that young people were returning to communities and using fishing as a safety net, but the social and cultural function of fishing was not being acknowledged by the authorities. An investment in a celebration of fishing heritage could provide this boost. Lastly, the role of women in fishing and in supporting well-being in fishing communities was largely invisible and the burden of coping largely rested on them, which could be supported and recognised through the creation of women's networks and better access to social benefits.

with local understanding of social structure and poverty, and is done with participation of communities. Overall, the types of methods and the way they are used must be selected based on context; private interviews may seem strange for highly communal societies, whereas diverse focus groups may not work in cultures which are hierarchical, and in which people are likely to defer to perceived leaders and spokespersons.

5.6 USING WELL-BEING ASSESSMENTS TO INFORM DECISION-MAKING

How a problem is framed shapes the choices made in conservation interventions (Coulthard et al. 2011). Currently, decision-making processes rely heavily on the natural sciences, and the usefulness of social data is often seen as enabling decision-makers to address direct and indirect 'threats' such as resource use (Stephanson and Mascia 2014). A well-being perspective allows a broadening of the decision-making process, and by focusing on social dimensions of systems, can elucidate connections between ecosystems and human development, and provide new interpretations of conservation problems. This can bring a pro-poor angle to interventions and better inform socially sustainable approaches. Although a complex and variable concept, using a framework and methods as described above enables well-being to be brought down to earth and gives it value as a practical tool within decision-making. Well-being is increasingly seen as the aim of development, shaping the design and objectives of interventions. For conservation, there is a need to systematically and purposively integrate well-being analyses into planning, and build the evidence base concerning the social impacts of different management interventions in different contexts. Understanding about well-being, gained through methods described above, can provide a starting point for incorporating relevant social dimensions into different stages of structured decision-making processes.

5.6.1 Defining Objectives and Targets

Decision-making requires that explicit objectives, by which management options can be evaluated, are agreed upon by stakeholders (see also Chapters 3 and 9). Including social outcomes as management objectives may also help decision-makers to reach a clearer definition of trade-offs between multiple objectives amongst different stakeholders (Halpern et al. 2013). Well-being analyses can elucidate local priorities, which aspects are most in need of attention and where protection and enhancement of nature, and aspects of management more broadly, can benefit components of well-being. What factors are currently negatively affecting well-being objectives and could be improved through better targeted natural resource management? Conservationists may aim to target aspects of well-being directly through their interventions, in partnership with more development focused organisations, or by sharing data (Stephanson and Mascia 2014).

Depending on the availability of primary or secondary data, spatial targeting across a landscape or region may focus on those most in need or avoid areas where well-being issues intersect with conservation. Most spatial prioritisations for conservation, which include social as well as biological layers, focus on economic costs (Naidoo et al. 2006). However, a recent paper demonstrated that a wider range of social values can be integrated into these prioritisations (Whitehead et al. 2014). This approach could be expanded further to encompass broader concepts of well-being through local stakeholder participation. Linking places to aspects of well-being, e.g. cultural sites (subjective) and livelihoods (material), could help conservation planners to identify socially feasible conservation solutions which support well-being and also to identify areas where there are likely to be conflicts between well-being and biodiversity priorities.

5.6.2 Designing Conservation Strategies and Negotiating Trade-Offs

After aspects of well-being to target have been decided, alternative strategies to address both these and biological aims need to be evaluated. Well-being targets linked to conservation goals can be incorporated into theories of change – conceptual models which outline the causal chain linking the intervention to specific outcomes and the assumptions being made (Leeuw and Vaessen 2009; Conservation Measures Partnership 2012). For example, an eco-certification scheme could lead to access to new markets and secure incomes. Improving the performance of governance structures for resource use could have the benefit of reducing corruption more generally. Consequences of particular strategies can be estimated based on available scientific evidence and local knowledge. Given the complexities involved in conservation and well-being dynamics, qualitative models which estimate the direction of change and highlight uncertainties and risks are more feasible than quantitative predictions. It is important to consider positive and negative feedbacks between intervention strategy, ecosystem and well-being components, and possible unintended consequences (Milner-Gulland 2012; Miller et al. 2012). For example, will increasing income or providing alternative livelihoods have repercussions for access to other resources without other measures being in place? Or will eco-certification requirements be too costly for small producers or produce greater incentives for corruption? It is vital that development of a theory of change and assessment of consequences is carried out with local communities and stakeholders through participatory and deliberative processes that enable collective consideration of issues. This early engagement in planning, with attention to equity and trust, is more likely to lead to long-lasting and robust decisions (Reed 2008).

If well-being is conceived of and experienced differently by different people, how can decision-makers hope to satisfy different stakeholders and environmental aims? Local needs for food and fuel could clash with conservation organisations' aim to protect forest habitat and endangered species, requiring trade-offs to be made between livelihoods and conservation. In other cases, the aims of some local people and conservation may align more closely, for example to counteract the influence of external influences such as commercial agriculture or mining, which can benefit some local players at the expense of others. Purposefully

---

Box 5.3 Taboo Trade-offs in a Kenyan Fishery

Daw et al. (2015) highlighted the importance of being aware of 'taboo trade-offs', which set sacred values (such as justice, honour or cultural identity) against secular values (such as economic gain). These trade-offs are psychologically difficult for people, and so are often ignored or avoided in negotiations. People may feel comfortable negotiating routine trade-offs between secular values, which concern interests and needs, or material aspects of well-being (Redpath et al. 2013). They may also understand the need to make 'tragic trade-offs' between different types of sacred values, or different people's sacred values. However, trading off routine and sacred values is 'taboo', meaning that fundamental, but unacknowledged, issues may impede negotiations.

Daw et al. (2015) developed a 'toy model' of a small-scale fishery in Kenya incorporating local ideas of well-being, fisheries data and stakeholder knowledge, which, alongside narrative scenarios, formed the basis for stakeholder discussion about trade-offs. This revealed that the management scenario, which was an apparent win-win for both conservation and profitability, would negatively affect marginalised women traders reliant on small, low-value fish, who would not normally be involved in management decisions, representing a taboo trade-off, which was not acknowledged until detailed probing revealed it. Instead women traders were predicted to benefit from systems optimised for food production (Figure 5.4).

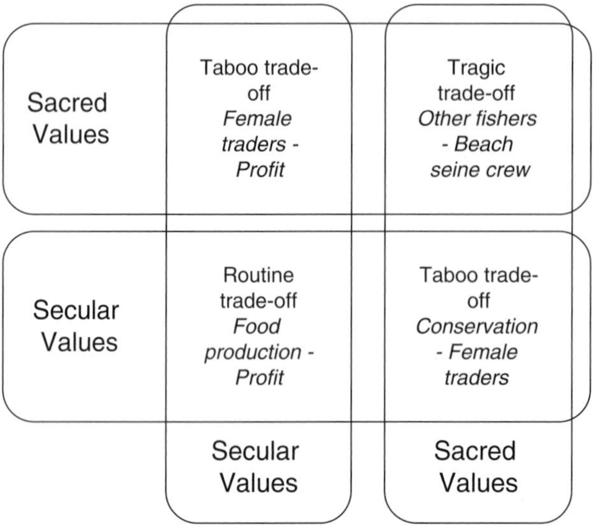

	Taboo trade-off *Female traders - Profit*	Tragic trade-off *Other fishers - Beach seine crew*
Sacred Values		
Secular Values	Routine trade-off *Food production - Profit*	Taboo trade-off *Conservation - Female traders*
	Secular Values	**Sacred Values**

Figure 5.4 Classification of trade-offs according to the values involved in which trade-offs pitting sacred against secular values are taboo; example trade-offs between different management objectives, the well-being of different stakeholder groups, and between objectives and well-being are shown in italics.

Source: Figure adapted from Daw et al. (2015).

incorporating different perspectives and priorities in decision-making processes is a way to open up negotiations on the hard choices and trade-offs, in a transparent way in the hope of building consensus (Coulthard et al. 2011; Box 5.3). Focusing on interests and needs, rather than values, may be more negotiable and support conflict resolution (Redpath et al. 2013). Conservationists need to be more explicit about both the benefits and costs of interventions, a process which if not done can lead to unrealised expectations and unresolved conflict (McShane et al. 2011).

Communities are far from homogenous entities, with differences in wealth, class, ethnicity, age and gender, and the impacts of any intervention on different parts of the community are likely to be uneven. Inclusion of different types of people in conservation planning and analysis of well-being allows decision-makers to interrogate who is winning or is likely to win and who is losing as a result of interventions. It is increasingly recognised that growing levels of inequality are significant in collective and individual ill-being, especially contributing to conflict (Alkire et al. 2012). Tailored management, to ensure that some people are not disproportionately impacted and are able to participate in decision-making, can reduce feelings of unfairness and resentment (Halpern et al. 2013). Indeed, perceived fairness has been found to be an important dimension of success for PES schemes regardless of tangible benefits, and is related to governance structures, suggesting that developing capacity within local institutions is needed (Sommerville et al. 2010).

5.6.3 Monitoring, Evaluation and Adaptive Management

Robust monitoring and evaluation of the impacts of conservation on the three dimensions of well-being can demonstrate success and ensure accountability and improve understanding of failures and problems in order to improve management. Uncertainty regarding the linkages between interventions, ecosystem change and well-being mean that adaptive management that responds iteratively to evidence and social change is vital for successful interventions. Understanding subjective feelings about the effect of natural resource management on well-being is important, even if an external evaluator or researcher may not agree with the person's viewpoint. Whether people associate changes in their subjective well-being with an intervention can have a profound impact on the outcome of that intervention. Perceived well-being may be at odds with objective measures, highlighting where there is dissatisfaction with elements of interventions. In villages involved in marine-protected areas (MPAs) in Indonesia, for example, there were negative changes in perceived well-being despite increases in wealth (based on material assets) during the course of the intervention, due to inequitable sharing of benefits, conflict and unmet expectations of the projects (Gurney et al. 2014).

Evaluating the social impacts of interventions post-hoc is perhaps where the majority of work on human well-being in conservation has focused, and this has largely involved snapshot methods based on semi-structured interviews, and with a strong emphasis on material aspects of well-being (de Lange et al. 2016). Few studies robustly attribute specific outcomes to an intervention. Box 5.4 describes an impact evaluation of interventions on locally relevant components of well-being in Cambodia, using quasi-experimental methods in which intervention villages and households were compared to controls through time, enabling robust attribution. There are, however, significant practical barriers to using such complex statistical methods, such as budget and technical skills, which necessitate alternative approaches such as participatory and theory-based methods in many cases. These methods focus more on understanding why interventions cause changes in well-being and may be better suited to providing evidence useful to managers at the site level (Woodhouse et al. 2015b). For example, examining a range of types of evidence for causal linkages can explain why an intervention appeared to improve one aspect of well-being but not another. Participatory approaches, which allow communities to assess impacts themselves, can suggest why some groups are expressing dissatisfaction and how they could be better targeted (e.g. Box 5.1).

Well-being is not a state but a process, in which interventions may affect people's interactions with the environment and each other, in turn impacting how well-being is defined and experienced – a phenomenon which must be taken into account when implementing adaptive management. For example, although in many coastal communities there is a strong attachment to fishing, its poor economic prospects and people's increasing monetary aspirations meant that artisanal fishers in Uruguay and Brazil did not aspire for their children to be fishers and some were starting to move away from the industry (Trimble and Johnson 2013). Expectations may also rise as conditions improve, perhaps as a direct consequence of the intervention, while when conditions are poor, people adjust their expectations to avoid disappointment (what economists call adaptive preferences). Impacts of natural resource management interventions will not be linear but change through the course of the project and beyond. For example, any initial gains in aspects of well-being such as fish catch, wealth and empowerment were lost after external support for MPAs in Indonesia was withdrawn, suggesting that interventions of this kind need to build capacity, gain broad-based support and sustain

---

Box 5.4 Evaluating the Social Impacts of Protected Areas and PES Schemes in the Northern Plains of Cambodia

Payments for ecosystem services (PES) is often hypothesised to improve local well-being due to the benefits provided (Pagiola et al. 2005), but this is rarely evaluated empirically. In the Northern Plains of Cambodia, two protected areas (PAs) were supported by the Wildlife Conservation Society from 2005, with the aim of protecting threatened species, preventing deforestation and agri-industrial development. Additionally, three PES schemes were established in some villages within the PAs from 2008 onwards. Clements and Milner-Gulland (2015) used a before–after, control–impact (BACI) design to evaluate the impacts of these interventions on human well-being. Four measures were used to capture components of well-being considered locally important and potentially impacted by the interventions: (i) poverty as measured by the Basic Necessities Survey (BNS), an index-based tool in which necessities are locally defined through a participatory process and scored at the household level (Davies and Smith 1998); (ii) agricultural productivity of rice, as the staple crop in the Cambodian diet as well as being socially and culturally significant; (iii) food security, measured as the difference between a household's annual harvest and its rice need for subsistence; and (iv) education levels of each household member. To measure the difference in impacts, PA villages were matched with control villages outside the PA, and then households participating in PES were matched with control households within the same PA villages. Social data were collected through household surveys across 20 villages in 2008, and the process was repeated for the same households in 2011. Data were disaggregated according to household livelihoods to elucidate variable impacts on different sectors of society.

Overall, the status of households in the area improved over the study period, as might be expected in a post-conflict situation. Average rates of change in basic necessities were similar between households in the PA and control villages, but there were significant differences depending on the main livelihood strategies households followed: Poverty improvements were faster for resin tappers in the PAs compared to the controls, and for households who had less than 1 ha of rice paddy, and so were amongst the least food secure in the community. Given that these two groups were key targets for conservation and well-being interventions, the result could be seen as a success.

Within PA villages, the two higher paying PES programmes improved BNS scores at a greater rate than in non-PES households, and these households were also able to better educate their children. These programmes are the Ibis Rice programme, which pays a premium price for rice to households following participatory land-use plan rules, and a bird-watching ecotourism programme. The Ibis Rice programme also increased rice harvests and improved food security, but was limited to those who had sufficient land to produce a rice surplus over their subsistence needs, suggesting elite capture. Ecotourism was also necessarily targeted at more educated and well-connected people. Involvement in the third scheme, which pays individuals for protecting nests of threatened bird species, had no added impact on income probably because the payments were small, but it was the only intervention which was egalitarian in terms of access. These results and insights can be used to adapt, target and structure the interventions for more equitable benefits in the future.

funding (Gurney et al. 2014). Evaluations may need to span long time scales to measure the sustainability of management strategies and consider the dynamics of changes; or at least evaluators and researchers should consider what kinds of longer-term impacts may appear in the future.

5.7 CHALLENGES AND FUTURE DIRECTIONS

Improving management decisions which support human well-being requires that much more effort needs to be invested in building a robust evidence base of which types of interventions work, and why. Although use of multi-dimensional concepts of well-being in impact evaluations of conservation (e.g. Leisher et al. 2012; Gurney et al. 2014), and in planning (Stephanson and Mascia 2014) is emerging, the focus remains on material assets and specific issues of particular interest to conservationists such as the impacts of wildlife on humans such as crop raiding. There does appear to be increasing momentum to address this gap, for example with the evaluation of the current evidence base for impacts of terrestrial protected areas on some well-being dimensions, which includes perspectives from diverse actors (Pullin et al. 2013), and efforts to map the current evidence available (McKinnon et al. 2016). More evidence is needed, however, for a range of interventions, and a common framework such as the one presented here (Figure 5.1) would allow some level of systematic comparison to be made between case studies. This would improve understanding about how different types of conservation interventions affect different dimensions of well-being, and the causal mechanisms at work. There is a risk, however, in making generalisations about which policies work, due to the diverse contexts in which interventions take place, meaning that the same approach leads to different outcomes for different people and places. The challenge is providing frameworks for integrating consideration of human well-being into decision-making, which draw upon the evidence base (quantitative and qualitative), but are sufficiently sensitive to allow translation to local contexts.

As the concept of well-being is gaining popularity in policy circles, it is inevitably being used as political rhetoric and for a variety of ends. Analysis of well-being is not a neutral, objective exercise, and different interests and ideologies influence the way it is understood and the way it is put into practice (Alkire et al. 2012). For example, an international NGO may want to show that its projects are making a difference, and to replicate its interventions and methods of measuring well-being, whereas national governments may want to show the current need of populations in the context of effective state governance in order to access international donor funding (Palmer Fry et al. 2015). There is a need to understand these perspectives; how power works to shape people's operationalisation of well-being. All decision-making is a political process, and well-being is itself a way of framing debate and evidence in this process. The framework and methods proposed here for conservation decision-making provide a starting point for the inclusion of local perspectives and participation, legitimising local forms of knowledge, which can get side-lined in policymaking, but which need to be integral to effective conservation (Adams and Sandbrook 2013). Ultimately, the question of whose well-being and preferences count is a moral and political issue, but a local perspective at least allows those with the most to lose to gain a voice in the debate with other often more powerful stakeholders including private companies, governments and international NGOs. There is a distinction, however, between knowledge mediated by external research and that articulated by people themselves, and the ideal is to move towards the latter (Brosius 2010). This diversity of well-being perspectives brings us back to the social dimension of WeD, and the wider societal question of how to reconcile and negotiate individual choices with larger-scale visions of a good society and desirable development pathways, including international interests, inter-generational equity and environmental sustainability (McGregor et al. 2008).

Given the complexity involved in the concept of well-being, many researchers and managers in countries and programmes which lack resources will be wondering how they can manage to examine and consider well-being. A multi-disciplinary approach to research and practice may require an expansion of project teams to include social scientists and more time to negotiate common goals and approaches. It is encouraging that there are calls for increasing collaboration between conservation and disciplines such as anthropology, which would go some way towards rectifying a tendency in conservation for social research to be fast and formulaic (Brosius 2006). However, these calls have been voiced for at least four decades without the fundamental barriers to interdisciplinarity being resolved (Pooley et al. 2014). Given the tight budgets of conservation implementers and the need for access to a range of specialist expertise, more collaboration between practitioners and academic researchers is needed. A strategy for multi-disciplinary practice, including discussing and negotiating questions and values up front and ensuring conceptual and data integration, would also be helpful (Pooley et al. 2014). Including in-country graduate students in the research team is a practical and cost-effective approach to conducting research, which has the added benefit of building capacity. There are also exciting opportunities emerging with new technologies, for example citizen science platforms on mobile phones, enabling communities to carry out research themselves to address their own priorities (Lewis and Nkuintchua 2012), with the potential for greater participation, legitimacy and more direct incorporation of local knowledge into decision-making.

5.8 CONCLUSIONS

Well-being can act as a lens through which better to understand people's lives, livelihoods and aspirations. It is certainly not a new concept, but conservationists have only recently started to engage with the idea, as the linkages between people and ecosystems become apparent. As this has happened, conservation and natural resource management interventions have evolved to incorporate multiple interacting goals including biodiversity, improved governance and poverty alleviation. This does not necessarily imply that conservationists entirely shift their mission focus but rather seek alignments with local well-being in their interventions, which ultimately provides a more sustainable solution. Connecting policy and decision-making processes with the details of local social realities and perspectives also provides a voice to local people. This can apply not only to materially poor areas of the world, but to all conservation interventions, which inevitably impact and involve nearby communities. However, given the fragility of some individuals' and households' security in situations of poverty, they have the most to lose from poorly planned interventions, yet potentially the most to gain from healthy and productive ecosystems.

Part II

Challenges in Implementation

Implementing Decision Analysis Tools for Invasive Species Management

JOSLIN L. MOORE, CHARLIE PASCOE,
ELAINE THOMAS AND MARIE KEATLEY

6.1 INTRODUCTION

While decision tools and processes, such as structured decision-making and adaptive management, are gaining widespread acceptance in the conservation literature, implementation on the ground is less common. This chapter describes how specific decision tools were developed and implemented over a seven-year period to assist national park managers in Victoria, Australia, to manage an invasive willow species (*Salix cinerea*), which threatens endangered alpine bog communities. Despite enthusiasm and commitment from all partners, implementation created a range of challenges for scientists and managers, including the need to clearly understand management objectives, effectively communicate research results and develop efficient data collection and transfer processes. Using the willow example as a case study, this chapter describes and reflects on these challenges and how they were overcome to help managers maximise the impact of their efforts.

Plant invasions are a substantial threat to biodiversity and ecosystem function worldwide and are a particular concern in protected areas that often have high conservation value. As a result, a large amount of protected area management effort is allocated to managing these species invasions. While there is increasing research on the impacts of invasive plant populations both outside and within protected areas, there is still a weak linkage with management (Hulme et al. 2014).

Adaptive management, a form of decision analysis that incorporates potential for learning into the decision-making and monitoring process (Walters 1986; Gregory et al. 2012), has been widely promoted by natural resource management and conservation scientists over recent decades (Hilborn et al. 1995; Shea K. and The NCEAS Working Group on Population Management 1998; Stankey et al. 2005; Williams 2001). Adaptive management, often described as 'learning by doing', is a process for decision-making under uncertainty that ensures the effects of management actions are monitored and used to update both knowledge and management decisions (Runge 2011). Despite incorporation of the term into the rhetoric of numerous government agencies, few examples of implemented adaptive management have been reported in the literature (Westgate et al. 2013).

Since mid-2007, quantitative scientists (led by Dr Joslin Moore) and park managers (led by Charlie Pascoe, Elaine Thomas and Marie Keatley) have joined forces, applying decision analysis to enhance the management of an invasive plant that threatens a high-value wetland vegetation community in north-eastern Victoria, Australia. The project has improved management outcomes and a strong relationship has developed between researchers and managers. However, the process has not all been smooth sailing. This chapter describes the ups and downs of the collaborative team's efforts to develop innovative science that addresses an applied environmental management problem.

6.2 BACKGROUND

Alpine bogs – also known as alpine wetlands, peatlands, mires or moss-beds – are characterised by a mix of wet heath shrubs, sedges, rushes, scale rushes and peat (*Sphagnum*) mosses (Tolsma and Shannon 2007). Alpine bogs are home to a rich profusion of wetland flora and provide a critical refuge for a number of endemic flora and fauna species. They require permanent water and impeded drainage to maintain a high water table (Department of Sustainability, Environment, Water, Population and Communities, 2013).

Alpine Sphagnum Bogs and Associated Fens (henceforth 'alpine bogs' or 'bogs') are an endangered plant community in Australia, listed under both state (Victorian Flora and Fauna Guarantee Act, 1988) and national (Environment Protection and Biodiversity Conservation Act, 1999) legislation. The community is geographically restricted; alpine and subalpine areas cover only 0.15 per cent of the Australian land surface (Williams and Costin 1994). Alpine bogs recover slowly after disturbance. The main threats have been identified as disturbance from fire and introduced hard-hooved animals (mainly feral horses, deer and livestock), climate change (through reduced water levels and increased fire frequency and intensity) and invasion of introduced plant species

(McDougall 2007; Department of Sustainability, Environment, Water, Population and Communities 2013).

The Bogong High Plains (1500–1884 m) is the largest contiguous alpine and sub-alpine region in Victoria, comprising approximately 18,000 ha of alpine and subalpine grassland, heathland, wet heathland, bog and snow gum (*Eucalyptus pauciflora* Sieber ex Spreng) woodland. Annual precipitation varies between 1200 and 2400 mm, falling as snow above 1400 m for three months of the year (Costin et al. 2000). The majority of the Bogong High Plains lies within the Alpine National Park managed by Parks Victoria. A small area (1,535 ha), including the township of Falls Creek, is managed as a ski resort by the Falls Creek Resort Management Board, a public management agency responsible for managing and promoting skiing and other recreational activity in the region.

Grey sallow willow (*Salix cinerea* L.) is a shrub willow of European origin, which was introduced into Australia more than 70 years ago and was widely planted to reduce erosion in waterways (Cremer et al. 1995). Willows are dioecious (have separate male and female plants) and, as both sexes of grey sallow were introduced to Australia, is one of a small but increasing number of *Salix* species that can produce seed in Australia. Insect and wind pollinated (Hopley and Young 2015), grey sallow produces small seeds that can disperse across long distances by wind and water (Cremer et al. 1995). The species is a serious invader in Victoria, New South Wales and Tasmania, where it is the target of a state-wide eradication programme (Holland-Clift and Davies 2007) and is also naturalised in Queensland. It has established widely in montane, sub-alpine and alpine vegetation in Victoria. As grey sallow can persist and produce seed in poorly drained wetland areas as well as riparian zones (core habitat for all *Salix* species), it is considered one of the most invasive willow species in Australia (Cremer 2003). All *Salix* species have very short-lived seeds (grey sallow maximum 8–12 weeks) and so do not form a persistent seedbank (Hopley and Young 2015). The seeds require high light and low competition conditions to establish. Grey sallow can also reproduce vegetatively and mature plants can resprout after fire (Pascoe, personal observation).

The montane and alpine regions of south-eastern Australia are subject to infrequent and sometimes large bushfires. Extensive fires occurred in the region in January 2003 (Alpine Fires) and in 2006–2007 (the Great Divide Fires). The 2003 fires burnt more than 3 million ha across Victoria, New South Wales and the Australian Capital Territory including more than 85 per cent of vegetation on the Bogong High Plains

(Williams et al. 2008). The Great Divide Fires were also substantial (> 1,200,000 ha) but their impact on the sub-alpine and alpine areas of the Bogong High Plains was less (Victorian Department of Sustainability and Parks Victoria 2008). Nevertheless, approximately 20 per cent of the Bogong High Plains burnt, the majority for the second time in four years. Overall, this second fire was less intense in the alpine bogs, probably because of lower fuel loads due to the short recovery time after the 2003 fires and milder weather conditions once fire reached the plateau.

Many of the alpine bogs were severely burned during these fires, especially during the 2003 Alpine Fires, leaving extensive open areas of moist ash bed – perfect conditions for the establishment of grey sallow. At the time of the Alpine Fires, grey sallow was widespread in the region, both within and outside the burnt area but uncommon in alpine vegetation (McDougall et al. 2005). Grey sallow seedlings were first noticed in bogs in January 2004, approximately 12 months post-fire (Figure 6.1). Seedlings observed in January 2004 probably germinated between October and December 2003. Neither Parks Victoria nor the many botanists who had been working on the Bogong High Plains prior to the fires anticipated the widespread establishment that was observed. Although a 1994 report commissioned by the Australian Alps Liaison Committee predicted widespread invasion into bogs and other suitable high-country habitat, recommending the removal of all willows, especially *Salix cinerea*, from the sub-alpine and alpine zones (Carr et al. 1994), this concern had not been widely promoted. For example, the 2003 Alpine Fires recovery plan did not identify grey sallow invasion as a key post-fire threat (Ministerial Taskforce on Bushfire Recovery 2003).

The source of the grey sallow seeds germinating on the Bogong High Plains after the 2003 Alpine Fires wasn't clear. The Bogong High Plains are surrounded by tall forests dominated by alpine ash (*Eucalyptus delegatensis* R.T. Baker) much of which is managed as a state forest by the Victorian government. While much is not part of the national park, these forests contain waterways that support populations of grey sallow that may act as seed sources for invasion of alpine areas. Given the prominence of wind as a dispersal vector for this seed, it was thought the predominant seed source for germination on the Bogong High Plains was the valleys and catchment headwaters to the north and northwest. However, it was known that mature grey sallows were established in scattered locations around the High Plains and a mature population was removed from the shores of Rocky Valley Dam in the summer of 2002–2003, just after the fires.

Figure 6.1 (a) An unburnt alpine bog on the Bogong High Plains in Victoria; (b) a team of contractors removing willow seedlings from an alpine stream in 2008; (c) a mountain stream with a dense infestation of mature willows in 2007, which may have contributed seed to the alpine infestation (photos: Joslin Moore).

Figure 6.1 (*continued*)

Grey sallow invasion management began on the Bogong High Plains in the 2003–2004 growing season and has been undertaken every year since (excluding the 2006–2007 summer when the Great Divide Fires limited the access). Parks Victoria employed contractors and volunteers to control grey sallow on and around the Bogong High Plains. Control in alpine bogs largely involved removal of seedlings established since 2003. In potential source populations, control involved removal of mature (reproductive) plants from upwind valleys (principally the Kiewa River and its tributaries) plus any grey sallow already established on the Bogong High Plains, as well as seedlings and juveniles from these potential source areas. Prior to the project, effort was split three ways towards these three main activities with approximately 30 per cent of effort allocated specifically to controlling grey sallow in bogs, 36 per cent allocated to control of source populations on the Bogong High Plains and 35 per cent allocated to controlling grey sallow in the rivers downstream (but upwind) of the Bogong High Plains.

Control of grey sallow was undertaken using a variety of methods and organisations, including contractors and volunteers, across a range of locations. For the first two years after the Alpine Fires, one group of contractors controlled willow seedlings within bogs and their surroundings by hand pulling. This was very labour-intensive as the seedlings were also bagged and taken away due to concerns that any material left behind might re-sprout. As the seedlings got larger, hand pulling was replaced by cutting and painting (cut stem and paint with herbicide), with the controlled biomass still being removed. By 2009, it was realised that biomass removal was not necessary and this practice stopped. Another group of contractors were deployed to manage the larger source populations in the waterways surrounding the Bogong High Plains and larger grey sallows on the Bogong High Plains but generally not within bogs. This team of contractors used a frilling and filling method (nick the stem and paint with herbicide) more appropriate for established plants with larger stems. The management programme was co-ordinated by different Parks Victoria staff each year until the summer of 2007–2008, when Ranger Elaine Thomas took over responsibility.

6.3 PROJECT ESTABLISHMENT

In June 2007, Dr. Joslin Moore was employed as a research fellow at the University of Melbourne, with funding from an Australian government research programme, to develop and implement an adaptive management case study in the alpine region. This meant that Dr Moore was able to focus exclusively on developing this project for the first three years (2007–2010). The first steps in developing an adaptive management framework, as with other decision theoretic approaches (see Dichmont and Fulton, Chapter 2, and Garrard et al., Chapter 3), are to identify the objectives of management, identify candidate management actions and develop a conceptual model of the system that links management actions to predicted outcomes.

When the project began, information regarding the ecology of grey sallow in Australia was very limited with no studies undertaken in alpine (treeless) vegetation. In addition, there was very little information regarding bog recovery rates post-fire (McDougall 2007) or the specific impacts of grey sallow on alpine bogs. Parks Victoria had gathered information regarding grey sallow establishment and the control programme was planned based on the following assumptions:

- Alpine bogs constituted a high conservation value asset of primary concern.
- The extent and locations of alpine bogs were well known and extensively mapped (McDougall 1982; McDougall and Walsh 2007).

- Grey sallows constituted a major threat to alpine bog condition and resilience to the impacts of climate change.
- Alpine bogs were largely resistant to grey sallow establishment, unless vegetation cover was disturbed (principally by fire).
- Alpine bogs would take more than twenty years for vegetation cover to completely recover post-fire (McDougall 2007).
- Pre-fire occurrence of grey sallow in bogs was negligible (alpine botanists working on the Bogong High Plains pre-fire rarely recorded grey sallow in bogs but were quick to detect the establishment of seedlings in January 2004).
- Grey sallow dispersal into alpine bogs on the Bogong High Plains was largely via wind, predominantly from the north to northwest (the predominant direction of warm summer winds).

In addition, Parks Victoria had identified the following knowledge gaps:

- The distribution and abundance of grey sallows of various age classes on the Bogong High Plains was incompletely known.
- Relationships between grey sallow age, size and maturity on the Bogong High Plains was not known.
- The locations of source populations were poorly known.
- The dispersal distance of grey sallow seed was unknown, making it difficult to identify regions that could potentially contain source populations.

Initial scoping, including a field visit to see the willow invasions and potential source populations, established a clear management objective to protect alpine bogs on the Bogong High Plains from the impacts of grey sallow invasion. However, it was not considered feasible to remove all potential source populations. As a result, we decided that the following key project questions would be addressed (paraphrased from the initial project agreement):

1. Was it more cost effective to control grey sallows at source or to wait for seedlings to establish in bogs and then control those?
2. Could management strategies be altered to increase knowledge and/ or rate of learning about key invasion and management processes (e.g. probability of seedling establishment)? Would this assist managers to make better decisions?

3. How should search and control efforts be distributed through space? For example, should effort be equally distributed throughout the region or focused on alpine bogs as the priority asset to be protected?
4. What level of management would limit ongoing seedling establishment in bogs and could this be achieved within a realistic budget?
5. For how long (and at what frequency) should monitoring of bogs and source sites continue after removal of grey sallow from bogs, given that seedlings may continue to establish until bogs fully recover from fire?

To address these questions, we undertook three major modelling phases (described below). Each of the modelling phases synthesised existing data and stimulated the collection of additional data. Models were used to summarise understanding of the system, associated uncertainties and identify key knowledge gaps which were then addressed using a combination of models and field studies. The philosophy of undertaking field studies motivated by models reflected an effort to gain maximum return on investment in terms of management relevance (Nichols and Williams 2006).

6.4 PRELIMINARY MODELLING

A preliminary model was developed to identify key factors likely to be important for the effective management of grey sallow invasion in alpine bogs (Moore 2007). A simple metapopulation model was used to ascertain the proportion of bogs occupied by grey sallows as a function of colonisation and local extinction rates. The colonisation rate represented the dispersal and establishment potential of willow seed from potential source populations and was reduced when effort was allocated to control these populations. The local extinction rate was purely a function of grey sallow control efforts within bogs.

This model was spatially implicit and provided the expected proportion of alpine bogs occupied, given an annual allocation of management effort between potential source populations (colonisation) and sink populations (bogs). The model's strength was that it made it possible to analytically determine the optimal allocation of control resources to potential source and bog populations that minimised the proportion of bogs occupied by grey sallow. Although there were no quantitative data to estimate the specific parameter values, it was possible to use credible parameter combinations to examine the effectiveness of different management strategies. For example, it was reasonable to expect control of the seedlings to be more cost-effective than control of large grey sallows in remote and inaccessible areas and that the available control budget was modest. These analyses indicated that a focus on willow removal from bogs was optimal if these assumptions held.

As with any model, this one included numerous simplifications and assumptions. Some were conservative and unlikely to fundamentally alter model conclusions. For example, the model assumed grey sallows that established in bogs were controlled before maturation and would not, therefore, become future seed sources. Because this assumption might result in an underestimation of the importance of seedling removal from bogs, including a maturation parameter was unlikely to result in a change in focus from the recommendation provided to Parks Victoria.

However, some other assumptions inherent within the model posed quite serious limitations on its ability to guide management decisions (especially for long-term strategies). For example, the model could not incorporate dynamic factors very likely to be important, including the cumulative effect of control on potential source populations (meaning it was likely the model overestimated the effort required to manage source populations), the fact that as bogs regained vegetation cover over time after fire, they became less easy for grey sallows to colonise, and uncertainty as to the locations of actual source populations. As a result, caution was required when making recommendations based on the model's results. Yet the model did clearly indicate that, in the short term, Parks Victoria should focus on removing grey sallow seedlings from alpine bogs rather than continuing to split its efforts between bogs and potential source populations. At this time, the overall strategy for management didn't change with the main outcome being the decision to develop more robust models and work to improve data collection and resolve key uncertainties.

In addition, during this initial modelling phase, researchers and managers reviewed and refined the critical knowledge gaps:

1. The distribution and abundance of grey sallow on the Bogong High Plains and in surrounding catchments.
2. The effectiveness of grey sallow seedling control (a new knowledge gap based on the preliminary modelling).
3. The effectiveness of control of potential source populations (a new knowledge gap based on the preliminary modelling).

4. Basic local grey sallow demographic data, most importantly reasonable estimates of seed dispersal distance, time to maturity on the Bogong High Plains, and the relationship between vegetation cover and willow establishment in alpine bogs.

Field studies, monitoring programmes and models were developed to fill many of these gaps and are described Section 6.7 that follows. Fieldwork and monitoring was undertaken by Parks Victoria and Moore's research team.

From this preliminary modelling and problem framing, two major decision models were developed. The first allocated annual grey sallow control effort across the Bogong High Plains. The second developed a management strategy for grey sallow in the region that would minimise its invasion on to the Bogong High Plains over the long term. These two projects ran concurrently from 2008 to 2010 and are described in the following sections.

6.5 SPATIAL ALLOCATION OF ANNUAL CONTROL EFFORT

One of the first issues to emerge was where to search for grey sallow on the Bogong High Plains and how much effort should be allocated to searching in any given area. A method to address this question had recently been developed by University of Melbourne researchers (Hauser and McCarthy 2009) and it seemed the perfect opportunity to apply their work to a real case study.

Hauser and McCarthy's method trades off searching costs with the costs of failing to detect individuals of a species when present. It enables optimal allocation of effort across space, with or without a budget. To implement the decision model, we needed a probability of occurrence map for grey sallow on the Bogong High Plains and estimates of willow detectability as a function of search effort. A decision model was developed for the entire Bogong High Plains (rather than just for alpine bogs) for two reasons: we did not want to pre-empt learning about habitat suitability by focusing only on bogs, and at this time Parks Victoria was still controlling grey sallow across the entire Bogong High Plains. However, we did take account of the focus on bogs by specifying a higher benefit of controlling grey sallow in bogs. This, of course, affected the optimal allocation of control resources.

Kate Giljohann fitted and validated an occupancy model for grey sallow on the Bogong High Plains as her honours year research project

(Giljohann 2009). We only had presence data available, so we used MaxEnt (Phillips and Dudik 2008) to fit a probability of occupancy and then reduced that probability in areas where previous control had been undertaken, assuming an average level of control effort to that undertaken previously. We then estimated willow detection rates and combined these to identify optimal allocation of control effort across the region (Giljohann et al. 2011). Model output was a map for a given budget (Figure 6.2), which could be updated annually. In addition, it is possible to weight different areas according to the conservation benefit of controlling grey sallow within them.

The modelling resolution was a 20 metre grid that would have been too fine a scale for field implementation. Therefore, the research team aggregated the time allocation to more reasonable units (person hours per hectare) to guide control effort, and used this as an indicative guide to highlight priority areas for willow control. Global positioning system (GPS) tracking of contractors enabled us to analyse how effort was allocated across the area. One result stood out – many willow control contractors were allocating more than the optimal amount of effort in each area (i.e. continuing to search for seedlings for too long) and would have had a greater overall impact if they had moved on to new areas sooner. We converted this finding into a rule of thumb: contractors should not search for grey sallows smaller than knee height (although they should control any they came across). From 2009 to 2012, the probability of occurrence map was updated annually to account for previous control efforts and a new optimal allocation calculated to meet the budget for the following year (Giljohann et al. 2009; Giljohann and Moore 2011a, 2011b).

6.6 LONG-TERM STRATEGY: STRUCTURED DECISION-MAKING WORKSHOP

Researchers were confident there would be very few circumstances under which allocating substantial effort to control potential source populations was likely to be efficient. However, modelling work had focused on relatively short-term outcomes (optimisation of willow control following the Alpine and Great Divide Fires) and didn't address long-term management strategies, given that fires were likely to occur in the future. To address this, we developed a longer-term strategy using a structured decision-making approach (see Garrard et al., Chapter 3).

It was a fortuitous coincidence for the project that Dr Michael Runge, an experienced practitioner in structured decision-making and adaptive

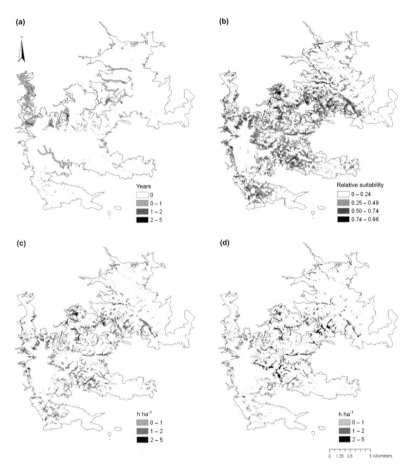

Figure 6.2 The Bogong High Plains study area illustrating the (a) estimated intensity of grey sallow willow control prior to development of the spatial prioritisation model (years 2003/2004–2007/2008), (b) the potential distribution of grey sallow willow accounting for control, (c) spatially prioritised control effort assuming an annual budget of 400 person days, with control weighted equally across all vegetation types and (d) the prioritisation when double benefits were assigned to control in bogs and wet heath vegetation (after Giljohann et al. 2011).

management from the United States Geological Survey (USGS) was on sabbatical at The University of Melbourne. He was able to help facilitate a structured decision-making workshop with agency staff that provided the basis for developing a long-term control strategy. The workshop included participants from Parks Victoria and other state agencies (then Department of Sustainability and Environment, North East Catchment

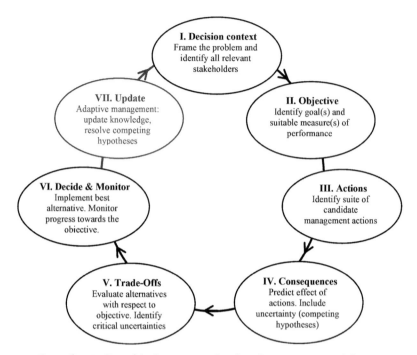

Figure 6.3 Outline of the key steps undertaken during a structured decision process. Steps I–III and step VI are values-based steps determined by the decision-makers. Steps IV and V (and VII if required) are science-based. After Moore and Runge (2012).

Management Authority) responsible for managing areas adjacent to the Alpine National Park. Dr Runge brought additional skills and experience to assist Parks Victoria and other land managers to structure and analyse the problem at hand. A workshop was held over two days in October 2008 – a very short timeframe for this kind of activity compared with similar five-day workshops carried out in the US. As a result, the entire process (Figure 6.3) wasn't completed, but the collaborative team worked its way through the first four steps and, crucially, identified the objectives and candidate management actions available.

The workshop was very successful; it enabled us to clarify management objectives and develop a shared understanding of the problem. This process confirmed an objective to protect the state and nationally listed Alpine Sphagnum Bogs and Associated Fens community by removing grey sallow. It clarified that the most crucial decision for managers was how to allocate control effort between grey sallow in bogs and various possible source populations.

Although the model was developed by the researchers after the workshop, being able to participate in its formulation was an important contributor to managers' understanding and acceptance of its results. The workshop particularly highlighted for managers the importance of clearly identifying the fundamental objective of management and associated measures of performance. In this instance, the fundamental objective related to maintaining and improving the condition of alpine bogs but there was no established measure for how to do this and grey sallow was only one of several threats to bog condition (others include changing climate, frequent fires and the impacts of feral horses, deer and past cattle grazing). The workshop therefore agreed that the fundamental objective for the management of grey sallow threatening bogs would be structured around the densities of grey sallow of different size classes in bogs.

Two major findings resulted from the decision process (Moore and Runge 2010a, 2010b; Moore and Runge 2012). First, optimisation showed that, in almost all scenarios, the optimal allocation of management effort was to focus on control of grey sallow in bogs (Figure 6.4), despite enormous uncertainty in almost all of the model parameters. Second, the value of information analysis showed there were limited opportunities to improve management through learning (maximum improvement of about 10 per cent, but for current budgets much less; Figure 6.5), and so a formal adaptive management approach probably wasn't warranted. The value of information analysis was very important because it showed that even though there was substantial uncertainty associated with the dynamics of the grey sallow infestation over time, this uncertainty did not change the best management strategy. Further analysis showed critical uncertainties for improving management decisions were the dispersal potential of grey sallow and the rate of recovery of vegetation cover in bogs after fire. However, learning about these factors would only result in modest improvements in management outcomes.

This doesn't mean there was no value in learning *per se*. For example, the large amounts of uncertainty meant we were unable to predict with any confidence whether any particular management strategy was likely to succeed (i.e. maintain very low densities of grey sallow in bogs over the long term), making it difficult to make recommendations regarding budgets or provide clear statements of expected outcomes. The analysis clearly showed that the parameter uncertainty needed to be reduced if Parks Victoria wished to make meaningful predictions of management

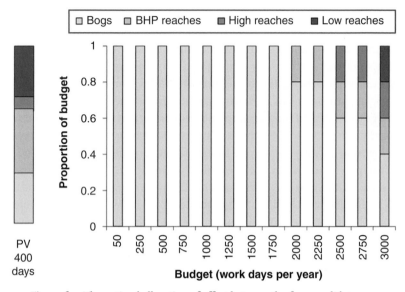

Figure 6.4 The optimal allocation of effort between the four candidate management areas across a range of budgets. The column to the left indicates Parks Victoria's allocation over the period 2004–2008.

outcomes. The development of the long-term strategy also highlighted that there was no process in place to monitor grey sallow distribution and abundance in bogs on the Bogong High Plains and thus evaluate management outcomes.

Changes brought about by development of the long-term strategy included focussing all control effort on alpine bogs from the 2010–2011 season, the development and implementation of surveys to monitor changes in grey sallow abundance in bogs over time and improved monitoring of control effort as a means to also monitor grey sallow abundance. Parks Victoria has also incorporated the work undertaken into their long-term seeding willow strategy for the region (Parks Victoria 2014).

6.7 DATA COLLECTION AND DATA MANAGEMENT

Over the life of the project, both researchers and Parks Victoria have invested in field studies and monitoring to address critical knowledge gaps and improve decision-making. The broad activities are summarised in the following discussion, with a focus on successes and

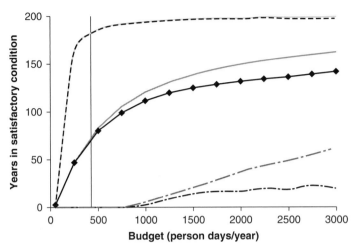

Figure 6.5 Summary of how management effectiveness and expected value of information changes with available budget. The black line shows the expected performance of the optimal action given best estimates for the parameters. The dashed black lines are the 90 per cent quantiles (representing uncertainty). The solid grey line shows expected performance if we knew the parameter values prior to allocating effort and indicates how much we could improve performance if we had perfect information. The dashed grey lines are the 90 per cent quantiles for perfect information. The vertical line indicates the resources allocated to control in 2008–2009 by Parks Victoria.

challenges. Note that the initial distinction between seedlings on the Bogong High Plains and adult source populations in the surrounding valleys has blurred over time, as mature plants have since been found on the Bogong High Plains and the post-fire cohorts of seedlings have grown and in some cases reached maturity.

6.7.1 Distribution of Grey Sallow on the Bogong High Plains and in Surrounding Catchments

The development of the spatial allocation model also produced a model of occupancy that summarised and interpolated known locations of grey sallow found during control works. The model revealed willow occupancy was strongly correlated with fire intensity and position in the landscape (a measure of soil water-holding ability).

Parks Victoria also made various efforts to map willow distribution in and around the Bogong High Plains using aerial surveys and remote sensing. These met with mixed success, being particularly poor for detecting small and/or scattered grey sallows. The Victorian Department of Environment and Primary Industries Index of Stream Condition project mapped willow (all species) along major waterways across the state, but this project covered only a small proportion of the Bogong High Plains region and only larger grey sallows were detectable. As a result, there remains no comprehensive mapping of grey sallows across the region.

6.7.2 The Effectiveness of Grey Sallow Control

The preliminary modelling highlighted that understanding the effectiveness of seedling control would be crucial for subsequent allocation of effort. Treatment effectiveness was measured as the detection rate, which is the proportion of grey sallows found per unit search effort (time) per unit area. This proved to be both challenging and difficult to measure yet remained one of the most important parameters for determining both annual distribution of control effort and the long-term control strategy (Moore 2008, 2009, 2013). Measuring effectiveness required having a good understanding of conditions prior to control, but it was very difficult to establish sufficient plots for control contractors to encounter without them being aware that they were being monitored. In addition, control methods changed over time, meaning that early effectiveness estimates were no longer relevant. Ensuring contractors remained ignorant of their being monitored by researchers was a high priority in the early days but, as GPS tracking of weed control contractors became standard (see Section 6.7.4), and the focus of control narrowed to alpine bogs, it became easier to direct contractors to control grey sallow in specific areas without concerns that they would behave atypically.

6.7.3 Willow Population Processes: Patterns of Establishment after Fire and Age at Maturity

While there was strong anecdotal evidence to suggest that the invasion of grey sallow into alpine bogs on the Bogong High Plains was triggered by bushfire, we had little information regarding seedling densities in relation to fire intensity. We undertook a series of surveys that supported the hypothesis that seedling establishment rates were higher in burned bogs. However, the surveys also indicated that grey sallow densities in unburnt bogs were not negligible, which challenged early assumptions about conditions for willow establishment. In 2011–2012, we undertook a study in bogs that had had no willow control to date and used growth rings to infer population structure and to examine the relationship between plant size and age (Moore and McAllister 2013). This showed that although there were peaks of recruitment three to four years post-fire, there was substantial ongoing recruitment up to nine years after fire. This suggested that the resistance of bogs with high vegetation cover to willow establishment was less than previously thought. It was also planned to use the study to identify age at maturity but only three flowering individuals were identified during the study, rendering it inconclusive.

6.7.4 Willow Control Effort

Information regarding previous control efforts existed when work on this project began, but it had been inconsistently collected and was held in a number of different places. One area that we worked hard to improve was recording of effort by willow control contractors.

Initially, contractors were asked to fill in paper data sheets describing control effort and numbers of grey sallow treated in each location. However, this proved onerous for contractors (e.g. they had to remove protective gloves to write on the sheets) and produced inconsistent records. In addition, contractors hadn't been adequately trained in project requirements. GPS data were also available, but their quality and meaning varied. In the early years, each contractor team (between three and six people) had only a single GPS unit between them, making it difficult to accurately map which areas had been controlled from track logs. Waypoints marked willow population locations but there was little information regarding the numbers or sizes of grey sallow associated with any specific waypoint.

From 2009 to 2010, the project moved to GPS-focussed data collection. Contractor personnel were tracked individually using GPS units throughout the workday with time and location data saved at regular (30- or 60-second) intervals. In addition, each contractor recorded a waypoint for each individual willow treated, enabling reasonably accurate estimations of willow density. This mode of data collection did not require contractors to remove safety gear or access recording sheets from their backpacks, so more information was recorded at a finer resolution and was substantially more reliable.

6.7.5 Data Management

Data management also emerged as a surprising challenge and one that often caused significant delays in information analysis. It was difficult to aggregate control information into a single format as it represented different kinds of activities, including surveys, opportunistic sightings, hand pulling of seedlings, frill and fill control, as well as cut and paint control with and without removal of the controlled grey sallows. Also, this work was undertaken at a time when Victoria was transitioning between standard mapping grids based on different geodetic datums (AGD 66 to GDA 94). This required data to be transformed between systems; however, haphazard record keeping in earlier periods meant substantial effort was needed to sort out the historical data.

New data also presented challenges. In particular, the conversion of raw GPS data to shapefiles (a natural choice when downloading data) resulted in loss of all-time information, which was crucial for evaluating control effort and linking that to the detectability studies. This meant that track log files had to be imported manually, which was very time-consuming. In 2013, the project employed a geographic information system (GIS) post-graduate student to write a programme to process GPS data, which greatly reduced data processing times.

In addition to these challenges, the University and Parks Victoria used different GIS software programs, so it proved cumbersome to transfer information between organisations. While all of this is very boring, it was crucial to the efficiency and effectiveness of data management and the data analyses that could be performed.

6.8 CURRENT STATUS

Control of grey sallows in alpine bogs continues. Since 2011–2012, the need for the spatial prioritisation of control effort has lessened; as of the summer of 2014–2015, all bogs on the Bogong High Plains have been searched once with all detected grey sallow removed. The large area of alpine bogs treated in recent years reflects the recommended focus (from the initial modelling) on control of grey sallows within bogs. The shift in effort away from potential source populations has enabled all of the 1350 ha of bogs to be treated and reflects a considerable change in management focus, as it is likely that it would have taken two to three times as long to reach all of the bogs if this change was not instituted.

The goal now is to design a follow-up treatment schedule that targets approximately one quarter of the Bogong High Plains' bogs each summer. This will enable removal of small grey sallow not treated during previous visits and minimise seed produced from them as they grow.

The monitoring of willow abundance in bogs (stratified random samples of 30–60 bogs were surveyed in 2009–2010, 2010–2011 and 2011–2012) suggested that willow abundance decreased in bogs across the Bogong High Plains but small sample sizes and the short time-frame mean that monitoring resolution was relatively coarse. Further monitoring of the bogs monitored during 2009–2012 undertaken in 2014–2015 (not yet analysed) will provide a more complete picture regarding the status of the willow invasion in bogs. The surveys are the primary mechanism for evaluating the status of grey sallow in bogs and hence the effectiveness of management. The intention is to continue monitoring the same set of bogs periodically (approximately every three years).

As populations are reduced within bogs, control effort will (subject to funding) move on to other wet areas on the Bogong High Plains, with an emphasis on areas in proximity to bogs. The degree to which control should be expanded outside bogs depends on patterns of seed dispersal. The team has recently secured funding to develop spatially explicit mechanistic models of seed dispersal across the landscape for a larger region that includes the Bogong High Plains to address this question. The value of information analysis indicated that dispersal had the highest value of information and this analysis has been used to attract co-funding from eight agency partners towards the project.

The looming question is when should the effort currently applied to willow control be refocused to manage other threats to bogs, such as disturbance due to exotic vertebrates. To answer this question requires quantifying the impacts of grey sallow on bog condition, information that is not currently available or being collected, and comparing this with the impacts of the other threats. In the meantime, Parks Victoria has implemented several other programmes, at varying stages of maturity, to address key threats, such as repeated fire, feral horses, sambar deer and a range of grassy and herbaceous weeds that also threaten bogs.

6.9 REFLECTIONS

Even though researchers and Parks Victoria staff were strongly committed to the concept of scientific management, it took time to build shared understanding and trust. The rewards, however, have been substantial. Researchers and managers reflect on their experiences of the project in the following.

6.9.1 Researcher's Perspective – Joslin Moore

This has been one of the most satisfying scientific endeavours I've undertaken – to see the science I've done put into practice has been highly rewarding, as has observing it improve the management of an important conservation area. I've also personally learned a great deal about collaborating and communicating with managers and how to make my science more relevant to their needs.

Like many academics, I've spent much time theorising about how to improve conservation management processes, but convincing managers to implement on-the-ground change based on theoretical insights hasn't always been easy. Practical management and academic work often seem worlds away from each other; they each approach a common problem from a different perspective and methodology. Even the language that researchers and managers use to speak about an issue can be different; what fires up an academic audience can fall completely flat when speaking to a meeting of managers.

Putting my findings in a more general context based on practical necessities and achievable outcomes was, however, a highly engaging and fulfilling process. I was delighted when the collaborative approach and workshops we employed for this project so successfully integrated scientific findings and management concerns, ultimately improving outcomes for all parties involved. And I've never been more convinced that an integrated, collective process is the way forward for projects of a similar ilk.

This project introduced me to structured decision-making for the first time and I became an immediate convert. I quickly realised how effective it could be to bring management decision-makers along in understanding a problem to be addressed and help them fully understand models and analyses. The process clearly separates decisions based on value judgements from those resulting from an improved understanding of the system and the logical consequences of actions to alter that system. These two aspects of decisions are often intermixed, which can result in a great deal of confusion on all sides. Clearly separating values and logical consequences simplifies decision-making and makes it easier to identify the actions most likely to produce the desired outcome. In addition, the process of defining the problem context and identifying objectives has proved very useful for managers. Clarifying the difference between fundamental objectives (the ultimate goal of management) and means objectives (that are useful only in the degree to which they contribute to achieving the ultimate goal) was also important. The workshop resulted in agreement between managers regarding the fundamental objective, which also provided researchers with clear direction regarding the problem to be addressed.

When I started the project, it appeared an ideal case study; the absence of a persistent seed bank, an apparently strong connection between grey sallow invasion and fire on the Bogong High Plains and the relatively small area occupied by the bogs meant that invasion management would be relatively straightforward. It seemed clear to me that control should be focused on the bogs. Reasoning and the preliminary model results suggested that in the absence of limitless resources there would only be a very small window of potential grey sallow dispersal distance where management of source populations would reduce further establishment in alpine bogs. And yet I wasn't having much luck convincing Parks Victoria or their partners of this. I attributed this to a lack of confidence in making strong early recommendations and an initial inability to clearly communicate model results. Although these conclusions appeared clear to me, I was unable to bring the managers along on the journey and communicate the logic of my conclusions.

I became more confident once we developed a long-term strategy in early 2009 using structured decision-making, but it still took some time for these recommendations to be implemented (which I interpreted as a combination of managers being unconvinced by my results and unrealistic expectations on my part). In addition, the recommendation to focus exclusively on the alpine bogs (symptom) rather than the root cause (source populations) did not sit well in a management context where resources are unreliable, suggesting the problem could well emerge again in the future if resources to address it are unavailable. I think this, combined with Parks Victoria's need to maintain engagement of other partners responsible for lower reaches, also contributed to the time it took for recommendations to be taken on board.

From a scientist's perspective, a graph is worth a thousand words. I still find it very difficult to understand that not everyone finds a graph as insightful as I do! I also overloaded my early messages with methodological detail, believing it necessary to explain how results were generated to minimise them being questioned. However, experience has shown that – as long as the detail is available in a report – focusing on results and findings rather than methods, it is a much more effective way to communicate with most managers. In addition, I discovered representing results as maps was an especially helpful way to communicate, being more consistent with the tools managers already use for planning.

Helping Parks Victoria improve its data management has been very satisfying; however, it was a constant challenge. The large volume of data, different GIS software in use within Parks Victoria and University of Melbourne, varying levels of expertise and limited availability of resources for curating the data all exacerbated data management problems. The substantial geographical distance (~350 km) between researchers and managers also made it more difficult to discuss data inconsistencies or share data management tricks over e-mail or telephone, especially when the sheer volume of data made data transfer complicated.

However, we also had plenty of successes. Moving from a paper-based to GPS-based control monitoring system for contractors was one outcome of which I'm most proud. Accounting for management imperatives and integrating them more fully into my thinking about how to solve problems was particularly satisfying; for example, I realised that tracking control effort was proving difficult because contractors simply couldn't fill out a paper log during the course of their work, we were able to develop a much more effective solution. In fact, taking the time to understand the practical problems at hand from a wide range of perspectives proved to be a lot of fun!

The project has ultimately taught me the importance of working with managers from the outset if I want to develop and apply models more successfully to practical conservation management. It's been a great experience for the whole group – from the close relationships we've formed to witnessing the practical extension of my team's work. Over time, I learned new ways to communicate more effectively and how best to get people on board with a more strategic approach. And I highly recommend the structured decision-making workshop model for reaching a workable consensus and allocating resources – I'll be running these from the outset of all new collaborative projects.

6.9.2 Research Manager's Perspective – Marie Keatley

Parks Victoria recognises that research and monitoring are essential parts of natural values management. Both assist us in dealing with uncertainty and in underpinning management decisions with credible, science-based information. Most research is undertaken via our

Research Partners Panel (RPP) – a collaborative partnership involving Parks Victoria, universities and other research institutions.

One of the RPP's strengths is that it allows robust and time-efficient project development. Briefs are relatively straightforward (e.g. focussing on background, objectives, milestones, outputs, personnel etc.), as the underlying contract addresses the tricky issues, such as intellectual property, confidentiality, commercialisation, termination of projects, etc. Briefs also define roles and responsibilities, helping us meet objectives, outputs, etc.

The most successful collaborations between Parks Victoria and researchers are those where mutual respect is present, where all recognise the expertise each person brings to a project (e.g. on-ground management and logistics, study design, etc.), and there is a shared interest in addressing the research questions (albeit from different perspectives). This project was an outstanding example of just such a successful collaboration. It also demonstrated how effective good communication can be – when people genuinely listen and are willing to discuss differences or change their approach if needed.

It does, however, take time to develop this kind of collaboration – and I believe face-to-face meetings remain the best way to achieve this, perhaps because there is time prior, during and afterwards to make personal connections (e.g. what did you do on the weekend?, etc.) and strengthen relationships. In this instance, the distances between all involved were large, so telephone conferences were sometimes necessary. Additionally, researchers' reports were technical but readable and they were always willing to present and discuss their results further.

One great success (although probably done imperfectly) was management's incorporation of recommendations based on research results. This was particularly challenging for some decisions. For example, not treating every willow in favour of focussing on those 'just' within bogs initially seemed counter-intuitive, but ultimately proved to be the optimal approach to meet our objectives, given resource constraints.

This collaboration changed the way Parks Victoria addressed a high-priority and expensive management issue; indeed science underpinned management decisions. An additional project legacy is that we now have a way to better quantify our management effectiveness.

6.9.3 Environmental Programme Manager's
Perspective – Charlie Pascoe

I found this project to be highly collaborative – more so than any other research project in which I have been involved. Part of the project's success was the mutual respect held for the needs and drivers of each party involved. There was a genuine eagerness on the part of researchers to understand the problem from a manager's perspective and a real desire to see science translated into management outcomes, rather than simply presenting the science and leaving it to managers to adopt (or abandon) it. In addition, managers understood the researchers' need to produce publications as a result of their work.

The researchers showed a great willingness and ability to work with managers to recognise limitations in particular management approaches and to identify, model and test potential alternatives. They also made a great effort to understand our day-to-day management issues and constraints, and to jointly determine ways to overcome some and realise that others were intractable and had to be accepted (e.g. climate, access and funding limitations). For example, the project helped make improvements in manager and contractor data collection techniques, so we could better enable task quantification and the work undertaken, and evaluate control efficiency and effectiveness.

The project achieved a number of significant shifts in management approaches. Initial modelling and the structured decision-making workshop convinced us of the need to focus more strongly on targeting those grey sallows that directly and immediately threatened alpine bogs, rather than dispersing our efforts more widely and trying to control potential source populations. Data demonstrating that it required more search effort to target small seedlings and juvenile grey sallow resulted in a refocussing of our efforts in controlling mature and adolescent grey sallow as a priority. And, finally, we shifted our annual allocation of control resources based on habitat suitability, past control efforts, seedling control effectiveness and the benefit of control.

But perhaps the most significant shift in system understanding was the realisation that grey sallows were far more established and widespread on the Bogong High Plains than previously thought. Surveillance and bog survey data showed grey sallow could establish in alpine bogs without a bushfire event, albeit at much lower rates than after fire.

For me, however, the most useful features of the research project have been the determination of search (at both bog and individual plant scales) and control effectiveness for different size classes of grey sallow, the structured decision-making workshop, the resource allocation model, and the monitoring protocol that allowed us to quantify willow abundance in relation to recent fire history and control effort. This monitoring will allow us to record changes in willow abundance over time to evaluate how effective of our control efforts are and demonstrate to our funding partners the effectiveness of their investments.

This project was not without its challenges. The distance between managers' and researchers' work locations made conducting face-to-face discussions and developing working relationships problematic. Obtaining and providing – in the required quantity, quality and formats – the data needed for modelling and evaluation was often difficult, as was determining and maintaining the right balance between research and management. I was keenly aware that every management dollar or hour allocated to research (including modelling and monitoring) was a dollar not spent on killing grey sallow.

Grey sallow invasion into alpine bogs is just one of many major management issues Parks Victoria is addressing in the Victorian Alps and one of many research programmes we are involved in. It was sometimes difficult to commit the time needed for an effective collaborative research–management partnership and keep up with all the research outputs and their management implications. Determining which knowledge gaps should be prioritised for research took some time and our inability to address some key gaps was frustrating. These included determining where the grey sallow source populations were located and what the relationship was between age of reproductive maturity and age/size of grey sallow on the Bogong High Plains (as information from lower elevations or overseas proved of little relevance).

It was also necessary to overcome a view among some managers, staff and willow control contractors that just going out and killing grey sallow was not the optimal way to use our available resources. For some, it went against the grain to retain some willow populations in or close to bogs for research and monitoring purposes and to ignore grey sallow in some parts of the landscape so that others in higher-priority locations could be targeted for control. However, for some of our partners and funders, our robust scientific approach and strong focus on measurable objectives and performance evaluation have been pivotal to our ongoing support and funding success.

Ultimately, involvement in the project has increased our focus on understanding the rationale for managing issues (i.e. managing the impacts of threats on priority assets, rather than just controlling threats) and for setting clear, long-term, fundamental and means objectives. It has also highlighted the value of data acquisition and management in understanding the current state of an issue and how management intervention changes this state over time.

6.9.4 Ranger's Perspective – Elaine Thomas

This project offered an entirely new way of interacting with researchers – in 25 years with Parks Victoria, I haven't experienced such a collaborative and rewarding process. I wish we did more of it!

Initially, balancing scientific and management objectives was, at times, challenging. However, it did make us think more carefully about how to use key data and analysis to allocate our limited resources more effectively.

When our willow programme first began, we treated invasive willow populations wherever they occurred. However, the project data made it very clear we could never hope to treat all grey sallow across all areas. So we began to sort out our fundamental objectives, leading us to focus specifically on alpine bogs as the key asset of concern.

To assist in this endeavour, the researchers created a map that we now use to show contractors exactly where we want them to concentrate their control efforts. This has proved a highly effective tool to achieve a more targeted approach to grey sallow management. In addition, the data collected by the project has allowed us to shift from using one GPS coordinate per contracted management team to using GPS as a counter that allows us to locate and log each willow in detail. The result is a significantly lower willow establishment rate, the ability to track results over time and a renewed determination to focus efforts where they count most.

For me, the most significant shift in system understanding occurred during the structured decision-making workshop. The maps created by researchers, based on fire history, presented at these workshops immediately made it clear where our control regime should be directed first and helped us to think about how we could better induct and instruct contractors to address our management goals.

There were, of course, challenges that arose from this new approach. For those involved in long-term willow management, getting our heads around the need to leave willow populations for research purposes was quite difficult! In fact, we did inadvertently control one area set aside for study.

Obtaining enough data for the project was also a complex undertaking, as was balancing the requirements of data collection and management versus doing the work. However, once detailed and actionable information was available, it was impossible to ignore the need to make a system shift to address the new findings.

Changing the mindsets of the willow control contractors who had long been focused on protecting natural areas from weeds in a particular way was sometimes difficult. The contractors had not been involved in the structured decision-making workshops often found it hard to understand the logic behind leaving certain populations unmanaged. It was my role to explain and reiterate the advantages of consolidating resources on specific, high-risk areas and the importance of meeting agreed targets. Yet, once the benefit of such work could be clearly identified by the reduction of new grey sallow willow populations, the task became easier.

Ultimately, I believe the project has set a new benchmark in the management of invasive species and has directly led to a positive change in Park Victoria's grey sallow management decisions. Improved data and analysis has reaffirmed the need to set objectives that are more focused on those assets we are trying to protect and to concentrate our efforts on those areas in which we can be most effective over time.

6.10 CONCLUSIONS

Overall, managers and researchers have found this effort to be a very valuable process. It remains a relatively rare example of models being directly used to guide both strategic and tactical management decisions. In addition, Parks Victoria has utilised the research results as a key input into the development of a cross-tenure, ten-year management plan for the control of seeding grey sallows on and around the Bogong High Plains and nearby Mount Buffalo. The project team (researchers and managers) received the inaugural Parks Victoria Nancy Millis Science in Parks award for research that had demonstrably improved park management.

The use of models and structured decision-making approaches to guide management is increasing and we think the success reported here is eminently repeatable. We consider the success of this endeavour can be attributed to a commitment from both researchers and managers to work together to solve the problem, the structured decision-making process that included managers in the decision-making process and facilitated understanding of the models developed, and our ability to explicitly incorporate uncertainty into the analysis.

Researchers and managers commenced their efforts with a willingness to bring science and management together to address this problem; it would have been impossible if one or other party had been unwilling. Both researchers and managers worked hard to understand different perspectives and imperatives and researchers were willing to let managers make the management decisions based on the insights generated from the analysis. Cultivating such an attitude is an excellent first step in integrating science with management. However, it remains challenging because the considerable investment required to build trust and understanding for collaborations of this kind are not factored into the work load of researchers or managers and this effort does not directly contribute to evaluation of workplace performance in either setting (Gibbons et al. 2008). Dr Moore's position for the first three years was relatively unusual in that she was funded to develop a collaboration of this kind and so was able to allocate considerably more effort to developing the collaboration than is usual for a researcher in an academic setting. After three years, her position changed to a more general research position and maintaining the level of interaction became more challenging. However, after reaping benefits from the initial relationship, Parks Victoria saw the value of contributing funding to enable the research team to continue to address key management questions.

Another strength of the process was the structured decision-making framework, which provided a mechanism for identifying fundamental objectives, and integrating model development and results into management. A particularly useful outcome was that fundamental and means objectives were clearly separated. The process also facilitated more effective communication of model results to managers, which then guided subsequent decisions (Addison et al. 2013). Structured decision-making also enables the values-based aspects of decisions to be clearly separated from system understanding and cause and effect, separating the 'values' and 'facts'. This separation results in greater clarity regarding the values driving a decision, which can resolve apparent conflicts or differences in opinion regarding the best management strategy to achieve a given objective. However, structured decision-making and adaptive management are not panaceas. They cannot resolve fundamental differences in values and are not considered appropriate tools for conflict resolution (Williams et al. 2009).

Another key to success was that the decision process incorporated the substantial uncertainty regarding the trajectory of the invasion and the expected effects of candidate management actions. Such uncertainty is ubiquitous in environmental and conservation management. Explicitly incorporating the uncertainty into the decision model enabled us to use value of information analysis and identify the critical uncertainties that affected the best management outcome. In the case of grey sallow management, uncertainty had little effect on the optimal management strategy despite significant uncertainty regarding management outcomes in the long term. This analysis avoided investment in learning about uncertainty that was superfluous to the decision at hand, increasing the efficiency of research.

This project demonstrates that models can be successfully applied to designing on-ground management plans via structured decision-making frameworks and can be particularly useful when uncertainty is high. These approaches have been widely used in the United States and are now becoming more common in other countries including Australia (Nichols et al. 2007; Runge et al. 2011; Tyre et al. 2011; Carwardine et al. 2012; Rout et al. 2014). Substantial progress has been made in developing modelling tools and frameworks to support these decision processes (Williams 2001; Rout et al. 2009; Johnson et al. 2011; McDonald-Madden et al. 2011). Application of these frameworks relies on the development of close linkages between researchers and managers and can be supported via research funding explicitly aimed at integrating models and management. The future looks bright for using models to improve management effectiveness and develop targeted monitoring programmes.

Using Management Strategy Evaluation as a Framework for Improving Conservation under Uncertainty: The Case of the Serengeti Ecosystem

ANA NUNO, NILS BUNNEFELD AND E.J. MILNER-GULLAND

7.1 INTRODUCTION

Conservationists and managers often deal with urgent issues, have to make hard decisions about which species or areas to protect, struggle to identify which threats are causing biodiversity change, have limited resources for intervention and have to decide between a wide range of management strategies given a limited amount of information (Wilson et al. 2009). In times of increasing demand for transparent and account-able criteria and processes in conservation, one important role for sci-entists is to provide robust advice to support management decisions (Pullin and Knight 2003; Halpern et al. 2013).

The robustness of conservation decisions is often affected by the social-ecological dynamics of the systems in which interventions occur, as has been increasingly recognised in conservation planning (Miller et al. 2012). Conservationists are also becoming aware of the need to account for trade-offs between conservation and human well-being (Milner-Gulland et al. 2014). Social-ecological systems (SESs) are com-plex adaptive systems composed of social and biophysical agents organ-ised in multiple subsystems that interact at several spatial and temporal scales (Ostrom 2009). Embedded into broader social, economic and political settings and related ecosystems, these subsystems cannot be fully understood in isolation (Matthews 2007); their reciprocal effects and feedback loops are fundamental to maintaining system structure and function in the face of disturbance (Liu et al. 2007). An integrated social-ecological perspective thus provides a better understanding of systems involving people and natural resources than focusing only on the effect of people on the environment or the effect of interventions on people (Miller et al. 2012). Ultimately, engaging with people and

Table 7.1 *Main Sources of Uncertainty*

Designation	Definition	Example
Process uncertainty	Due to variation in the system itself	Population fluctuations due to climate variations from year to year
Observation uncertainty	Due to the process of measurement	Sensitive nature of the activity leads to harvest underestimation when interviewing users about offtake
Structural uncertainty	Due to lack of understanding of the true dynamics of the system	Functional form of density dependence
Implementation uncertainty	Related to translation of policy into practice	Institutional inertia and non-compliance with management rules

Source: Based on Milner-Gulland and Rowcliffe 2007; Bunnefeld et al. 2011.

their well-being in conservation programmes will increase legitimacy, improve effectiveness and allow positive outcomes for people as well as nature (Milner-Gulland et al. 2014).

Natural resource managers and conservationists are, however, often confronted with the challenges of uncertainty (Harwood and Stokes 2003). The outcomes of management interventions are frequently constrained by factors that may be difficult to account for, potentially explaining many of the failures in conservation and natural resource management (Regan et al. 2005; Holland and Herrera 2009). Managed systems are subject to natural variation, the data collected might be biased, the managers often have incomplete knowledge about the systems and shifts in social, political and economic institutions affect how people use natural resources over time (Nicholson and Possingham 2007; Gavin et al. 2010; Fulton et al. 2011c). Regan et al. (2002), Walker et al. (2003), Ascough II et al. (2008) and Kujala et al. (2013) provide detailed discussions and typologies of uncertainty. In this chapter, we use the categorisation and definitions described by Milner-Gulland and Rowcliffe (2007), who consider process uncertainty, measurement uncertainty (thereafter called observation uncertainty), structural uncertainty and implementation uncertainty as the main types (Table 7.1).

Conservation decisions in developing countries may be particularly prone to great uncertainty, given frequent lack of local capacity and resources, political instability, institutional complexity, poor governance and data unavailability (Danielsen et al. 2003; Clements 2010; Waldron et al. 2013). The consequences of making wrong decisions in such contexts may be particularly severe due to the high levels of biodiversity, reliance of local communities on natural resources for subsistence, potential socio-economic impacts to already impoverished communities and complex feedback between conservation and poverty (Myers et al. 2000; Ferraro et al. 2011; Nielsen et al. 2012).

Using the social-ecological dynamics surrounding the conservation of harvested protected wildlife in the Greater Serengeti Ecosystem, Tanzania (hereafter 'the Serengeti'), as a case study, we adopted a conceptual framework developed in fisheries specifically to deal with decision-making under uncertainty but still underused in conservation: management strategy evaluation (MSE; see Dichmont and Fulton, Chapter 2). In this chapter, we use the conservation of harvested ungulate species in the Serengeti as an example to discuss the potential applicability of MSE as a decision-support tool in the study area, and illustrate challenges and opportunities for robust decision-making under uncertainty, based on our experiences and lessons learnt whilst conducting research about the Serengeti. In particular, we focus on the following issues:

1. What opportunities and barriers are there for implementing MSE in the Serengeti?
2. How would an ideal MSE look from the Serengeti perspective?

7.2 CASE STUDY: THE SERENGETI

Well known for its charismatic wildebeest (*Connochaetes taurinus*) migration and for having some of the largest herbivore and carnivore populations in the world (Sinclair 2012), the Serengeti is an iconic social-ecological system. The Serengeti national park was proclaimed in 1951 and is now one of the most visited protected areas in the world (UNDP 2012). Its importance for biodiversity conservation, development and cultural heritage is widely acknowledged (Shetler 2007; Sinclair et al. 2007). The importance of the wildebeest migration, estimated to currently encompass around 1.3 million animals (Hilborn and Sinclair 2010), has often been demonstrated, both for its ecological significance as a keystone species and as a source of tourism revenue (Sinclair 2003; Norton-Griffiths 2007; Holdo et al. 2011).

When a section of the Serengeti was proclaimed a national park, local communities residing within currently protected areas were evicted to adjacent land. All natural resource use within the national park has been prohibited since its establishment (Shetler 2007). Currently, livelihood strategies of local communities are predominantly based on a combination of farming, livestock herding and bushmeat hunting (Loibooki et al. 2002). The importance of bushmeat for the local economy has been suggested to be considerable, but it is difficult to quantify (Barnett 2000; Knapp 2007, 2012). Hunters must obtain a licence for hunting according to quotas set annually, but illegal bushmeat hunting and consumption is widespread throughout the Serengeti (Loibooki et al. 2002). Bushmeat hunting has been perceived as a threat to wildlife in the system for several decades (Watson 1965; Arcese et al. 1995; Hilborn et al. 2006) and ongoing initiatives aimed at controlling illegal hunting include, for example, law enforcement, access to micro-credit for environmentally friendly enterprises ('COCOBAs') and wildlife management areas (WMAs). Due to the illegal and sensitive nature of bushmeat hunting, it is hard to quantify compliance with the laws, catch composition and hunting effort. Therefore, the uncertainty around the magnitude of, and trends in, offtake is an essential consideration for the management of protected wildlife resources in the area (Loibooki et al. 2002; Knapp 2012). Ultimately, this uncertainty affects the ability to assess the effectiveness of strategies aimed at controlling hunting and socio-economic impacts of conservation interventions on local communities.

Assessing the impacts of bushmeat hunting on migratory and resident wildlife populations has also been difficult for three main reasons: (1) challenges to estimating rates of hunting mortality, which requires quantifying illegal offtake; (2) difficulties in disentangling the role of hunting mortality from among other potential drivers of change, such as climate and land use change; (3) observation uncertainty affecting how monitoring data and wildlife estimates relate to actual wildlife abundance, and the managers' ability to detect abundance trends under limited budgets and with observation error (Figure 7.1). Given its immense area (around 25,000 km²) and abundant wildlife, it comes as no surprise that monitoring such a system has several difficulties. Every three to five years, migratory and resident ungulate population sizes are estimated in the Serengeti. Migratory wildebeest are monitored through aerial point sampling, which requires conducting flight transects, taking aerial photos every 30 seconds and then counting the juvenile and adult wildebeest in these photos (Hilborn and Sinclair 2010). Systematic

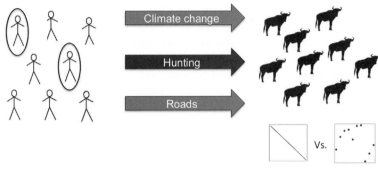

A. Assessing poaching prevalence and offtake

B. Linking wildlife population change to specific threat

C. Detecting true trends from monitoring data

Figure 7.1 Key challenges affecting the managers' ability to assess the impacts of bushmeat hunting on wildlife populations: (A) challenges to estimating rates of hunting mortality, which requires quantifying illegal offtake and identifying 'rule-breakers' (illustrated inside circles); (B) difficulties in disentangling the role of hunting mortality from among other potential drivers of change, such as climate and land use change; (C) observation uncertainty affecting how monitoring data and wildlife estimates relate to actual wildlife abundance, and the managers' ability to detect abundance trends under limited budgets and with observation error.

reconnaissance flight surveys are used for surveying resident species, such as impala, and flight transects are conducted with two observers in the plane recording the number of impala seen within each transect sub-unit (Norton-Griffiths 1978). But uncertainty about how the abundance estimates differ from the true population size, and how to robustly detect trends over time when multiple threats (e.g. poaching and road development) might be affecting wildlife populations are important questions faced by managers and decision-makers in the area (Nuno, Milner-Gulland, et al. 2015).

Moreover, in addition to the national park, this system also includes protected multiple-use areas and village areas with agricultural and live-stock systems, and with a range of different restrictions on hunting and settlement (Figure 7.2), including the Ngorongoro Conservation Area, which was established as a multiple land-use area without hunt-ing while accommodating the existing Maasai pastoralists; Ikorongo, Grumeti and Maswa Game Reserves, which allow licensed hunting but not human settlement; community-managed areas where wildlife use is encouraged in order to generate income for the villages (WMAs); and the Loliondo Game Controlled Area, which allows human settle-ment and licensed hunting (MNRT 1998; Polasky 2008). These

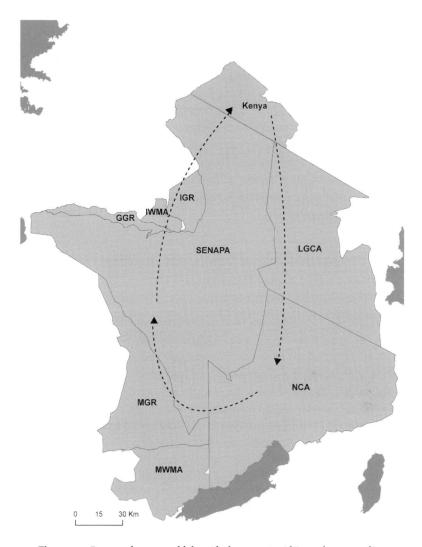

Figure 7.2 Protected areas and lakes (darkest grey) within and surrounding the Greater Serengeti ecosystem. SENAPA = Serengeti National Park, LGCA = Loliondo Game-Controlled Area, NCA = Ngorongoro Conservation Area, MGR = Maswa GR, GGR = Grumeti Game Reserve, IWMA= Ikona Wildlife Management Area, MWMA= Makao Wildlife Management Area, and IGR = Ikorongo Game Reserve. Dashed arrows indicate broad wildebeest migration patterns.

various protected areas are managed by a range of governmental, non-governmental and private sector organisations, and, when making decisions about the Serengeti, a great number of interests are at stake; 106 groups of institutional stakeholders were identified in a study by the Serengeti Ecosystem Management Project (SEMP 2006). Within such a large stakeholder pool, reaching decisions about potential management strategies is particularly challenging; multiple potentially conflicting objectives might include biodiversity conservation, tourism revenue and poverty alleviation. The institutional complexity and social interactions between different actors are likely to affect conservation decisions and their effectiveness, making implementation uncertainty a major consideration.

7.3 OPPORTUNITIES AND BARRIERS FOR IMPLEMENTING MANAGEMENT STRATEGY EVALUATION

As part of an interdisciplinary collaborative project (FP7 HUNTing for Sustainability) and AN's doctoral studies, during four years (2009–2013), we were involved in research focused on the management of social-ecological systems under uncertainty, and the potential application of MSE using the conservation of harvested protected wildlife in the Serengeti, Tanzania, as a case study. This section briefly describes our approach, whilst using our experiences to illustrate and reflect upon some of the opportunities and barriers to developing and implementing a MSE approach in this study area.

7.3.1 Why an MSE for the Serengeti?

The difficulties and complexities of managing social-ecological systems, including those related to monitoring and implementation uncertainties described in the previous section, are not unique to the Serengeti; they are a common challenge to robust conservation and management interventions worldwide. Tools for dealing with those types of issue are, however, still generally under-researched or underused. MSE is a powerful conceptual and operational framework developed in fisheries to facilitate management under uncertainty (see Dichmont and Fulton, Chapter 2) and has great potential for use in conservation. Its strength comes from its incorporation of multiple sources of uncertainty, being explicit about the links between monitoring and management decisions, as well as allowing decision-makers to consider various, often

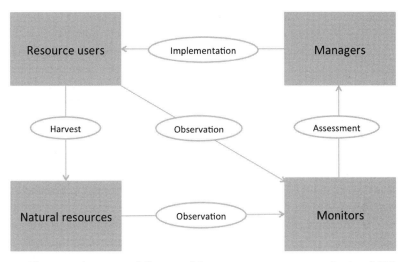

Figure 7.3 A conceptual diagram of the management strategy evaluation (MSE) framework used in this chapter.

conflicting, management objectives as defined by different stakeholders (Kell et al. 2007; Punt and Donovan 2007; Bunnefeld et al. 2011). The conceptual frameworks of MSE can be designed to emphasise the perspectives of different groups within the system (e.g. 'resource users', 'managers' and 'monitors'; Figure 7.3).

The tool's full potential in conservation remains generally unaddressed, particularly given its flexibility to incorporate all relevant system components and actors in a single modelling framework and potential wide applicability when resource users are included (Bunnefeld et al. 2011; Milner-Gulland 2011). The MSE framework could contribute to a better consideration of social-ecological feedbacks, increased predictability and robust decision-making in conservation planning.

Because of its potential general applicability, with expected benefits both for people and wildlife, and for its academic novelty, we adopted an integrated MSE approach as the modelling framework for the FP7 HUNT project (Milner-Gulland, 2011). Unlike most fisheries MSEs to date (but see Dichmont and Fulton, Chapter 2), we included a resource-user component to explicitly incorporate harvester decision-making and behaviour. This enabled us to consider how resource-user decision-making and behaviour may affect the success of different interventions. Also, in order to more realistically represent interventions that account for measures of human welfare and resource-user behaviour, in this integrated MSE framework, we included monitoring both of the status of biological populations and the local communities (Figure 7.3).

This case study is very different from those usually considered for MSE, which generally focus on setting harvest quotas (e.g. Bunnefeld et al. 2013; Edwards et al. 2014; Punt et al. 2016). However, we felt it would be useful to explore whether MSE could be adapted to focus on the implementation of conservation policies other than quotas, which would directly or indirectly affect hunter decisions (Milner-Gulland et al. 2010). In addition, other advantages of the MSE approach that made it worth exploring are: allowing stakeholders to recognise trade-offs and risks associated with different scenarios; incorporating assessment of uncertainty into the definition, development and selection phases of the MSE (Punt and Donovan 2007; Mapstone et al. 2008); involvement of multiple stakeholders in the establishment of the criteria, definition of scenarios and final scenario choices, stimulating discussions between and within stakeholders and decision-makers (McAllister et al. 1999); generating interest and buy-in because it gives stakeholders the information most relevant to their current decisions (Ives et al. 2013). The use of MSE in this system would thus be a major development, and one with great potential to improve management and to provide a template for further application of the approach in conservation. Because we were involved in an international collaborative project including researchers from multiple fields (e.g. economics, political science, sociology and ecology) using bushmeat hunting in the Serengeti as a case study, this represented a great opportunity to build upon multidisciplinary findings and integrate them into a unified framework.

7.3.2 Our Approach and Some Lessons Learnt

When we started planning our research on MSE for the Serengeti, our initial goal was developing an integrated model including key components illustrated in Figure 7.3 that could be used to explore and inform realistic management decisions about bushmeat hunting in the area. This goal was not achieved but several lessons were learnt throughout the process; hopefully our experiences can provide useful insights for reflecting about conservation and management in such complex social-ecological systems.

Whilst some of the conceptual work behind our MSE research had started some time before the project, meetings with project partners and a few stakeholders at an early stage of the project (February 2010) were crucial for identifying key conservation issues, gaps in knowledge and data availability in the study area. From discussions with people working on the ground, village residents surveyed during a pilot study, and other researchers, we soon realised that there was a lot of uncertainty associated with two major components of the model: monitoring of trends in wildlife numbers and the prevalence and drivers of illegal hunting. There was also limited evaluation of policies affecting hunter decisions, and institutional barriers were potentially affecting conservation implementation and links between conservation science and practice. To address these issues, which we felt was essential for developing a realistic MSE approach that was relevant for local decision-makers, we used simulation modelling to investigate potential biases in monitoring and subsequent detection of wildlife trends; specialised questioning techniques to survey local communities about engagement in illegal hunting; and semi-structured stakeholder interviews to investigate issues with conservation implementation in the Serengeti. In the following, we briefly describe our research for each one of the key steps (Figure 7.3), illustrating different ways of dealing with uncertainty-related issues in conservation and resource management.

7.3.2.1 Harvest and Population Dynamics

The seasonally available migratory ungulates, such as wildebeest, represent the bulk of harvested wildlife, but poaching affects a wide range of resident ungulates, such as impala (*Aepyceros melampus*) and topi (*Damaliscus lunatus*) and non-target species, such as spotted hyena (*Crocuta crocuta*) (Hofer et al. 1996; Loibooki et al. 2002; Holmern et al. 2007). We developed a model of the population dynamics and harvesting of two representative ungulate species. The migratory wildebeest population is iconic of the Serengeti and has been extensively studied over the last 60 years (Mduma et al. 1999). The resident population of impala found in the Grumeti-Ikorongo Game Reserve (Figure 7.2) has received considerably less attention, but represents a suite of resident ungulate species important both for local livelihoods as bushmeat, and as constituents of the Serengeti mammal fauna.

After deciding on our target harvested species, the next step was developing a model to simulate their population dynamics. Based on the available data and scientific literature, we developed post-breeding, age-structured, two-sex matrix models to represent ungulate population dynamics (Caswell 2001). The development, structure and parameterisation of these models is fully described in Nuno et al. (2015).

This population dynamics model was then used to produce expected abundance and structure of both wildlife populations over time under 'baseline conditions', i.e. without harvest. In order to investigate potential harvesting effects, illegal bushmeat hunting was then simulated ('poaching scenario') by assuming a 10 per cent harvest rate for wildebeest, to be precautionary, and a 5 per cent rate for impala, which is less heavily targeted by poachers (Rentsch 2011). While these are simplified hunting conditions, this type of scenario-based analysis can be used to investigate the sensitivity to harvest and ecological conditions. For example, our results suggested that, under the simulated conditions, both species would decline on average by 43–50 per cent in 50 years, with wildebeest populations declining non-linearly while about half of the impala simulations showed non-linear declines and half showed linear declines.

7.3.2.2 Wildlife Monitoring

Uncertainty about how wildlife abundance estimates differ from the true population size, and which type of monitoring errors should be minimised first, are important questions faced by managers and decision-makers in the area and elsewhere (Nuno et al. 2013). MSE can be a useful tool for improving monitoring under uncertainty, because it incorporates not only the dynamics and abundance of natural resources but also the observation (i.e. monitoring) of those same resources (Figure 7.3), allowing recommendations about data robustness and monitoring conditions to be made. This rationale is similar to the 'virtual ecologist' approach (Zurell et al. 2010), where simulated data and observer models are used to mimic real species and how they are observed.

Using this approach, we started by simulating 'true' scenarios of wildlife abundance (taking into account, for example, animal distribution, population structure and herd size) and then simulated each step in the monitoring process (e.g. defining number of transects and time between photos) and potential errors (such as miscounting juveniles hidden behind adults and missing animals at further distances) to investigate how each of these factors may affect the final estimates. This incorporated four main components: (a) a spatial distribution model, which provided the 'true scenario' against which simulated monitoring data were compared; (b) an 'observation model', which simulated monitoring of these populations; (c) a data analysis component, which estimated wildlife abundance from simulated monitoring data, the 'assessment model'; and (d) an assessment of survey accuracy and precision, in which discrepancies between 'true' and 'observed' population sizes and their drivers were investigated (see details in Nuno et al. 2013). This allowed us to investigate which components of monitoring should be prioritised in the Serengeti to improve survey accuracy (the difference between the estimates and the 'truth') and precision (uncertainty in the estimates), and showed how different monitoring budgets could affect the quality of the estimates obtained (Nuno et al. 2013). Our results suggested that the relative importance of each process affecting precision and accuracy varied according to the survey technique and biological characteristics of the species; while survey precision was mainly affected by population characteristics and sampling effort, the accuracy of the survey was greatly affected by observer effects, such as detectability of juveniles and herds.

7.3.2.3 Measuring Illegal Hunting

Due to the illegal and sensitive nature of bushmeat hunting in the Serengeti, there is enormous uncertainty surrounding hunting prevalence and hunting household characteristics. For example, previous studies estimated that 8 to 57 per cent of households in the Western Serengeti engage in bushmeat hunting, with these values highly variable between studies (Loibooki et al. 2002; Kaltenborn et al. 2005). However, non-response and social desirability bias are well-known problems when conducting social surveys about sensitive topics, and might explain some of the issues with the existing data about hunting in the Serengeti; interviewees may not be willing to discuss participation in illegal activities (Groves 2006), or might lie to project a favourable image of themselves (Fisher 1993). Specialised questioning techniques have been developed in several disciplines to ensure respondent anonymity, increase willingness to answer, and critically, make it impossible to directly link incriminating data to an individual (Nuno and St John 2015).

Given the novelty of applying these specialised questioning techniques, we started by exploring the feasibility of applying some of these techniques in the study area by testing the willingness of respondents to give sensitive information, and their understanding of the survey, depending on the technique employed (Nuno 2013). Then, we assessed the prevalence of illegal hunting using the best performing of these techniques (the unmatched-count technique [UCT]), as well as identifying the socio-demographic characteristics of non-compliant households (Nuno et al., 2013). Eighteen per cent of households admitted to being involved in hunting. Our results suggested that poaching remains widespread in the Serengeti, despite ongoing interventions, and current alternative sources of income may not be sufficiently attractive to compete with the opportunities provided by hunting.

7.3.2.4 *Assessment*

An assessment model, which aims to simulate the process of estimating trends from monitoring data, such as wildlife abundance or poaching prevalence (Figure 7.3), is a crucial part of the MSE approach; by simulating the process by which the status of the system under consideration is assessed, it allows monitoring data to be linked to specific management objectives, and providing recommendations about potential management and conservation interventions to be made.

Building upon our modelling work, we simulated multiple scenarios of population change (e.g. 'poaching scenario' and 'climate change scenario') and wildlife monitoring in the Serengeti ecosystem, and investigated monitoring effectiveness under uncertainty, defined as the ability of the monitoring programme to detect trends robustly. We developed a modelling framework in which 'true' population dynamics under different scenarios of change were placed within a monitoring framework that estimated trends in wildlife abundance based on simulated monitoring data. This enabled us to evaluate monitoring effectiveness, depending on the type of monitoring and its budget (Nuno et al. 2015). We found that as monitoring period and frequency increased, observation uncertainty was more important in explaining effectiveness, and type I (rejecting the null hypothesis when it is true, such as when a species is reported to be declining but is actually stable) and III (correctly rejecting the null hypothesis but incorrectly inferring the direction of the effect) errors had low prevalence for both ungulate species under the simulated conditions. This improved our understanding of the effects of monitoring conditions on perceptions of observed trends, ultimately producing advice on management decisions based upon those data. This model was only developed for wildlife monitoring; an integrated 'virtual monitor' approach could also be used to provide a comparison of trends obtained from monitoring both social and ecological dimensions of the system.

7.3.2.5 *Implementation*

A main advantage of using an integrated MSE framework is that implementation uncertainty, related to the translation of science and policy into conservation practice, can be explicitly considered. For example, instead of implicitly assuming full compliance by harvesters and perfect implementation, we can consider how harvester decision-making may affect the success of different interventions. Similarly, it is important to understand how national-level policy might translate into on-the-ground implementation by conservation and park management agencies.

While we were successful in obtaining further insights into the socio-economic drivers of harvest and poaching prevalence, we were not able to make predictions about how resource user behaviour would change under social and environmental change (including interventions). This would be needed for to develop a fully operational MSE model. Several socio-economic studies in the area have focused on identifying who engages in certain behaviours and potential drivers of that behaviour, but there is still a need for integration of existing theoretical and empirical understandings of the incentives for non-compliance into predictive studies of how approaches to reducing rule-breaking behaviour might work. Tools from experimental economics such as choice experiments (Moro et al. 2013), experimental games (Travers et al. 2011) or scenarios (Cinner et al. 2011) could produce these insights.

Nevertheless, we did use MSE as conceptual framework to describe the current network of relationships between management actors, enabling reflection on the potential blockages to implementation of effective policy (Nuno et al. 2014). We used this framework to map and understand linkages within this SES, identifying challenges and potential barriers to successful conservation implementation in the Serengeti. We demonstrated how MSE could provide a useful framework to better understand social dynamics and feedbacks when integrated with other tools, such as key informant interviews and social network analysis, to then guide institutional change for more effective management. Our results suggested that the links between system components and actors are currently not well established and fully functional in the Serengeti, decreasing the robustness of the system and effectiveness of conservation interventions. Collaboration is very reliant on the connectedness of one individual (from a non-governmental organisation [NGO]), which means that the system may be vulnerable to the loss of this person. Close attention to improving communications between different interest groups is a key consideration for the design and implementation of future interventions in the area.

7.3.3 Some Lessons Learnt

As we conducted our research in the Serengeti and focused on different components of an integrated MSE approach (Figure 7.3), a key realisation was that MSE consists of much more than a modelling tool for decision support. Whilst improving management is the ultimate goal of an MSE, the framework has advantages even when that goal is not met, which we outline in the following.

7.3.3.1 MSE as a Unifying Framework

Academically, the integration of social and ecological considerations in conservation and resource management is an ongoing challenge. For planning and implementing effective conservation interventions, holistic approaches are needed that account for multiple system components and feedback dynamics between them, allowing managers and decision-makers to evaluate trade-offs between multiple criteria and consider several potential management interventions. Whilst there are several frameworks for conceptualising social-ecological systems, such as Ostrom's SES framework and the human–environment system framework (Binder et al. 2013), and social-ecological systems models (Schlüter et al. 2012), MSE is particularly useful for this type of case study due to its focus on well-defined typologies of actors and common operational steps within natural resource management and conservation (i.e. resource use, monitoring, assessment and implementation). Because a MSE approach can be designed to include separate but linked models of the social and ecological aspects of the system, and their interactions, it is a powerful approach to understanding system dynamics. Moreover, MSE's focus on uncertainties and on evaluating management options means that it is better adapted to answering real-world questions (see Dichmost and Fulton, Chapter 2). It is also a useful component of adaptive management, providing a virtual test of potential management strategies before they are implemented in the real world. For example, the lack of integrated approaches that consider conservation, development and tourism together was identified as a major barrier to successful implementation in the Serengeti by key stakeholders (Nuno et al. 2014), while the need for local communities to be able to evaluate different options for resource ownership has been identified as one of the challenges to co-management in the Serengeti (Kideghesho and Mtoni 2008). An MSE approach could thus be used to integrate multiple perspectives and social and ecological considerations within a unified framework before implementation of the intervention, and promote consensus within a co-management committee, such as the Serengeti Ecosystem Community Conservation Forum.

7.3.3.2 *MSE as a Diagnostic Tool*

As mentioned in the earlier discussion, using MSE as a general framework for our work in the Serengeti was useful for identifying key components and system actors within a social-ecological system, as well as pinpointing key types and sources of uncertainty affecting management decisions, which we then addressed in multiple ways as described in previous sections. This makes it relevant to end-users by capturing key linkages they care about as well as being useful for visualising different stakeholder roles within the system. For example, by presenting a simple schematic of the system to key stakeholders in the Serengeti and asking for their feedback, we were able to identify key issues affecting conservation implementation in the area, many of which related to institutional complexity and poor science-practice linkages (Nuno et al. 2014). An MSE approach is thus also useful for diagnosing areas where uncertainties are most important to the qualitative outcomes, or where conflicts are most critical, either to get more data/understanding or to focus on in subsequent discussions. The emphasis on the MSE process (e.g. design, deliberations and diagnosis) instead of only on its ultimate goal is an essential advantage that should be fully exploited. The qualitative application of MSE for generating information for decision-making and planning has, however, been given very little attention. An exception is Smith et al. (2007b), where the operating model used to test alternative strategies was replaced by projections based on expert judgement; this work helped stakeholders confront a range of problems and issues in the fishery and was used for restructuring the fishery to achieve the changes that were identified as needed.

7.3.3.3 *Tool Flexibility*

Despite having been originally developed as a tool to explore and inform management decisions about harvest quotas in fisheries, the application of MSE to several different case studies for the conservation or management of terrestrial and marine resources, such as trophy hunting in Ethiopia (Bunnefeld et al. 2013), management of lion hunting (Edwards et al. 2014), control of overabundant wildlife in Australia (Chee and Wintle 2010) and evaluation of marine spatial closures with conflicting fisheries and conservation objectives (Dichmont et al. 2013) demonstrates its flexibility in terms of management or research questions, and system dynamics, structure and composition. Moreover, an MSE approach is not restricted by limited data availability (although that certainly restricts the research or management questions that can be answered). For example, our Serengeti wildlife monitoring work was based on previous studies in the area, insights from experts and broader studies on monitoring issues, but interestingly access to actual monitoring data was very limited because our requests to a local partner agency were not answered. Data accessibility can unfortunately be an important issue affecting conservation decisions worldwide. The presence of an observation model at the heart of an MSE can thus be particularly useful for providing recommendations under uncertainty, demonstrating the flexibility of this approach in terms of data requirements and how to make the most out of whatever information is available (e.g. Edwards et al. 2014).

7.3.3.4 *Limited Feedback between Monitoring and Management Actions*
A few key factors affected our ability to develop a realistic, relevant and functional MSE that could actually be used to inform management decisions in the area. The minimum requirement for MSE to be an appropriate modelling framework is that there is are potential or actual links between monitoring and management decisions, i.e. that data being collected are, or could, be used to inform decisions about system management. However, the links between system components and actors (monitoring, assessment, implementation) are currently not well established and fully functional in the Serengeti (Nuno et al. 2014). In our studies, improving implementation (rather than research, monitoring or assessment) was perceived by stakeholders as a key priority, particularly given the amount of research already conducted in the area. This suggests that actually applying the knowledge accumulated over the last decades in the Serengeti is still challenging. The lack of monitoring and evaluation of existing interventions, leading to uncertainty about the effectiveness of particular interventions aimed at reducing the exploitation of bushmeat species by local people (patrolling, micro-credit schemes) also makes it difficult to learn from previous and ongoing interventions. If these links and feedback effects are not effectively considered, a MSE approach in the Serengeti can never be converted from an academic exercise to a meaningful decision-support tool.

7.3.3.5 Challenges in Interdisciplinary Collaborations

The research described in this chapter integrates approaches from both the natural and social sciences, and our work is generally interdisciplinary. Nevertheless, there is only a certain amount of research that a single group can conduct in a limited period of time; being integrated into an interdisciplinary project with other groups represented a great opportunity for capitalising on people's skills and findings through team-working. However, while a number of collaborations and cross-disciplinary publications arose from this project, most work happened in parallel without integration, with some barriers relating to methodological challenges, timing and length of the project, disciplinary prejudices and interdisciplinary communication. This is a familiar story for multidisciplinary environmental and conservation projects worldwide (Pooley et al. 2014). For example, issues of time and phasing were pertinent due to the need to both collect and analyse data on household decisions in order to construct meaningful models of household behaviour (Moro et al. 2013; Moro et al. 2015). It was also particularly challenging for us, as modellers, to bridge the intellectual and disciplinary gulf to social anthropologists, who distrusted the necessarily reductionist approach implied by MSE as a framework. This meant they were unwilling to share their insights and results, which would have enabled us to construct a more realistic model of the institutional and social structures within which resource users operated. As a result, the initial goal of developing realistic simulation models that accounted for household behaviour was not achievable within the three-year project period. The time and technical requirements of developing and implementing a MSE approach should not be underestimated, particularly if data collection is also required and the modelling expertise is still being developed (as in our case). Also, early and deep engagement between social and natural scientists, and understanding by both of the role and value of each within the project, are essential to meaningful collaboration.

7.3.3.6 Stakeholder Engagement and Representation

In hindsight, local stakeholder representation was considerably restricted at the start of the project, as discussions about the MSE approach only happened with staff from Frankfurt Zoological Society (FZS) and Tanzania Wildlife Research Institute, and other researchers. Although we decided to focus our research on a specific household behaviour (bushmeat hunting) within a defined area (Western Serengeti) to make the approach more tractable and implementable, study participants in an institutional analysis exercise still listed 13 institutions operating in the bushmeat hunting system in the Serengeti (Nuno et al. 2014). Most of these stakeholders were not part of the project. Furthermore, our analysis of stakeholders and implementation issues should have been conducted at the start of the project, in order to identify key representatives and assess their concerns and priorities, besides facilitating engagement and buy-in. If our MSE approach was ever to be converted into a decision-support tool, these social considerations would need to be better understood and taken into account at a much earlier phase, particularly given that this was our first time working in the study area. We believe this is one of the main requirements for successful adaptation of this approach to conservation issues, where stakeholders often hold very different values, and trade-offs between biodiversity conservation and development are often controversial (e.g. discussion on proposed road in the Serengeti: Homewood et al. 2010; Holdo et al. 2011a; Fyumagwa et al. 2013; Hopcraft et al. 2015). It is important also to note that building these relationships takes time; it was probably unrealistic to expect that full stakeholder engagement could be achieved within a three-year project, starting from scratch, and without prior experience of participatory modelling (such as is routine in MSE for fisheries; Dichmont and Fulton, Chapter 2). Therefore, if academic researchers are keen to implement MSE within the standard project period, they need to be embedded within existing institutional and collaborative structures, in which all relevant stakeholders are represented and are willing to engage. Prior experience of working with a range of stakeholders is also needed, or else the services of an experienced facilitator should be employed.

7.4 AN IDEAL MANAGEMENT STRATEGY EVALUATION APPROACH FOR THE SERENGETI

MSE as a quantitative tool in the Serengeti would be most constructive if used to improve the implementation of conservation policies designed to affect resource users' decisions. For example, bushmeat hunting in the Serengeti is a conservation issue that has received the attention of local and international actors for several decades and is currently perceived as a substantial threat to the system; when asked to list top threats to the Serengeti, poaching was one of the most frequently mentioned by key stakeholders, as well as increasing human population growth and land-use conflicts (Nuno et al. 2014). This topic is thus of great management and conservation relevance and tools to improve conservation implementation would be welcomed in the area.

Developing a fully operational quantitative MSE model that could be used to evaluate management strategies for the conservation of harvested protected species in the Serengeti would require the steps outlined below; these have many similarities with the stages of structured decision-making described by Garrard et al. in Chapter 3.

Step 1: Stakeholder Analysis, Engagement and Representation

Because the ultimate goal of MSE is informing management decisions, a fully operational and successful MSE requires stakeholder representation and engagement from the start (Dichmont and Fulton, Chapter 2). Based on our institutional and stakeholder analysis (Nuno et al. 2014), group representatives should be identified and invited to attend workshops, semi-structured interviews and/or form a working group where discussions would take place, making sure the MSE approach addressed their concerns and priorities. For example, facilitated workshops with institutions based in the Western Serengeti, such as Grumeti and Ikorongo Game Reserves, village representatives, Tanzania National Parks (TANAPA) and FZS, could be undertaken to explore and deliberate about specific targets and thresholds.

Step 2: Specification and Quantification of Management Objectives

While there are broad socio-economic and conservation objectives shared by stakeholders in the Serengeti (Nuno et al., 2014), further work must be done on setting specific management targets. For example, conservation, development and tourism are perceived as key action areas in the Serengeti, but trade-offs between them have been poorly considered in a structured way due to the lack of pre-defined quantitative and/or qualitative management targets that can be used to evaluate interventions and make conservation decisions. This task is, however, complicated by a lack of baseline data and lack of agreement between stakeholders.

Within facilitated workshops with representatives from multiple stakeholder groups, exercises on priority setting and choice of indicators should be undertaken; given the proposed focus of the MSE on bushmeat hunting, we suggest that targets should be set related to biodiversity (e.g. number of wildebeest), human well-being (e.g. household income, and other measures – see Woodhouse et al., Chapter 5), and management resource expenditure (e.g. money spent on each of the management strategies). Discussions about the choice of indicators and decisions about thresholds are key, and we anticipate that finding scientifically acceptable and agreeable thresholds could be challenging, given the diversity of stakeholder values and perceived priorities in the area; the magnitude and complexity of this task should not be underestimated.

Step 3: Development and Parameterisation of the MSE Model

Our research described in this chapter focused on developing operating, observation and assessment models for the biological component of the system (wildebeest and impala) so that these could be easily incorporated in a full MSE model. Key aspects still to be developed and incorporated in a MSE framework for the Serengeti remain on the social side: (a) modelling hunter resource use, and their decision-making under changing conditions (including implementation of new management strategies); (b) modelling the implementation of management advice for different strategies, following the assessment of system state; (c) modelling the uncertainties around monitoring hunter behaviour.

(a) Modelling Hunter Decisions

The next requirement for continued development of an MSE model for the Serengeti is a link between system state (including conservation interventions) and resource user behaviour. A resource user model would require, for example, developing a household utility model to investigate trade-offs between livelihood options, such as farming and hunting, in their contribution to maximising well-being (which could be used as one of the socio-economic objectives). This approach has been used for bushmeat hunting in the past (e.g. Barrett and Arcese 1998; Damania, Milner-Gulland and Crookes 2005; Holdo et al. 2010). The impact of alternative management strategies on the factors underlying livelihood decisions (e.g. changes in crop prices, protein availability, credit availability or risk of capture when hunting) would then feed through into changes in the balance of livelihood activities.

Given the recent work on potential economic effects of policies to mitigate bushmeat hunting and consumption in the Serengeti (Rentsch and Damon, 2013; Moro et al. 2013, 2015) and previous work on the trade-offs between farming and hunting in the area (Barrett and Arcese 1998; Johannesen 2005), developing a household utility model would be a logical next step to expand past MSE-related research. One of the biggest challenges to realistically modelling human behaviour in the study area would be incorporating intertemporal choices, i.e. how individuals trade-off costs and benefits in time, which is still generally poorly understood (Keane et al. 2008), and for which no empirical data is available in the Serengeti. While simplified assumptions could be made about intertemporal choices, for example, with individuals having a single, fixed discount rate for all situations, the reliability of these assumptions should be investigated, particularly given the rapid socio-economic changes undergoing in the area. Data on time-preference could be collected using socio-economic surveys with discount rate elicitation questions, such as series of binary choices involving real or hypothetical monetary payments that occurred at different points in time (Teh et al. 2014).

(b) Modelling Implementation of Management Advice
After the assessment of the system state (e.g. wildlife trends, compliance with hunting regulations), this information should be used by managers and conservationists in the area to inform decisions about which strategies to implement, if any action is required. Institutional and implementation uncertainties in the Serengeti, related to the translation of policy into practice and arising from interactions between different groups and the different sets of rules governing their behaviour, greatly affect conservation outcomes and managers' ability to design effective strategies (Nuno et al. 2014). To simulate and explore how science and policy translates into actual conservation action by local actors in the Serengeti and how this could be improved, information about how different stakeholders interact (obtained from our social network analysis) and how these interactions influence the decision-making process could be used in a model of management decision-making. For example, we could consider the linkages between institutions and organisations operating in the area, incentives for cooperation and collaboration, as well as barriers to scientific information uptake in structured way. This would require obtaining more detailed information about linkages and decisions over time, and the incentives for working collaboratively (e.g. Gordon et al. 2013).

(c) Modelling Monitoring of Hunter Behaviour
Ideally, developing a MSE model component that focussed on monitoring of resource use and users would require a similar approach to that used for wildlife monitoring (see previous section); simulated data and

observer models should be used to mimic real human behaviour and how resource users are observed. Our research using specialised questioning techniques provides insights about socio-economic characteristics of hunters and potential mismatches between true and observed behaviour due to the illegal nature of the activity. However, it would be naïve to assume that a single 'perfect' technique can be identified and used to provide a reliable estimate of what is actually happening. Ground-truthing, validation studies and the use of complementary methods for triangulation may help overcome the constraints inherent to each survey technique. Comparative studies are particularly limited in the area (and generally) and deserve further attention; only through robust comparison of several monitoring techniques (both for wildlife and resource use) will we be able to assess their inherent biases and evaluate how, and when, to minimise them. This would be particularly useful for developing a MSE model that effectively incorporates monitoring of resource users, as that requires a better understanding of not only discrepancies between true and observed behaviour, but also of their potential drivers (e.g. survey technique, question sensitivity, socio-demographics and enumerator effects). This model development is a specialist technical task, but it still needs to be transparent and informed by the stakeholder working group. It is important that they trust the datasets being used and are able to contribute their own data and expertise. Stakeholders also need to understand and approve the assumptions being made in model construction. If this doesn't happen, then later presentation of model outputs will be met with scepticism and the recommendations will be less powerful.

Step 4: Identification, Simulation and Evaluation of Candidate Strategies
We suggest that the management strategies to be considered should be centred on influencing household decision-making and illegal bush-meat hunting. For example, a comparison could be made between investing in law enforcement and more indirect interventions such as livelihood enhancements (e.g. access to microcredit), and improving access to other protein sources (e.g. domestic meat). These represent actual challenges and decisions currently being made in the area and, given the ethical and logistical implications of experimenting on wild-life and local communities, exploring these alternatives within a MSE approach should be recommended as a first step before actual implementation in the study area. These simulations need to be done under

a range of conditions, representing both potential future states of the world (e.g. a range of human population density estimates, presence or absence of a road, climate change), and key structural uncertainties (e.g. in the functional form of the utility function).

It is also important to note that different management strategies are currently devised and implemented by different agencies (e.g. law enforcement is the province of TANAPA and livelihood enhancements tend to be done by a range of more or less independent NGOs). Therefore, part of the power of MSE, as a participatory process, is to get all stakeholders to realise that their interventions are part of a broader picture, and that it would be more effective to consider them as an integrated whole, rather than implementing them independently. This step of quantifying, and then implementing, different combinations of strategies within the MSE framework is an important part of promoting debate and mutual understanding between actors. Considering together what the potential states of the world are that the strategies should be tested under, and which uncertainties should be represented, can bring people together and focus on what people agree about, rather than their differences of opinion. This is likely to be helpful in the Serengeti, given that our research suggested that people agreed about what the issues were, but less so about what the priority actions were to tackle them; the MSE process helps them to build a foundation of consensus on these issues, and demonstrates the outcomes of different actions under a range of circumstances.

Step 5: Summary of Performance and Selection of the Management Strategy

After running models for each candidate strategy (e.g. enforcement, access to microcredit and increased availability of other protein source), model outcomes need to be summarised in a way that is accessible to a range of different stakeholders. This can be challenging when there are several performance metrics, representing different goals, which are likely to trade-off (e.g. human well-being and wildlife numbers). This is why time spent at steps 1 and 2 is vital, in order that at this stage, pre-defined and pre-agreed metrics already exist (e.g. number of wildebeest, household income and money spent on each of the management strategies). Communication and visualisation of the achievability of different management targets under different circumstances, the predictability of these outcomes, and their trade-offs, are essential for engaging stakeholders and providing relevant information for their decisions. At this stage, facilitated workshops with stakeholders should be organised to share findings based on simulations and show potential outcomes for multiple scenarios. Depending on the level of stakeholder participation during model development, this step may be repeated based on their feedback (e.g. if they would like to test alternative scenarios) or be used to support final decisions for implementation. It is not the job of the scientist to provide an 'optimal' solution (another distinguishing feature of MSE from other modelling approaches) but to lay out the consequences of different strategy combinations for decision-makers in an objective way. From this point on, an ideal MSE approach would lead into actual decisions and data being collected on any subsequent outcomes, so that it could inform more robust future decisions as a component of adaptive management (Keith et al. 2011).

7.5 CONCLUSIONS

There are a number of challenges to successfully developing and implementing a MSE model to aid conservation in the Serengeti. While some of them would require applying considerable effort in terms of promoting closer collaboration and collecting socio-economic data, the flexibility of MSE means pragmatic decisions could be made in terms of specific questions being addressed, emphasis on certain system components, and spatial and temporal scales. The uptake of scientific recommendations based on a MSE model would, however, require fundamental changes in the way scientific information is perceived and used, and much closer links between monitoring and management decisions (Nuno et al. 2014). For a MSE model to be more than an academic or thought exercise in the Serengeti, a shift in perceptions towards holistic approaches in conservation and a recognition of the power of exchanges between simulation modelling and field experiments would be needed.

The Serengeti has many critical issues and challenges that need to be addressed for its better management and full functionality as a resilient SES. Instead of focusing on MSE as a quantitative modelling tool, its potential as a conceptual framework promoting a participatory approach to conservation might be even greater. For example, while applying MSE to conservation in the Serengeti may be complex and challenging given its institutional complexity, poor governance, number of stakeholders involved and controversial trade-offs between poverty and conservation, the exercise alone of engaging stakeholders around discussion about, and planning for, MSE could be very useful. Given experience in the fisheries sector (see Dichmont and Fulton, Chapter 2), MSE is worth a strong consideration as a robust operational framework for guiding conservation implementation. This is particularly true in difficult and complex systems like the Serengeti, where management decisions are hindered by the need to consider multiple conflicting objectives and many types of uncertainty.

ACKNOWLEDGEMENTS

A.N. was supported by the Portuguese Foundation for Science and Technology (FCT) (doctoral grant SFRH/BD/43186/2008) and Defra Darwin Initiative funding. We thank the participants in the FP7 HUNTing for Sustainability project for their contributions to the research underlying this chapter.

The Use of Quantitative Models in the Harvest Management of Wild Ungulates, Carnivores and Small Game: Using Norway as a Case Study

ERLEND B. NILSEN

8.1 INTRODUCTION

One of the central aspects of conservation biology is the relationship between human exploitation and the conservation of these exploited resources. Management of harvested species is often controversial, and, in general, the controversies can be divided into two components. First, there is often disagreement about the specific management goals or targets. Well-known examples include large carnivore management in Europe, where carnivores are mainly conserved in what has been termed the coexistence model (Chapron et al. 2014), implying that they are sharing the landscape with a range of human activities. Second, there are often controversies and disagreements about the target system or current state of the population. In general, management of such complex systems calls for management schemes that are open and transparent; quantitative models lend themselves well to such situations because one can formulate the problem explicitly and point the discussions towards uncertain elements. Thus, there are clear links between these controversies and the modelling tools that have been proposed for their management.

Because there are competing goals among groups of stakeholders, models being used to manage wildlife species might benefit from being able to optimise several criteria simultaneously. Such criteria might relate to both the abundance and distribution of controversial species. As an example, Norway is divided into eight management regions for large carnivores, each with politically determined management goals (Linnell et al. 2010). Within each region, politically appointed regional management boards are responsible for management, including the spatial distribution of harvest quotas. In principle then, the board should do so in the light of the trade-off between those who prefer to keep low numbers of carnivores to prevent livestock losses and those who prefer higher densities to maximise other criteria. Other examples include the management of moose (*Alces alces*) that represent both revenue in terms of income from the harvest and nuisance in terms of damage to economically important tree species (Nilsen et al. 2009b). Here, there is often an asymmetric distribution of costs and benefits among the landowners, as some landowners will benefit from a high moose abundance whereas others will not. In other cases, the trade-offs might be less clear-cut, as might be the case for small game management.

While the traditional focus has been on maximising the sustainable harvest off-take, recent focus on ecosystem services (ES) has highlighted the cultural value associated with wildlife presence in the landscape (Bradbury et al. 2010; Daniel et al. 2012). Traditional natural resource management models most often rely on maximising one objective function (e.g. maximising mean annual yield), but such objective functions might be inappropriate in situations with recreational fisheries or hunting (Wam et al. 2013). Indeed, as the examples above make clear, there often is not a single best management practice on which all stakeholder groups can agree. Shifting the focus towards the ES concept opens up new opportunities for the evaluation criteria. Such an approach is appealing, but also challenging, as there might be complex trade-offs between competing interests, different ES might be difficult to compare directly (e.g. due to the difficulties of measuring the monetary value of cultural ES), and because cultural services are expected to be fluid and change frequently (Daniel et al. 2012).

Using quantitative models as a tool to guide decisions in harvest management has been advocated for many decades. Such quantitative models could be based on simple deterministic population models, but following seminal work on harvesting stochastic resources (Lande et al. 1994, 1995), it became clear that the solutions from the deterministic models would often be sub-optimal (and in fact unsustainable) when taking stochasticity into account. Importantly, such uncertainty does not only relate to the population dynamics, but also to the other processes inherent in the management cycle (Williams et al. 2002; Bunnefeld et al. 2011; Bischof et al. 2012). Four main sources of uncertainty can be recognised (Figure 8.1, following Williams et al. 2002 and Nichols et al. 2007). First, there is uncertainty in how a given system functions and responds to management actions (known as ecological or structural uncertainty). Second, environmental stochasticity always represents an

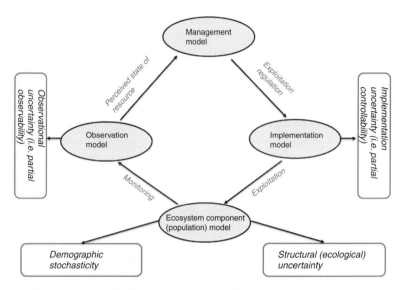

Figure 8.1 Generalised management cycle, illustrating the incorporation of uncertainty within a management strategy evaluation (MSE) model. Each of the sub-models (blue boxes) are represented by models with various levels of complexity, which are associated with different types of uncertainty.

important source of uncertainty (Lande et al. 2003). Third, management decisions are often only partially followed by the practitioners (known as partial controllability), as, for example, hunting regulations are not always respected (Liberg et al. 2012) and pre-described quotas are not always filled (Bischof et al. 2012). Fourth, managers do not directly observe the state of the system but do so only through more or less rigorous monitoring programmes with their associated uncertainties (known as partial observability). When management models include considerations about these four sources of uncertainty and are used to simulate different management scenarios, they are known as 'management strategy evaluation' models (MSE; Figure 8.1) (Bunnefeld et al. 2011; Milner-Gulland 2011). While such models have been well known in fisheries for more than a decade (Dichmont and Fulton, Chapter 2), they have only recently been introduced to the management of terrestrial biodiversity (Bunnefeld et al. 2011; Schlüter et al. 2012).

In this chapter, I first discuss how the social-ecological system associated with the species at stake influences the choice of optimising criteria and trade-offs that should be considered in the modelling work. Then, I briefly introduce the Norwegian game species that I will compare and contrast under the current state of knowledge. In particular, I will examine to what extent quantitative statistical or mathematical models are used in their management. The suite of species and systems presented here does not include all game species in Norway, but they represent gradients in scientific, social and governance factors, such as level of specific knowledge, number of hunters involved, harvest decision jurisdiction (i.e. local, regional or national) and level of social controversy.

8.2 CONTRASTING SOCIO-ECOLOGICAL SYSTEMS CREATES CONTRASTING TRADE-OFFS

The two Norwegian ungulate species I consider in this section are roe deer (*Capreolus capreolus*) and moose (Table 8.1). Large herbivores represent substantial resources in many parts of the world, supplying local communities with goods and economic income (Fitzgibbon et al. 1995; Storaas et al. 2001). However, there are also a number of challenges associated with the management of ungulates in areas where their abundance has increased: abundant ungulate populations might have a major impact on vegetation and habitats important for conservation (Ripple and Beschta 2003; McGraw and Furedi 2005) and might represent a considerable nuisance, causing vehicle accidents (Putman 2003; Mysterud 2004; Seiler et al. 2004), and damaging commercially important timber stocks (Hörnberg 2001; Skonhoft and Olaussen 2005) and agricultural crops (Putman 1986; Putman and Moore 1998; Schley and Roper 2003). Typically, models that consider the costs related to high abundances of ungulates as well as the revenue from the harvest will find optimal densities to be lower than in situations where they are not considered (Skonhoft and Olaussen 2005). Complicating the situation further, due to the migratory or nomadic behaviour of many ungulate species, such damages are rarely symmetrically distributed among the landowners. This creates further challenges in the management (Skonhoft 2005; Nilsen et al. 2009b). Nilsen et al. (2009b) presented a bio-economic model for moose management in Norway, where two sub-populations of moose are subject to different site-specific mortality rates caused by the spatial distribution of territorial wolf packs, coupled with the seasonal migration of moose. In general, they found that failure to cooperate in what they called the unified management scheme resulted in moose populations that are too high, which increased the moose damage and increased the asymmetry among landowners.

Table 8.1 *Summary of Case Species, Including Annual (National) Harvest Bags and Scale of Management Decisions for the Five Game Species (Roe Deer, Moose, Wolverine, Lynx and Willow Ptarmigan) Considered in the Chapter*

Species	Harvest Bag[a]	Management Scale[b]	Comments
Roe deer	28,300	Local and municipality	Few national regulations regarding management targets
Moose	35,670	Local and regional	Few specific regulations regarding management targets
Wolverine	38	Regional. Appeals handled by Ministry	Regional and national management targets decided by the Parliament
Lynx	94	Regional. Appeals handled by Ministry	Regional and national management targets decided by the Parliament
Willow ptarmigan	134,400	Local	Few specific regulations regarding management targets

[a] Arithmetic mean for the years 2007–2013.
[b] The scale at which management decisions are taken. Local means local (single) landowners.

Concurrent with the increase in ungulate abundance, there has been a change in the attitude towards large predators (Mech 1996), resulting in increasing numbers and distribution of large predatory species in some areas such as Europe (Swenson et al. 1994; Wabakken et al. 2001; Smith et al. 2003; Chapron et al. 2014). In this chapter, the two carnivore game species I consider are the lynx (*Lynx lynx*) and wolverine (*Gulo gulo*) (Table 8.1). The lynx is the only wild cat species in Scandinavia, and its diet is usually dominated by wild ungulates such as roe deer (Odden et al. 2006; Gervasi et al. 2014), but high predation rates on sheep (*Ovis aries*) and semidomestic reindeer (*Rangifer tarandus*) have been reported (Mattisson et al. 2011; Odden et al. 2013). In Norway, the lynx is distributed across most of the country and its abundance is regulated through a quota harvest system (Linnell et al. 2010).

In contrast to ungulate management, the objective in carnivore management is rarely to maximise the yield in terms of number of animals harvested. Rather, the general trade-off is found at the intersection between securing viable populations and (to some extent) ensuring their ecological functioning, and the costs associated with livestock depredation and competition over game animals (Linnell et al. 2005). In addition, for some species and in some regions, fear of carnivores might affect management decisions (Linnell et al. 2005). As large carnivores usually live at low densities and have large spatial requirements (Carbone and Gittleman 2002), collaboration across national borders (i.e. transboundary management; Linnell and Boitani 2012) is often the only meaningful way to manage and monitor these populations (Gervasi et al. 2015). Low acceptance of management goals and regulations could have detrimental consequences for carnivore conservation. For example, poaching has been reported to be more socially acceptable in some rural areas in Norway where the potential for conflict is highest (Gangaas et al. 2013). Such effects have been reported to limit or slow down the recovery of wolves in Scandinavia (Bull et al. 2009; Liberg et al. 2012). In some cases, the carnivores have even become a symbol of larger political segregation between urban middle class citizens and the rural working class (Skogen and Thrane 2008). It is clear that against this background, any management model that does not consider the socio-political setting will fail to achieve its targets.

In contrast to carnivores and ungulates, the social-ecological settings surrounding game bird management in Scandinavia is relatively benign. Nevertheless, potential conflicts exist. Our example species in this game class is the willow ptarmigan (*Lagopus lagopus*) (Table 8.1). There is an increasing awareness about the role that birds play in terms of offering cultural ecosystem services (Bradbury et al. 2010), and there is increasing focus on the ecosystem processes that are supported by game birds, mainly because they represent important food sources for birds of prey (Nystrom et al. 2005, 2006). In light of the ongoing population decline of many alpine birds in Scandinavia, including willow and rock ptarmigan (*Lagopus muta*) (Lehikoinen et al. 2014), the effects of recreational hunting on bird population abundance and their ability to deliver these services has frequently been debated in the media during the last few years. Should the current population trends continue, such controversies could be expected to increase in the future. A very different type of conflict, however, is related to the way quotas and hunting permits are allocated among the hunters. In Norway, hunting regulations take many forms, such as daily bag limits, seasonal bag limits, season length and number of permits sold. Based on a survey among ptarmigan hunters in Norway, Andersen et al. (2014) show hunters, in general, were supportive of some types of regulations whereas they did not approve others. Further, based on the same survey, Wam et al. (2012) subdivided the hunters into three groups depending on their preferences with respect to daily harvest bag size and the number of other hunters in the area. Based on a bio-socio-economic model, they showed that disregarding hunter preferences from the model resulted in a management model that would not be acceptable by hunters, because it would result in overcrowding and very low bag limits. Should the current population declines continue such that the resource become more limiting, the controversies are predicted to increase in the future.

Based on this brief review, it is clear that the social-ecological setting framing the harvest management in Norway differs considerably between some of the main game species in Norway. As a consequence, the objective functions to maximise, as well as the trade-offs that need to be built in to the quantitative management models, are very different for the different systems.

8.3 COMPARING THE USE OF MODELS IN UNGULATE, CARNIVORE AND SMALL GAME MANAGEMENT: NORWAY AS A CASE STUDY

The construction and presentation of statistical and mathematical models related to the management of wildlife species has a long tradition. Among the case studies considered here, there is great variability in the extent to which such models are available. Table 8.2 summarises the data and state of knowledge available for each of the case study species. In particular, I will focus on whether these models have been directly used when allocating harvest quotas.

For the Eurasian lynx (*Lynx lynx*) population in Norway, a Bayesian state-space harvesting model has been developed (Nilsen et al. 2011). The model was used as a forecasting tool, and the posterior probability distribution of population sizes under different harvesting off-takes were displayed. The model was constructed to serve as a guiding tool for the managers during the quota setting process, partly to reduce the controversy over quota setting (Nilsen et al. 2012a). During the first years after the model was published, it was regularly cited and indirectly used when deciding harvest quotas, but the impact was not as direct as the model and results allowed for. Later, the monitoring programme was adjusted to accommodate cross-border collaboration with Sweden. This resulted in a discontinuity of the time series data used to estimate the

Table 8.2 *Summary of Knowledge Base, Structured around the Four Sub-models in Figure 8.1*

Species	Population Dynamics Model	Monitoring Model	Harvest Decisions*	Implementation Model	Stakeholders' Preference on Management Options
Roe deer	Fairly well studied in some parts of the distribution (Nilsen et al. 2009a; Gervasi et al. 2012)	No monitoring data available	• Local authorities. • No general model used to guide quota setting	Not well studied	Not well studied. Few strong controversies
Moose	Many studies to build on and several harvesting dynamics models published (Sæther et al. 2001; Nilsen et al. 2005)	National monitoring based on hunters' observations (Solberg and Saether 1999)	• Local and authorities • Various models used, but rarely based on a quantitative model as a single tool	Not well studied, but overall quota filling can be assessed from official statistics	Few strong controversies, but exceptions exist in some regions
Wolverine	Demographic data available, as well as CMR analysis based on faecal DNA samples (Gervasi et al. 2015).	National monitoring programme. Based on den site monitoring and non-invasive DNA-methods	• Regional authorities • Quotas frequently appealed to the Ministry • No formal model used to guide quota setting	Formal analysis presented (Bischof et al. 2012)	Not well studied, but frequent controversies among stakeholder groups
Lynx	Demographic data (Andrèn et al. 2006; Nilsen et al. 2012b) and time series analysis based on monitoring data.	National monitoring programme. Based on snow tracks from family groups (females with kittens). (Nilsen et al. 2012a)	• Regional authorities • Quotas frequently appealed to the Ministry • Some reliance on quantitative models but mainly as rules of thumb	Formal analysis presented (Bischof et al. 2012)	Frequent controversies among stakeholder groups

(continued)

Table 8.2 (*continued*)

Species	Population Dynamics Model	Monitoring Model	Harvest Decisions*	Implementation Model	Stakeholders' Preference on Management Options
Willow ptarmigan	Several studies to draw on, including full-scale harvest experiments (Pedersen et al. 2004; Sandercock et al. 2011).	National monitoring included in general bird surveys (Kålås et al. 2014). Several local and regional initiatives that are coordinated nationally	• Local authorities • Some controversies, especially when abundance is low • Some reliance on quantitative models but mainly as rules of thumb	Some results presented in various Norwegian reports and in Brøseth and Pedersen (2000)	Knowledge based on questionnaires to hunters and landowners (Wam et al. 2013). Some controversies due to interference with other ecosystem processes

Note: The column 'Population Dynamics Model' relates to the current knowledge about the demography, and to which extent such models are already available. Column 'Monitoring Model' describes briefly the current monitoring programmes for the focal species that would be used to formally construct the monitoring model in a complete MSE model. Column 'Harvest Decision' refers to the (a) management authority responsible for deciding harvest quotas and (b) to what extent a formal models are used to guide quota setting. Column 'Implementation Model' describes to what extent the relationship between quotas and actual harvest bags have been described, analysed and published. Column 'Stakeholders' Preferences on Management Options' indicates very briefly the current situation with regard to stakeholder positions related to quota setting and harvest management.

parameters of the model, and for the last couple of years, the model has not been formally applied. Another harvesting model, based on modelling the total reproductive value of the lynx population rather than the population size, has also been developed and published in the scientific literature (Sæther et al. 2010), but has not been, to my knowledge, so far directly used in the quota setting process.

For the willow ptarmigan (*Lagopus lagopus*), an extensive large-scale harvest experiment was carried out to assess the effects of harvest on the annual and seasonal survival and rate of population change (Pedersen et al. 2004; Sandercock et al. 2011). This work has resulted in general recommendations to the management authorities with regard to harvest levels and impact, but so far no formal quantitative model has been tested or utilised in practical management settings. A bio-economic model optimising hunters' satisfaction under different harvest levels and number of permits has been developed (Wam et al. 2012; see the earlier discussion), but so far this model has not been directly implemented in willow ptarmigan harvesting in Norway. Several other models have been developed based on data from neighbouring Sweden (see e.g. Aanes et al. 2002).

Moose (*Alces alces*) is perhaps the most investigated wildlife species in Norway, and several high-impact studies have been carried out (Solberg et al. 1999; Saether et al. 2007; Fryxell et al. 2010). In addition, several quantitative harvesting models have been developed and published, dealing with moose harvesting under different settings and constraints (Sylvèn 1995; Sæther et al. 2001; Nilsen et al. 2005, Skonhoft 2005; Nilsen et al. 2009b). While some of these models have had impact on the general quota sizes and in particular quota allocation in terms of sex and age frequencies, the models have rarely been directly used in practical management. On the contrary, a range of different models is used locally, but no systematic review exists of their origin, similarities or robustness.

For roe deer (*Capreolus capreolus*) and wolverine (*Gulo gulo*), no quantitative models have been established or used to any great extent in their management. For roe deer, several high-impact studies on their life history, demography and population dynamics have been conducted (Nilsen et al. 2009a; Gervasi et al. 2012), but so far this work has not resulted in any quantitative harvest models that can be used directly by management to aid in the harvest decisions. For the wolverine, annual hunting quotas are decided by politically elected regional management boards. Currently, no quantitative models are used to guide in the quota setting process, and no systematic review is available to assess how the quotas are set given the current population state.

Due to varying levels of research effort, the knowledge base is uneven across the five case study species and there is a substantial variation in the degree to which quantitative models could be used to inform harvest management. However, even formal quantitative models that have been published in the scientific literature are not used extensively in game management in Norway. In any case, there are no quantitative models that include all the four sources of uncertainty described in the introduction. Currently, little is known about the extent to which the four forms of uncertainties (see Figure 8.1) are taken into account in the harvest management. A formal review of the issue is outside the scope of this chapter, but judging from the impression one gets from reading the scientific literature, there are far more quantitative harvest models that address environmental stochasticity (and to some extent demographic stochasticity; see Lande et al. (2003)) than there are models that include the full range of uncertainties, including partial controllability. It is equally clear that for most species addressed in this chapter, the candidate models discussed above mainly consider uncertainty relating to environmental stochasticity (and to some extent demographic stochasticity), whereas the other sources of uncertainty (structural uncertainty, partial controllability and partial observability) have been given attention to a much lesser extent. In this section, I will briefly discuss the published sources for information that would be needed to build a full MSE model for the species considered in this chapter.

Recent case studies on a range of species, including lynx and wolverine from Norway, indicate how the managers are indeed experiencing only a partial control over the harvest off-take. For instance, in a recent study, Bischof et al. (2012) estimated the degree of quota filling for four species of carnivores (Eurasian lynx, wolverine, brown bears, *Ursus arctos,* and grey wolf, *Canis lupus*) in three countries (Norway, Estonia and Latvia). They reported substantial variation in the degree of quota filling (from 40 per cent for wolverine in Norway to nearly 100 per cent for lynx in Latvia). In Norway, there was a positive relationship between the instantaneous potential to fill a quota slot and the relative availability of the target species for both wolverine and lynx. Failing to take such species- and system-specific quota filling rates into account might lead to outcomes that are not foreseen when allocating quotas. For the other species in this chapter, no similar analysis has been conducted. For the wild ungulate species, the data to perform analysis on a seasonal basis are readily available but such analysis has to date not been presented. Nevertheless, a similarly clear distinction with respect to quota filling appears to exist between moose (very high degree of quota filling) and roe deer (very low degree of quota filling). If such differences are not accounted for, quantitative harvest models are likely to result in models that are less robust.

There is a rich literature on monitoring of wildlife species, and I will not cover the statistical and logistical challenges here. Models that take the uncertainty in the monitoring data available to the managers into account, known as adaptive harvest management (Nichols et al. 2007), represented a great leap forward compared to traditional resource management models. Formulating the harvest management model explicitly in terms of the monitoring data available for the managers has the advantage that uncertainty in these data are transferred to the uncertainty in the recommendations of forecasts. For the species considered in this chapter, there is a great variability in which extent formal monitoring data is available to the managers. For the two carnivore species considered (lynx and wolverine, respectively), the monitoring is a part of the National Monitoring Programme for large carnivores, and substantial resources are allocated to this task annually. Indeed, for the lynx, these monitoring data have been incorporated into a state-space harvesting model (Nilsen et al. 2011). Nilsen et al. (2012a) examined the correlation between the population trends obtained through the official monitoring programme with those of an independent population trajectory arising from a virtual population reconstruction, and found, in general, a very good agreement. Note, however, that this comparison was done at a national scale, and that due to demographic stochasticity and sampling error, the correlation is expected to become weaker when analyses are repeated at the regional scale at which management decision are taken currently.

8.4 CONCLUSIONS

Based on this review, it seems clear that game management in Norway is not heavily reliant on the use of quantitative (population) models. For many species, harvesting models exist and have been published in the scientific literature, but only rarely have they been directly implemented in the management routines. One should not underestimate the impact that some of these studies might have had on the overall harvest management and quota setting mechanisms. The current situation might probably resemble the findings presented in Sutherland et al. (2004), in which informal knowledge is mixed with the general recommendations stemming from the quantitative models discussed in this chapter.

On studying the historical records of ecological research, it is found that the most basic ecological research has its foundation in an applied problem (Krebs 2001). However, as the term *applied ecology* implies, the application of ecological theory and knowledge is a core element of the field. When I published my first paper in applied ecology (Nilsen et al. 2005), we did not actively work to get our model implemented in actual management practices. Later, when I think about it, this seems to be a common finding; there is a lot of scientifically sound applied ecological work that could potentially be used more directly by wildlife managers, but unless the scientists engage with management, somehow the work is less likely to be of any immediate utility. There is clearly a possibility to implement quantitative models more directly in the management cycle.

While quantitative models have indeed had influence on the management of wildlife species in Norway, there are few records where such models are used as the only tool in the management process. Further, there are currently no cases where models considering the full range of uncertainties (as outlined in Figure 8.1) have been applied. This situation does not seem to be unique to wildlife management in Norway; MSE models have only been introduced to terrestrial (harvest) management and conservation recently (Bunnefeld et al. 2011). As this brief review has elucidated, such models could indeed be constructed for a range of species and systems with very different social-ecological settings. For some of the systems, little is known about parts of the management cycle outlined in Figure 8.1, and many of the sub-models would then probably have to be specified in very general terms.

Communicating uncertainties related to natural resource management with various stakeholders is challenging, and might in fact be one of the reasons why more quantitative models have not been directly implemented. As anyone with some experience with models that contain multiple sources of uncertainty (as do the MSE models sketched out in Figure 8.1) knows, the error bars related to the outcome of multiple model runs can be depressingly large even in cases where we claim to have a good understanding of the system. As any scientists who have presented their work for the media also know, such uncertainty tends to fade away when the numbers go public. Thus, in many cases, establishing new and creative way to communicate the results from the models would be worthwhile. Engagement between scientists and stakeholders might help in creating a common understanding about what one can expect in terms of precision and outcome when using quantitative models for harvest management. In a recently published paper, Elston et al. (2014) used a stochastic population dynamics model to inform the debate about hen harrier–grouse management in northern England. Importantly, stakeholders were involved in the process, commissioned the work and agreed upon the underlying principles. Such engagement between scientists and stakeholders may be necessary to promote more use of quantitative models in harvest management.

Linking Biodiversity Indicators with Global Conservation Policy

EMILY NICHOLSON, ELIZABETH A.
FULTON AND BEN COLLEN

9.1 INTRODUCTION

Around the world, natural ecosystems, ecological processes and bio-diversity are in decline, and with them many of the goods and services that humans rely on (Walpole et al. 2009; Tittensor et al. 2014). Numerous international agreements have been adopted by governments and non-governmental organisations to stem these losses, including the Convention on Biological Diversity (CBD), which comprises a set of targets, the Aichi Targets, under a strategic plan to stimulate effective and urgent action to stem biodiversity loss (Convention on Biological Diversity 2011). Many indicators have been developed by scientists to measure the state of biodiversity, the pressures driving its change, the responses of management and policy and the changes in benefits accrued by humans from biodiversity (Walpole et al. 2009; Butchart et al. 2010; Collen and Nicholson 2014; Tittensor et al. 2014). The policies that are required to halt declines in biodiversity and achieve conservation objectives, such as the Aichi Targets, are less clear.

Effective conservation policy requires an explicit understanding of the links between the desired outcomes of conservation, how those outcomes can be measured and the proposed actions needed to achieve them. There are a number of ways in which this might be achieved. One of the most promising is to project forward the modelled impacts of alternative policies on both biodiversity and on the indicators that will be used to monitor their impacts, ideally using quantitative process-based models (Perrings et al. 2011). This has the dual benefit of enabling the impacts of policies to be evaluated for their effectiveness, and also

Emily Nicholson and Ben Collen contributed equally to the chapter evaluating whether the indicators can detect changes needed to inform policy (Nicholson et al. 2012; Collen and Nicholson 2014).

Remarkably, many of the indicators used to track biodiversity around the world remain untested in their ability to reflect trends of interest, such as declines in threatened species or ecosystem function (Mace et al. 2010; Nicholson et al. 2012), rendering changes in indicators either difficult to interpret, meaningless or, at worst, misleading with respect to change in biodiversity. A recent review by Tittensor et al. (2014) found that only a minority of potential indicator metrics were suitable for monitoring progress towards global conservation targets, based on criteria for temporal and spatial coverage, relevance to conservation targets, and scientific credibility (Tittensor et al. 2014). As a consequence, only sixteen of the twenty Aichi Targets have any indicators available with which to measure progress, while multiple targets rely on very few biodiversity indicators; most of these have not been subjected to quantitative performance testing.

The lack of systemic evaluation of indicators, conservation targets and the actions needed to achieve them raises several questions to which conservation science can contribute:

- How can predictive models best be used to inform conservation targets, policies and management, and the indicators used to measure their performance?
- How can indicators be tested in order to evaluate whether they are fit for the purpose of monitoring change in biodiversity?
- Is the current set of biodiversity indicators fit for purpose?

In this chapter, we address these questions, focussing on those biodiversity indicators used at the global level for reporting on biodiversity change, in particular those associated with the CBD's Aichi Targets; the points raised are pertinent to a variety of other conservation policies and indicators. We argue that indicators can best inform policy when part of an indicator-policy cycle (Figure 9.1; Nicholson et al. 2012) that links conservation targets, policy evaluation, implementation and monitoring. A key element of an indicator-policy cycle is rigorous evaluation of whether indicators are fit for purpose, including how indicator structure and uncertainty in data affect conclusions. We illustrate our argument and the potential for application of this framework with several biodiversity indicators used at a global level.

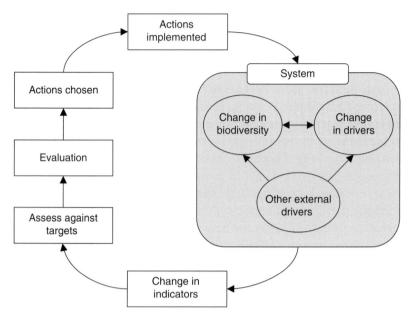

Figure 9.1 Indicator-policy cycle, which is both a conceptual model for use of indicators within a decision-making framework linking targets, actions and indicators, but also forms the basis for quantitative modelling for evaluating conservation targets, the policies required to meet them and indicators for measuring their performance. Adapted from Nicholson et al. (2012).

9.2 INDICATOR-POLICY CYCLE: LINKING TARGET, POLICY, ACTION AND MONITORING

The indicator-policy cycle, described in Nicholson et al. (2012), places indicators for measuring change in biodiversity and the impacts of policy on biodiversity, within the cycle of decision-making and implementation. The cycle (Figure 9.1) draws heavily on management strategy evaluation (see Dichmont and Fulton, Chapter 2), in particular its application in indicator testing, such as Fulton et al. (2005) and Branch et al. (2010), and other structured and decision-theoretic approaches used in adaptive management and evaluation of monitoring (Walters 1986; Shea et al. 1998; Nichols and Williams 2006; McDonald-Madden et al. 2010; Gregory et al. 2012), including structured decision-making (see Garrard et al., Chapter 3). Such a conceptual model linking targets, actions and indicators can be used as a quantitative model for evaluating targets, the policies required to meet them, and the indicators for measuring progress towards targets and policy effectiveness.

There are multiple sources of uncertainty inherent in the indicator-policy cycle that could influence outcomes, including model error in assessing impacts of policies or management actions, unexpected impacts of policy, and imperfect implementation of policies (see a more comprehensive list with examples in the supporting information in Nicholson et al, 2012). One important source of uncertainty is the relationship between an indicator and the underlying trends in aspects of biodiversity that are of interest. Many trade-offs exist in indicator design: for example, an indicator might be a very good proxy for biodiversity, but the data required could be very difficult or expensive to collect. Alternatively, a metric might be readily estimated with available data, but a poor proxy for the aspect of biodiversity of interest. An excellent example of this can be found in indicators of protected area effectiveness and policy, where there is a disconnect between the goals for protected area coverage and means of measuring their effectiveness (Box 9.1).

Thus far, global biodiversity indicators have largely been used for tracking the status of and trends in biodiversity and drivers of loss (Mace and Baillie 2007; Butchart et al. 2010; Secretariat of the CBD 2010). In order to evaluate their future performance, scenario modelling has been employed to project how indicators might measure impacts over the long term. Most such studies model the underlying data that feeds into the indicators, re-creating the indicator based on modelled projections of future biodiversity. (See the following discussion for examples.) However, in a mid-term analysis of progress towards the CBD's Aichi Targets, Tittensor et al. (2014) used statistical models to project forward likely trends in fifty-five indicators, based on recent trajectories of the indicators themselves, rather than the data that underpin them.

Two recent studies used general scenarios representing socio-economic development pathways, under which projected biodiversity change was evaluated rather than specific policies (Leadley et al. 2010; Pereira et al. 2010; Visconti et al. 2016). Visconti et al. (2016) projected trends in two widely used biodiversity indicators (the Red List Index and the Living Planet Index – see sections that follow) under different climate and land-use change scenarios. They used species-specific ecological models of response to climate and land-use for 440 terrestrial carnivore and ungulate species globally, to estimate distributions and population size, with which they estimated the two indicators. Leadley et al (2010) performed an extensive review to collate existing model-based scenario projections, also summarised in Pereira et al. (2010). They synthesised the results of the reviewed studies with four measures of biodiversity change. Two measures related to changes in forest cover and projected changes in distribution of species, functional species groups or biomes, based on global vegetation models. The other two measures related to species extinction and abundance, based respectively on species-area curves and mean species abundance (simulated using the GLOBIO model, Alkemade et al. 2009), dependent on models of environmental change, rather than species-specific models such as those used by Visconti et al. (2015). Metrics such as mean species abundance and projected extinctions based on species-area curves typically do not account for species-specific responses to threats and drivers (Visconti et al. 2015), and are also difficult to monitor. For example, mean species abundance is a theoretical variable rather than projected abundance of particular species (Leadley et al. 2010). As a consequence, it cannot feed back into a monitoring loop to improve models, indicators or policy, to allow modellers and decision-makers to learn and update their knowledge.

Three other examples relate to more specific policy scenarios, which were projected with the explicit aim of testing the indicators used to measure change (Branch et al. 2010; Nicholson et al. 2012; Costelloe et al. 2016); these are also discussed further in Box 9.1. Relatively simple models of trends in mammal abundance were used to project alternative protected area policies in sub-Saharan Africa (described in Nicholson et al. 2012; Costelloe et al. 2016). The modelled changes in abundance were used as underlying data to model changes in two indicators, the Red List Index and the Living Planet Index, to aggregate and illustrate the change across the species. This study is also described briefly in Box 9.1. Nicholson et al. (2012) performed similar analyses with a fisheries policy case study, using ten ecosystem models to project the impacts of two alternative policies (halting and halving bottom trawling) on species' biomass trends. The modelled species trends were extrapolated to species that underpin the Living Planet Index, to project changes in the index under each scenario. Branch et al. (2010) evaluated the Marine Trophic Index, modelling four realistic fishing scenarios with models of twenty-five ecosystems. These examples show the clear potential of indicators in communicating the projected impacts of alternative policies, and also some areas in which indicators can be developed, if they are to be used to help monitor the impact of various policies on biodiversity change.

Box 9.1 Protected Area Policy and Indicators for Measuring Change

Protected areas remain at the centre of conservation strategy (Jenkins and Joppa 2009). Declines in biodiversity within protected areas do, however, continue in many areas around the world (Craigie et al. 2010; Laurance et al. 2012; Jokinen et al. 2014). Factors such as governance, amount of funding, and capacity to control the effects of threatening processes affecting species in and around protected areas may all influence their effectiveness in conserving biodiversity. The CBD in Aichi Target 11 sets out that 17 per cent of land area should be in the effectively managed protected areas by the year 2020 (Convention on Biological Diversity 2011). The current set of indicators judged to be of sufficient quality, scope and coverage to be measure progress to Target 11 are: (i) coverage of protected areas, (ii) protected area coverage of bird, mammal and amphibian distributions (effectively a gap analysis of species), (iii) coverage of ecoregions (marine, freshwater and terrestrial), (iv) funds directed towards protected areas, and (v) management effectiveness (Tittensor et al. 2014). The first three concern different metrics of the spatial coverage of protected areas; the fourth establishes the ongoing commitment of funds toward them. Only the last of these five indicators addresses the effectiveness of management, and is a cumulative count of protected area sites in which effectiveness has been assessed once using a wide variety of measures and assessment methods, making comparisons difficult. The indicator is unable to show change in effectiveness over time (i.e. whether park management and biodiversity outcomes are improving), or the proportion of protected areas considered to be effective (which could inform priority areas for effort and resources). Moreover, the area under protection (the focus of the target) does nothing to indicate the worth for conservation of the areas being protected.

Model-based analyses reinforced the need for better indicators of management effectiveness: Costelloe et al. (2016) projected changes in mammal populations in sub-Saharan Africa in response to potential policies for protected areas; they compared scenarios for increasing coverage to 17 per cent to meet CBD targets, improving management effectiveness (halting declines within protected area boundaries), and a combination of the two. They found that only increasing management effectiveness had a substantial improvement over business-as-usual and expanding protected areas without effective management (see Figure 9.2), when measured by two biodiversity indicators: the Living Planet Index, a measure of change in abundance; and the Red List Index, which measures change in extinction risk. Protected area coverage alone is insufficient to measure progress in protecting biodiversity (Costelloe et al. 2016).

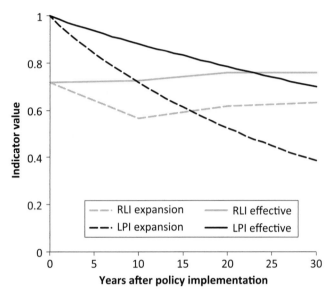

Figure 9.2 Different behaviour of two indicators, the Red List Index (grey) and Living Planet Index (black), under two conservation scenarios – expansion of protected areas (dashed line) and effective protected area management (solid line). Both indicators differentiate between the scenarios, showing effective management has greater biodiversity benefits than expansion, but the RLI is less sensitive than the LPI. Adapted from Costelloe et al. (2016).

9.3 HOW CAN INDICATOR PERFORMANCE BE TESTED?

One of the advantages of modelling policy impacts on both biodiversity and the indicators used to measure it, is that it allows an evaluation of whether the indicators are fit for purpose. Several criteria have been proposed and applied for assessing indicators in ecology, biodiversity conservation and fisheries science, such as a strong theoretical basis, sensitivity to change, public awareness and cost (e.g. Buckland et al. 2005; Rice and Rochet 2005; Jones et al. 2011; Vačkář et al. 2012; Tittensor et al. 2014). Evaluations using scenario models and empirical data take indicator evaluation one step further, by testing the performance and behaviour of indicators under a range of conditions.

Within fisheries management, there has been great interest in testing indicators, largely within a management strategy evaluation framework (e.g. Fulton et al. 2005; Branch et al. 2010; Smith et al. 2011a; Fay et al. 2013). Typically, this involves the development of models that capture the key processes, features and dynamics of the study system, to simulate and predict the impacts of management scenarios. Model outputs are sampled mimicking the way data are collected in the real world, and the 'data' used to calculate the indicators. The model is treated as the 'truth' against which the sampled data and subsequent indicator values are compared. Models are ideal for this purpose, providing a 'virtual truth' that is not available in real-world examples, where knowledge is inevitably incomplete. This framework can be used to examine both the structural elements of the indicators (how well do they reflect aspects of biodiversity of interest), and also the impacts of the quality and quantity of data available to estimate them (such as geographical or taxonomic biases), and combinations of the two.

Model-based studies complement empirical analyses that use existing time-series of biodiversity data and indicators (Branch et al. 2010; Link et al. 2010; Hornborg et al. 2013). Such approaches have been used extensively in fisheries, where in some cases multiple data types and sources are available. For example, in Branch et al. (2010), times-series for catch, long-term trawl surveys and stock assessments were combined with ecosystem models to probe the Marine Trophic Index, while Hornborg et al. (2013) used multiple data sources to evaluate the same indicator. In biodiversity monitoring, it is rare to have multiple independent data sources on the same ecosystem in a way that allows testing of indicators in such a manner.

Model-based analyses can also be used to assess the capacity of sets of indicators to measure change in different components of biodiversity, as is recommended to represent change in different aspects of biodiversity and impacts of different threatening processes (Fulton et al. 2005, 2015; Smith et al. 2011b). Comparative analyses have been employed to evaluate the different performance indicators used in fisheries management at local scales (Fulton et al. 2005; Fay et al. 2013). Link et al. (2010) used existing time-series to analyse the extent to which indicators respond in a predictable manner to pressures (e.g. fishing and environmental drivers) and interventions (proposed management actions), to enable decision-makers to tease apart the relative impacts of different drivers of change (Link et al. 2010). To our knowledge, no analyses have evaluated sets of indicators to ask whether current biodiversity indicators suffer from similar structural or data biases which would impair their ability to detect trends of importance.

9.4 ARE CURRENT BIODIVERSITY INDICATORS FIT FOR PURPOSE?

Remarkably, few biodiversity indicators have been systematically and rigorously evaluated, so for the most part, whether many indicators are fit for purpose remains unknown. Here, we outline how indicator structure and data bias, quality and quantity have been found to affect indicator performance, and in sections that follow provide detailed descriptions of three indicators that have been subjected to performance testing: the mean trophic level, adopted by CBD as the Marine Trophic Index, the Red List Index and the Living Planet Index.

The design and construction of an indicator determine the way it responds to change in different aspects of biodiversity, including its sensitivity to change. For example, evaluations of the Living Planet Index, based on ecological and mathematical theory, found that it exhibits many useful properties for representing change in species abundance (Buckland et al. 2005, 2011; McCarthy et al. 2014). In contrast, Nicholson et al. (2012) and Costelloe et al. (2016) found that the Red List Index exhibits some counter-intuitive behaviour due to the underlying data: the International Union for Concservation of Nature (IUCN) Red List status of species, a snapshot assessment of extinction risk. The IUCN Red List criteria measure declines in abundance over species-specific timeframes; if declines stabilise, a species can return to a low-risk category after prolonged periods of decline (though see Keith et al. 2004; Stanton 2014). As a consequence, the Red List Index has the potential to exhibit a shifting baseline over the long term (Costelloe et al. 2016).

Indicators can fail to represent trends of interest because of bias in the data used to calculate them. This can include bias due to the data type available; for example, the Marine Trophic Index is based on data on the tonnage of species caught in commercial fisheries, rather than biomass of the ecosystems, because catch (or at least landings) data are widely available (Pauly et al. 2013), with substantial consequences on its reliability as an indicator. The Living Planet Index uses data only on vertebrate abundance (Collen et al. 2009a). Though proof of concept exists to extend it to invertebrates (Dirzo et al. 2014), whether sufficient data exist to create a robust and representative index remains in question. Similarly the Red List Index currently includes only amphibians, birds, corals and mammals (Butchart et al. 2007, 2010), though representation is growing. Taxonomic bias in data can stem from the types of species that are targeted for monitoring and study; the vast majority of biodiversity data is focussed on vertebrates, rather than plants, invertebrates and fungi, which provide the bulk of the world's species. Geographic bias stems from uneven distribution of research and time series both globally (for example, an under-representation of data from tropical regions in the Living Planet Index dataset, Collen et al. 2009a) and locally (e.g. accessible areas close to roads are disproportionately surveyed in a landscape, Grand et al. 2007). While there are developments to expand coverage of some indicators (e.g. a sampled approach to Red Listing to broaden taxonomic coverage: Baillie et al. 2008; Collen et al. 2009b; Collen and Baillie 2010), a large investment of both time and money would be required to achieve a reasonably representative set of indicators (Scholes et al. 2008; Pereira et al. 2012).

A further problem with indicator data is the length of time-series from which to elicit trends: the Living Planet Index extends back to the 1970s, and the Marine Trophic Index to the 1950s. Recent analyses have extended the Red List Index for some mammals by adding retrospective Red List assessments to those done in 2008 (Di Marco et al. 2014); however, such analyses are not comprehensive across taxa, giving only recent RLI values for the taxonomic groups assessed, which themselves comprise only a subset of biodiversity (mammals, birds, amphibians and corals).

Data biases have substantial consequences for the patterns of biodiversity observed and captured by indicators, both temporally and spatially, and for subsequent interpretation of trends and the resultant conservation decisions (Grand et al. 2007; Branch et al. 2010; De Ornellas et al. 2011). There has been relatively little analysis of the impacts of these biases on the performance of biodiversity indicators in representing trends of interest, with some exceptions mostly within the sphere of fisheries science (e.g. Branch et al. 2010; Nicholson et al. 2012; Hornborg et al. 2013; Costelloe et al. 2016). Such in-depth stress tests of other biodiversity indicators are urgently needed but have only just begun, and so far on a limited subset.

9.4.1 Marine Trophic Index

The Marine Trophic Index (MTI) was embraced as a CBD indicator in the early 2000s. It is calculated using the mean trophic level of fisheries catch or landings data, weighted by biomass (Pauly et al. 1998; Pauly and Watson 2005); it is therefore also referred to as the mean trophic level, particularly in the fisheries literature. The MTI demonstrates that since the 1950s, landings have comprised smaller, shorter-lived species of fish as well as invertebrates from the lower parts of food webs (Pauly and Watson 2005). Because the MTI was seemingly well established scientifically and supported by an extensive database (The Sea Around Us project, www.seaaroundus.org/), probably the best data available to support any of the CBD indicators, it was earmarked as 'ready for global use'. It is a recommended indicator for Aichi Target 6 (Convention on Biological Diversity 2011), but has not been updated since 2005, and so was not included in the mid-term review of target achievement (Tittensor et al. 2014).

In-depth analyses probing the MTI, however, have found that the indicator failed to reliably detect changes in marine ecosystems (Fulton et al. 2005; Branch et al. 2010; Hornborg et al. 2013; Shannon et al. 2014), for two main reasons: first, because it is based on inherently biased data; and second, because it is sensitive to factors other than the state of the ecosystem.

MTI is designed to be calculated using data on total catch, that is, landings (fish returned to port) and discards, rather than just landings (Pauly and Watson 2005), though in most cases only landings data are available. The assumption is that catch data (and to some extent landings) track underlying biomass trends, an assumption that has been undermined (Branch et al. 2011; Pauly et al. 2013). Hornborg et al. (2013) used long-term empirical datasets from Sweden to analyse MTI trends, and found poor correlation between ecosystem MTI (based on fishery-independent data from the International Bottom Trawl Survey) and landings MTI (Swedish landings data from the International Council for Exploration of the Sea [ICES]). They concluded that 'the trend in landings MTI appears to be, at most, a weak measure of ecosystem state and pressures on biodiversity in the area'. Branch et al. (2010) used a combination of ecosystem models and multiple sources of empirical data (catch, trawl surveys and fisheries stock assessments; Figure 9.3), and found that the inherent bias in the type of data used to calculate it rendered catch MTI is a poor proxy for ecosystem MTI. Furthermore, MTI is also sensitive to the species included within the datasets (Figure 9.3), and estimates of species' trophic level (Branch et al. 2010).

Catch and landings, and thus MTI based on these data, are influenced by multiple factors, including changes in management, fishing technology and profit (Branch et al. 2010; Hornborg et al. 2013). Thus the mean trophic level of catch can decrease due to better management of an ecosystem and improvements in its sustainability (Garcia et al. 2012), although the decreases in MTI are generally interpreted as

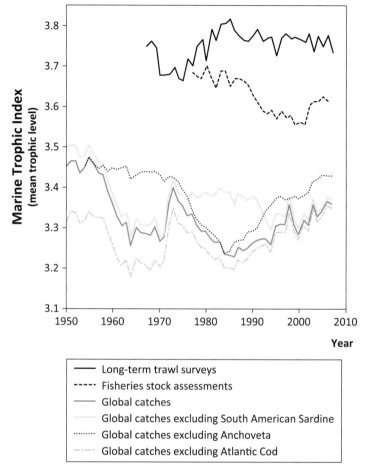

Figure 9.3 Both the absolute value and trends in the Marine Trophic Index (MTI), known in fisheries science as the mean trophic level, were found to differ greatly depending on data source (Branch et al., 2010). The index was also sensitive to the species included in the catch data, showing here, for example, the impacts of excluding key targeted species. This sensitivity to data source and type renders the indicator an unreliable measure of ecosystem MTI. Figure adapted from Branch et al. (2010).

a negative signal of ecosystem health (Hornborg et al. 2013). For example, Hornborg et al. (2013) point out that decreases in landings MTI in Sweden were influenced by management to protect and rebuild fish stocks.

These flaws in MTI as an indicator have been detected because the MTI has been placed under much greater scrutiny than any other CBD indicator, which are yet to face such rigorous testing; limitations in other CBD indicators may also be found if tested in this way.

9.4.2 Red List Index

The Red List Index (RLI) measures overall extinction risk of sets of species and tracks changes in that risk (Butchart et al. 2004, 2007). It depends on data on risk classification from the IUCN Red List of Threatened Species, specifically the status of the component species, assessed against a set of quantitative criteria that assess population size, range area and rate of decline of both. The index is a function of the proportion of species in each threat category at given points in time, and changes due to improvement or deterioration in the status of individual species. The RLI was adopted as a CBD indicator and underpins measures of progress towards six of the twenty Aichi Targets (Tittensor et al. 2014).

Analyses have shown that the RLI also has some potential issues related to the design of the indicator, in particular due to the data that support it (Nicholson et al. 2012). Because the RLI is built on threat classifications as presented in the IUCN Red List, it is affected by the structure of the IUCN classification system. The IUCN Red List criteria were designed for snapshot assessments of threat status, rather than for tracking long-term trends in extinction risk. Specifically, population declines (criterion A of the IUCN Red List criteria) are measured over a biologically relevant timeframe of the longer of 10 years or three generations (up to a maximum of 100 years). As a result, declines prior to the assessment window are 'forgotten', resulting in a shifting baseline (Nicholson et al. 2012; Costelloe et al. 2016). This is illustrated well in the analyses of Costelloe et al. (2016), who modelled protected area management on mammal populations; their projections of the Tsessebe (*Damaliscus lunatus*) under business-as-usual showed dramatic decreases in abundance across most of Africa, with the exception of Southern Africa, where the population continued to increase slightly (Figure 9.4). As a result, the Red List status of the species in 2020 was projected to be 'Critically Endangered' due to large declines (89 per cent decline over three generations), but returning to 'Least Concern' as the population stabilised, albeit at much lower levels; these correspond to

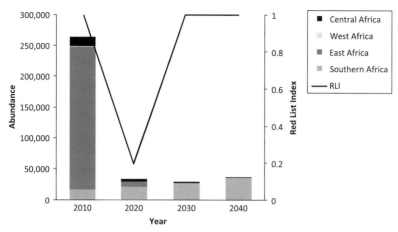

Figure 9.4 The behaviour of the Red List Index (RLI) for a single species, the Tsessebe (*Damaliscus lunatus*), projected by Costelloe et al. (2016). The data for a single species demonstrates show how counter-intuitive behaviour can arise in the Red List Index, due to shifting baseline effects (see also Box 9.1 and Figure 9.2). Although the species' total abundance has decreased greatly, the RLI improves (increases) twenty years after policy implementation, because declines are measured over a biologically relevant timeframe. Adapted from Collen and Nicholson (2014) and Costelloe et al. (2016).

RLI values for the species of 0.2 for Critically Endangered and 1 for Least Concern (Figure 9.4).

In terms of extinction risk of a particular species, such an approach is correct. If a population declines rapidly, and stabilises some time later at a level much lower than it started at, then its extinction risk changes back to a low level (assuming that the newly stabilised population is large enough not to trigger a risk category based on population size alone). However, the expectation is perhaps that an indicator should not 'forget' change from a previously larger population size (Collen and Nicholson 2014), because of the ecosystem-wide implications of large shifts in abundances. Furthermore, the RLI relies on changes from relatively coarse threat classifications, and therefore can change slowly and is not very sensitive to change in abundance or ecosystem composition, particularly in common species (Costelloe et al. 2016); change in abundance, used in indicators such as the Living Planet Index, may in some cases provide a more sensitive and reliable metric over short timeframes (Figure 9.2).

The RLI suffers from taxonomic bias, with implications for indicator performance. It is currently based on only four taxonomic groups, mammals, birds, amphibians and corals, though the development of a sampled Red List Index is underway to reduce taxonomic bias (Baillie et al. 2008; Collen et al. 2009b; Collen and Baillie 2010). For example, the RLI of pollinators is the only indicator for CBD Target 14 – ecosystems that provide essential services are restored and safeguarded (Tittensor et al. 2014). This index is simply a subset of the overall RLI for mammals and birds (i.e. those species that are recognised as being pollinators). If the job of the indicator is to track essential services such as pollination, there is a pressing need to expand the group of species to include invertebrate pollinators (Potts et al. 2010) as well as the plants that they pollinate.

9.4.3 Living Planet Index

The Living Planet Index (LPI), which is based on the geometric mean relative abundance of vertebrate populations, is one of the few other indicators to have faced substantial testing from multiple directions. The mathematical and statistical properties have been examined both through theory and by exploring empirical datasets (Buckland et al. 2005, 2011; van Strien et al. 2012). Analyses of its mathematical structure showed that it is related directly to extinction risk (McCarthy et al. 2014); this supports its use in monitoring change in extinction risk, such as under Aichi Target 12: 'By 2020 the extinction of known threatened species has been prevented and their conservation status, particularly of those most in decline, has been improved and sustained'. However, analyses of the way in which trends are aggregated under the LPI have shown it to be sensitive to the emphasis placed on data from different areas and sources (Collen et al. 2009a; Costelloe et al. 2016).

Like other indicators such as the Red List Index, the LPI suffers from taxonomic and geographic bias in data (Collen et al. 2009a). Bias in the data that underpin the LPI has been found to potentially mask trends in vertebrate biodiversity in some regions, due to a disproportionate amount of data on birds in available times-series, relative to other elements of the vertebrate fauna (Nicholson et al. 2012). Further biases that are likely to affect indicator performance include spatial biases – for example, the LPI data are biased geographically, with more time-series data available from temperate regions than tropical regions (Loh et al. 2005).

9.5 CONCLUSIONS

Conservation science is a relatively young field of research and practice. As it has matured as a discipline, there has been an increasing emphasis on rigour, transparency and consistency (Mace 2014); for example, the Red List of Threatened Species has recently celebrated its fiftieth anniversary, but it was only in the early 1990s that the first formal, quantitative set of criteria based on ecological theory were developed (Mace and Lande 1991; Mace et al. 2008). Meaningful conservation targets, policies to meet them, and indicators to evaluate policies and measure progress towards targets must rely on a rigorous scientific underpinning if they are to achieve their goal (Mace and Baillie 2007). Structured approaches such as management strategy evaluation provide an excellent framework for comprehensive and systematic testing of policies and indicators, and ultimately decision-making.

The goals and expression of biodiversity targets shifted between the CBD targets of the 2000s and those of 2010, from vague to more specific and achievable, or at least measurable targets (Perrings et al. 2010), but a strong link to the policies needed to achieve them at different spatial scales is still lacking. Testing the modelled performance of alternative management actions prior to implementation should be the gold standard for conservation decision-making. Like policies, indicators need to be tested to evaluate whether they are fit for purpose. If the right information to guide conservation policy cannot be gleaned from existing metrics, then gathering new monitoring data on a global scale for an array of new metrics could be a costly but necessary endeavour. The inconsistent delivery of standardised monitoring means that a set of agreed metrics of biodiversity is urgently required (Pereira et al. 2013). Striking the right balance between expanding existing datasets and developing new, more appropriately designed monitoring programmes and metrics, and between scalable measures for monitoring that appropriately balances local and global priorities, provide clear challenges to conservation science, but will be vital if our measures of biodiversity are to robustly support conservation decisions.

Whether adapting existing indicators or developing new ones, the conservation science behind indicator development must be rigorous. The types of tests we describe above can explore whether indicators are telling what we want to know, and what we think they are telling us. Such testing was mentioned in the selection of indicators of the CBD 2010 target, with all indicators being 'identified for immediate testing'

(Balmford et al. 2005). Yet, with few exceptions, the indicators remain largely unevaluated in their capacity to report meaningfully on conservation targets and the means of achieving them; this remains a critical task for conservation science if it is to influence progress in conservation and inform the policies that will stem from international processes, rather than simply report further biodiversity loss.

Synthesis: Moving Forward Together

E.J. MILNER-GULLAND, EMILY NICHOLSON
AND NILS BUNNEFELD

10.1 THE ROLE OF MODELS IN MODERN CONSERVATION

Conservationists and natural resource managers are dealing with complex social-ecological systems, standing on ground that is constantly shifting on different spatial and temporal scales, where the stakes are high and it is impossible to please everyone. Dichmont and Fulton (Chapter 2) remind us that under these circumstances, decision-makers are attempting to solve 'wicked problems'. These are problems with a high level of complexity and multiple subsystems and dependencies; high uncertainty around the consequences of actions and the system dynamics themselves; and divergence in values, perspectives and strategies (Head 2008). All the case studies in this book could be seen as wicked to a greater or lesser extent, and this is representative of the wider field.

In such complex circumstances, it can seem unrealistically simplistic to use structured frameworks incorporating quantitative models to guide decision-making. However, the case studies in this book point to the huge utility of using structured, model-based approaches to solve real-world problems in conservation and natural resource use. They show how these approaches can help to separate facts from value judgements, set clear objectives and (perhaps surprisingly for the uninitiated) bring people together towards a shared understanding of the issues and motivate a collaborative process to search for solutions. This approach can also provide a rigorous scientific basis to decision-making, which can give it more credibility to external observers.

Modelling in this new sense is not about an academic scientist working alone to produce a black box model, which he or she then publishes as a journal article in the hope that implementers will adopt the findings –

maybe tweeting about it or looking for other ways to disseminate the findings to relevant implementers and considering the job done. This is the way in which many academics are used to seeing their role as conservation modellers, the editors included (e.g. Milner-Gulland et al. 1992; Milner-Gulland 1994; Nicholson et al. 2006). Sometimes, as Nilsen (Chapter 8) describes, academic modelling can filter through to decision-makers from the academic literature. But now there is an increasing push to bridge the research–implementation gap, and ensure that scientists (who are generally funded from the public purse) are genuinely having impact in the real world (Sunderland et al. 2009; Arlettaz et al. 2010).

This book provides a wealth of experience and examples of how modelling can be done in a way that means it contributes to improved real-world conservation and resource management. The chapters show how important it is that all interested parties reach out; it's not just the job of the scientist but also of the potential users of science. The word 'participatory' is becoming so widely used that it risks becoming an empty buzzword (and one that can cover up inequalities and marginalisation; Chapter 5). However, the strong message from this book is that people of different expertise, perspectives and goals need to come together in order to produce meaningful models that can truly support decision-making. These models can support implementers by helping them to organise their thoughts, think their priorities and constraints through to their logical conclusions and explore the implications of their potential actions, as well as making explicit the uncertainties and their implications (as particularly highlighted in Chapters 2 and 3).

Generally, participatory modelling is done at the beginning of a management process, or when change is needed, and may start with a workshop using a structured decision-making (SDM) framework to define the problem. This can then lead on to a management strategy evaluation (MSE) of the alternatives, using the decision framework developed earlier. Many insights arise during these developmental stages; thus an approach of rapid, iterative prototyping is valuable (Chapter 3). A well-developed decision framework and analysis lead to implementation, which leads into ongoing adaptive management and a cycle of monitoring and evaluation (Chapter 2). A structured approach can work at the local level (such as the MSE case studies in Chapter 2), or at the level of global policymaking through an indicator–policy–cycle (Chapter 9). Moore et al. (Chapter 6) show how this approach worked particularly well, in terms of improving both scientific understanding and scientist–practitioner collaboration, when the science moved in cycles between modelling and data gathering, with reassessment of the evidence in between.

10.2 LESSONS FROM THE CASE STUDIES

Our contributors have accumulated many years of experience in this approach to modelling, and write insightfully about their own experiences – both from the perspectives of newcomers who are hitting rocky patches for the first time (such as Nuno et al.; Chapter 7) and people who are decades down the road (such as Dichmont and Fulton; Chapter 2). Some key points they highlighted concern the importance of participation and commitment; understanding how trade-offs, power and politics play out; identifying and overcoming the scientific and technical challenges and thinking long term, including looking to the future.

10.2.1 Participation and People

Almost all the chapters highlight the absolute need for participation of the fullest range of stakeholder voices from the start, if the decision-making process is to be both effective and legitimate. However, there are big challenges, and sometimes these are underappreciated; as Nuno et al. (Chapter 7) highlight, the process of stakeholder mapping and engagement can be long and difficult, yet is not often thought of as a vital first stage of the SDM process. Not every interested party can be involved in participatory modelling, because groups need to be manageable in size and appropriate in composition. This requires representation of group viewpoints by individuals. Dichmont and Fulton (Chapter 2) point out that the fisheries sector, where MSE was developed and is now widely embedded in management, benefits from good institutions which are able to represent interest groups, and that translating the approach to other sectors can be challenging when these institutions are not present or widely accepted. Marginalised voices are easily excluded (Chapter 5). Even if they are in the room, they may not feel able to voice their thoughts or may not be listened to.

Once the composition of the group is decided upon, it is important that there is mutual respect for what each person can bring and awareness of the competing priorities. For example, Moore et al. (Chapter 6) highlight the need of academics to publish novel research, and of managers to act and to spend money wisely. Personal trust and familiarity need to be built among participants who may have very different backgrounds and experiences. The label of 'expert' can be a powerful barrier between scientists and other people without a strong academic background or interest in research; humility and respect for the expertise that has brought each person to the room are vital, but not easily engendered when the modeller can be seen ex ante as so pivotal to the process and so technically skilled. Experts, however, should not be unassailable, not least because their judgement is not necessarily any better than that of anyone else concerned about a problem (Burgman et al. 2011). Again, fisheries is a sector in which scientists, managers and resource users have been working together for many years and from which lessons can be learnt (Chapter 2).

Although we have up to now been using the words 'scientist', 'modeller' and 'academic' relatively loosely and interchangeably, it is also vitally important to understand that a range of academic expertise is needed to solve the wicked problems that conservation and natural resource managers face. This is becoming more and more strongly emphasised over time, particularly in the conservation literature, and yet truly interdisciplinary research, with understanding and respect between academic disciplines, is still not easy to achieve. Pooley et al. (2014) highlight some of the reasons for this and come up with very similar suggestions to those of our case study authors – in particular, engaging early and explicitly with conceptual and methodological differences and agreeing ground rules on ways of working together at the start. One of the major disciplinary omissions from conservation and natural resource management is the humanities and the qualitative social sciences (Pooley 2013); this needs to change if conservation is to be effective, because understanding people's cultural background, historical context and ethical standpoint is fundamental to changing human behaviour. However Nuno et al. (Chapter 7) mention the challenges of modellers and social anthropologists finding common ground when the academic languages they speak and their world views are so very different. This needs to be addressed if the full range of expertise is to be brought to bear on how to make decisions in a way that will lead to sustainable and acceptable outcomes – such as that of the anthropologists writing in Chapter 5.

10.2.2 Trade-Offs, Power and Politics

Once an issue in conservation or resource management has made it to the stage at which a structured approach to decision-making is being considered, there is almost inevitably a trade-off being made between someone's needs and wants and someone else's. It may be that an unacknowledged trade-off is causing the difficulties, for example land appropriation from poor rural farmers by conservationists or commercial concessionaires may lead to resentment and conflict (Chapter 5; Homewood et al. 2009, Harrison et al. 2015). Conservation requires hard choices, and it is vital that these choices, and the accompanying trade-offs, are made explicit; otherwise a structured decision-making approach cannot succeed. An interesting insight into the underlying causes of resistance to management actions comes from Daw et al. (2015), highlighted in Chapter 5. This is the concept that trade-offs can be tragic: between two sets of 'sacred' deeply held values; routine, between two utilitarian 'secular' needs; or taboo, between a sacred value and a secular need (Tetlock 2003). Resource managers may make the error of assuming that the trade-offs they are aiming to resolve are routine, and therefore amenable to rational solution. Conservationists perhaps better understand that some of their management decisions involve tragic trade-offs (between the world views of hunters and animal rights activists, for example). However, both need to be more alert to the possibility of taboo trade-offs, which can be hard to address in decision-making when people are reluctant to talk about them, because they are uncomfortable to acknowledge. An example might be between the practical, modelled approach to minimising the risk of invasion of grey sallow willow into alpine bogs in Victoria, Australia, by using a targeted approach to seedling removal, and the strong feeling of the invasive control contractors that they should act to remove invasive seedlings when they see them regardless of whether this is the best use of their time and resources (Chapter 6). Another might be balancing the strong cultural feelings about hunting in Norwegian society with the damages done to landowners' property by wildlife (Chapter 8). These issues emphasise yet again the importance of a nuanced, qualitative understanding of the system as a foundation for decision-making, and properly inclusive participation in decision-making processes (Chapter 5).

One approach to ensuring that trade-offs are considered within the appropriate framing from the beginning, highlighted by Moore et al. (Chapter 6) is to focus on fundamental objectives (the ones which are most values-driven) during the SDM processes, rather than on means objectives (things that appear to need to be done in order to get to an end-point). Often in highly charged debates, the argument is about means objectives rather than fundamental objectives, and this can quickly lead to stalemate as there is no way to bridge between world views. For example, the current debate about whether or not to trade in rhino horn (e.g. Biggs et al. 2013) is an argument about a means objective, which bypasses fundamental issues about what society's objectives for rhino conservation are. A workshop taking participants through the framework of SDM can be an opportunity to explore the fundamental objectives of management, and whether they can form the basis for further discussion or not. Nuno et al. (Chapter 7) find the MSE conceptual framework itself a useful starting point for discussion of the opportunities and constraints for participatory decision-making in the Serengeti, even in the absence of modelling; this would be worth investigating in other contexts.

Another interesting issue, brought up by Chee et al. (Chapter 4), is the power dynamics between the individuals attending workshops and participatory forums, and the rest of their organisation. Chee et al. find that these individuals generally come away with positive feelings towards a modelling approach, and a commitment to implement it for decision-making, but may find themselves unable to do so. This might be due to organisational constraints (funding or time limitations), political manoeuvres by others within an organisation with different views or managers not liking to lose their decision-making power and feeling threatened by the transparency inherent in structured decision-making processes. These issues are hard to resolve post-hoc, and so need to be addressed within organisations early on, when the commitment to engage is first made. Sometimes that commitment may be made lightly, and change is then not evident, even when the need for change is clear to all (Chapter 4). At the next scale up, Nuno et al. (Chapter 7) highlight the lack of engagement between the government department which produces the monitoring data for the Serengeti, and the department which manages the National Park; an approach like MSE could only work if the decision-making processes of each reflect the needs and insights of the other. There's a need for realism about whether a participatory process to develop an MSE model would actually change the fundamental political landscape within which these two departments operate. Dichmont and Fulton (Chapter 2) reflect on similar issues arising when attempting to implement MSE at the large catchment level, with fragmentation of responsibility, sectoral divides and the lack of an overarching governance framework hampering decision-making.

10.2.3 Challenges for the Modeller

So far we have emphasised the social, institutional and governance issues which make carrying out structured, participatory decision-making a challenge. However, this is not to neglect the issues that face scientists when attempting to collect data and build meaningful models to support the process. Repeatedly through the book, the authors warn us not to underestimate the technical difficulties in data acquisition, storage and processing, as well as the modelling itself: Moore et al. (Chapter 6) describe the major breakthrough of getting global positioning system (GPS)-located data on where invasives control contractors were going, but the accompanying difficulties of data processing across agencies with different software and approaches to data manipulation; Nuno et al. (Chapter 7) highlight the need to fill some fundamental and substantive data gaps with extensive fieldwork before starting on an MSE model, while Dichmont and Fulton (Chapter 2) explain the challenges of modelling a complex and dynamic social-ecological system at the appropriate resolution. Having said this, sometimes developing simple conceptual models can produce useful insights into uncertainties and provide enough clarity around the issues to allow a decision to be made without substantial technical and time investment (Chapter 3).

Many of the models used in MSE and to underpin decision-making in conservation science still focus on environmental uncertainties, rather than also thinking about observation and implementation uncertainties. Nilsen (Chapter 8) highlights this as a concern for wildlife management in Norway, a country at the forefront of modelling the population ecology of hunted species. This may be because observation uncertainty has not been considered a process that is worth modelling in its own right, rather than just as a source of variability in the data. However, the biases in observational data (for both ecological and social systems) can be both substantial and dynamic, meaning that trends in relative values can be very misleading and therefore a poor basis for decision-making at both local (Keane et al. 2011) and global scales (Chapter 9). Implementation uncertainty, also often modelled as a simple stochastic process, is also likely be hugely influential in determining what works and what doesn't (Fulton et al. 2011a).

Once the modelling is complete, the medium by which scientists communicate with decision-makers is critical in order that messages are well understood and can be used. Moore et al. (Chapter 6) talk about this from the perspective of both the modeller and resource manager, both of whom comment on the importance of communication that makes sense to the recipient rather than necessarily the provider. The modeller highlights her realisation that maps are much better means of presenting findings than graphs, and the manager comments on how very useful for management those maps were.

10.2.4 Thinking to the Future

All the case studies highlighted the substantial investment of time and resources that is needed to achieve better decision-making for natural resource management. This means years, not months, and a commitment from all sides to make the process work. The commitment needs to be there from the beginning of the process and for a realistic length of time, perhaps five to ten years. The relatively simple system which Moore et al. (Chapter 6) describe required five years of intensive engagement, including three years of full time work for the scientist, in order for change to be realised. Dichmont and Fulton's chapter is a summary of decades of slow and careful progress towards a more inclusive and transparent management approach. Expectations need to be clear from the beginning: that there will be ongoing and potentially substantive benefits from this new approach into the long run, but that this requires a large investment of staff time and resources early on. If this is not apparent, or accepted, by all parties with power to implement or impede management, then people may be delegated to participate in a hollow process, which creates unfulfillable expectations on all sides. To set against this, Dichmont and Fulton (Chapter 2) chart major impact from the MSEs in their two Australian case study fisheries; the Northern Prawn Fishery was able to move to self-management, with the fishery actively managing itself with government oversight. In the South-East Shark and Scale Fishery, in four years what had been seen as the 'blue sky' best-case but unrealistic management option became a reality through a participatory MSE process. This relatively quick outcome was possible, however, because it built on a long history of joint working between scientists, fishers and managers, and so the stakeholder engagement and trust-building elements were already present.

Another important message was the importance of thinking longer term about the management process, not just about the current decision-making challenge. MSE and other forms of SDM need to become part of ongoing adaptive management, not an one-off exercise, if they are to have power to improve sustainability in the context of wicked problems. During the initial period in which commitment to change and to new ways of thinking is high, there is a window in which new systems for ongoing monitoring and evaluation can be put in place. As in the example given by Nilsen (Chapter 8), models that are not updated with new information are soon obsolete and irrelevant. More than that, management strategies themselves become obsolete in the face of new external and internal drivers of change. Nicholson et al. (Chapter 9) give the example of global conservation policy, which works at time steps of four to five years, and where scientists currently just chart how far off the negotiated targets conservation outcomes are; there is an urgent but unfulfilled need for an ongoing cycle between understanding the system, developing and monitoring appropriate indicators, reporting progress and changing approaches to improve their effectiveness.

10.3 HOW FAR INTO CONSERVATION CAN THIS APPROACH BE TAKEN?

10.3.1 Moving into More Complex Situations

The case studies in this book tell us inspiringly how models can be used to support and enhance decision-making in the real world, for conservation and other natural resource problems. Using real examples, our authors have shown that it can be done. The most successful examples to date, however, are for resource harvesting in developed countries, addressing management at the level of the individual stock, and in some cases for simpler problems than the classic wicked problem. For example, the change in management of invasive species in a nature reserve was, as Moore et al. (Chapter 6) eloquently explain, difficult and slow to achieve, despite the lack of human users of the resource with livelihoods dependent on the outcome, the single target species and the comparative ease of working in a rich country. The problems which Dichmont and Fulton (Chapter 2) address are substantially more complex, but still focus on management of a fisheries resource in a developed country. They then describe how much harder it was to extend MSE to a multi-sector, multi-jurisdiction system of coastal management. This was true both technically, in terms of developing meaningful systems models, but also in terms of engagement and uptake from sectors without the institutional history of working in this way. Nuno et al. (Chapter 7) highlight the challenges and possibilities of applying MSE to conservation problems in poor countries, where capacity is low and data are poor. These problems require management strategies other than just controlling harvesting, including influencing human decisions more indirectly through community development projects, ecotourism or addressing crop raiding. If the approaches showcased in this book are to have widespread uptake within conservation, they need to be shown to work for the whole range of conservation problems and situations.

There is no conceptual reason why MSE should not work in a range of conservation situations (Bunnefeld et al. 2011). It could also work at a range of scales from the local (e.g. Edwards et al. 2014 for lion trophy hunting) to the global (Chapter 9). However, the lessons from Dichmont and Fulton (Chapter 2) about the degree to which system complexity hampers both technical progress and uptake require respect. It's easy to conceptualise how an MSE might work in a complex, data-poor situation, but that does not necessarily translate into operationalisation in a way that can produce real-world impact. Analogously, Maxwell et al. (2015) explore why global conservation targets are not made SMART (specific, measurable, achievable, relevant, timebound) in order to improve their effectiveness, and suggest that this is because of the need for negotiated targets which allow wriggle room, through being ambiguous in definition or quantification, or clearly unachievable so that failure is implicitly acceptable.

We have already underlined the need for qualitative understanding of the multiple dimensions of well-being in order to make decisions that are legitimate and long-lasting (Chapter 5). The question remains, however, of how, or if, this depth of nuanced understanding fits within a more structured approach, which by its nature tends to simplify. How can you explore trade-offs between the clearly stated objectives of different well-defined user groups when the reality is so much messier? Might it even be counterproductive to try to fit a well-being approach into a quantitative framework, tempting users to move away from qualitative depth into simple metrics that mask the true picture? Thinking about how SDM frameworks and quantitative models can support conservation efforts in places with power inequalities, weak tenure, low capacity and poor data (where the majority of conservation is focussed) is a critical need if these approaches are to be widely used in conservation. These are situations in which simplistic application of structured approaches can be part of the problem not the solution, by promoting a top-down way of thinking about management issues, thereby opening the process up to domination by voices which can more easily engage with external bodies.

The nearest we have to answers to these questions are the data-poor examples in Chapter 2, but coastal Western Australia is very different to the forests of the Congo basin or the plains of Northern Cambodia (Chapter 5). There is a crying need for the application of approaches like MSE in new and more challenging contexts, so that the power and limitations of the approach can be explored. There is huge and unrealised potential here, if MSE is used as a guiding and structuring framework for qualitative reflection, participatory monitoring and transfer of management responsibility from higher-level authorities to the communities whose well-being is most dependent on nature (Figure 10.1).

10.3.2 Supporting Conflict Resolution

Another pertinent set of questions is around the degree to which these approaches are useful in situations of conservation conflict, defined by Redpath et al. (2013) as 'situations that occur when two or more parties with strongly held opinions clash over conservation objectives and when one party is perceived to assert its interests at the expense of another'. Moore et al. (Chapter 6) suggest that this is not the approach to take for conflict resolution when a commitment to work together towards solutions is not yet present. Redpath et al. (2004) used decision modelling in an attempt to resolve the long-running and emotive conflict between grouse moor owners and bird conservationists over the management of hen harriers in Scotland. At the time, Redpath et al. felt that the exercise had been successful in helping the two groups better understand the positions of the other, the range of views that exist within and between groups, the scientific evidence and pointing towards potential approaches that both might be prepared to engage with. However ten years on, and despite a lot of effort being expended in participatory modelling (e.g. Elston et al. 2014), stakeholder forums and other forms of mediation, the conflict still persists (Redpath et al. 2013). Even in situations like this, however, when participatory structured decision processes don't precipitate the change which all sides recognise as necessary, all parties tend to agree that the process is still useful (cf Chee et al.'s results in Chapter 4). It helps them to separate facts from values, to see the world from other perspectives and to clarify the issue, their underlying objectives and potential strategies. It seems, therefore, that so long as people are prepared to commit to sitting around a table together and constructively approaching a shared problem, the process can be beneficial, even

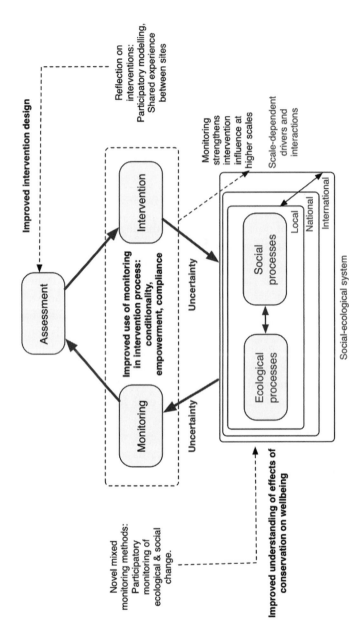

Figure 10.1 An example of how MSE could be used to structure new ways of improving participatory governance of natural resources in a conservation context with poor governance and capacity. By combining an MSE approach with new ways of monitoring the system in a bottom-up way, by local people according to local priorities, the MSE approach can promote positive change.

if it doesn't move the situation on as far as might have been hoped. More work is needed on the circumstances under which conflict is likely and a structured decision process might help, and MSE could be a tool for exploring this.

10.3.3 New Approaches to Predicting Human Behaviour

Another interesting avenue to pursue could be linking the SDM and MSE frameworks with approaches that focus more on individual decision-making. The approaches we have discussed in this book were implemented at the collective level, but in many parts of the world the important need is to engage with the individuals who choose to hunt or fish, or to clear forest (Chapter 7). Their motivations are complex and context-dependent, strongly affected by social norms and the constraints that they face in adopting a given behaviour. The link between knowledge and understanding of a problem, attitudes towards it, behavioural intention and actual behaviour is not clear-cut. Approaches from psychology such as the theory of planned behaviour, which provide frameworks for analysing behavioural change under these circumstances, are starting to be more widespread within conservation science (St John et al. 2010; Figure 10.2). However, currently few MSE models exist that incorporate human behaviour into the operating model (e.g. Milner-Gulland 2011 including individual behaviour, Fulton et al. 2011b incorporating fishing fleet behaviour), and these model behaviour as rational utility maximisation, which is not necessarily appropriate in more complex situations. Understanding how changes in well-being affect behavioural choices, and how those choices would change under different management strategies, is fundamental to an expansion of MSE to conserving nature in areas where individuals are the prime decision-makers. As yet, this territory remains unexplored.

One strength of MSE modelling is its predictive nature; it enables the exploration of 'what-if' scenarios in a safe virtual environment. Conservation is currently more reactive than predictive; hence there is little emphasis in designing interventions to avoid unintended consequences, and little empirical evidence to support such interventions (Milner-Gulland 2011; Larrosa et al. 2016). Bringing behavioural economics and decision science into understanding how people will react to different management interventions is necessary if decision-theoretic approaches like SDM and MSE are to produce meaningful results in systems where the drivers of human decision-making are largely not

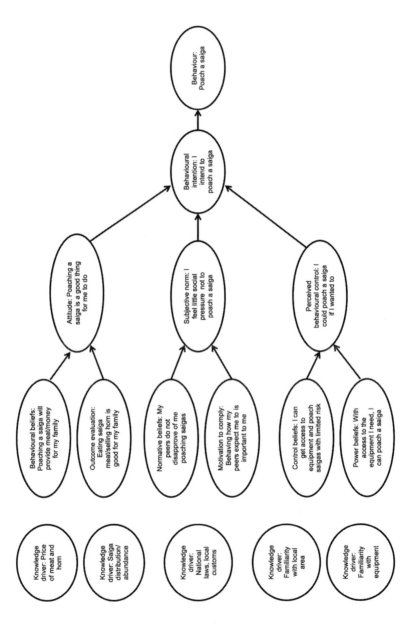

Figure 10.2 The theory of planned behaviour, as applied to poaching of the critically endangered saiga antelope.

financial. Chapter 7 moves us towards this territory, but there is a long way to go.

10.4 DECISION-MAKING IN A DYNAMIC WORLD

10.4.1 Integration into Adaptive Management

Everything changes, and models or decision-making frameworks that don't adapt will soon be obsolete (as highlighted in Chapter 8). The key to the ongoing usefulness of quantitative decision-making frameworks is therefore their integration into adaptive management. This means that the decision-making process would take place on a cycle which depends on both how quickly the system is changing, and cost and capacity issues. In some cases, when systems change quickly and substantively, the intervention will need to be thoroughly reassessed on a regular basis; in other cases, occasional realignment is all that will be needed.

Highly trained scientists may not always be available, however, and indeed, if the intention is empower resource users to continue to manage their own resources alone, frameworks are needed that can easily be adapted and can be used by the untrained. In an ideal world, perhaps the best option would be to plan for ongoing interaction between scientists and implementers, with commitment from both sides to keep working together. This can be challenging both for academic scientists, who must fulfil their need to produce novel, publishable research, and for implementers, who may just wish to get on with things independently, without relying on external support on an ongoing basis. This leads to the question of how best to ensure that a balance is struck between 'gold standard' decision-making processes, such as several of our contributors have engaged in (particularly Chapters 2 and 6), and more basic, preliminary approaches that can nonetheless provide useful insights for management. An iterative approach like rapid prototyping (Chapter 3) can help to determine where investments in the development of a decision-making framework will be most valuable. This process can allow someone with relatively minimal training to realise that they can, in fact, resolve the decision on their own, or it can lead them to realise they need to access expert facilitation and technical advice in order to overcome the challenges the decision poses.

One key reason why quantitative modelling is shunned in conservation, and certainly not taken up to the extent that it is in fisheries management, is a systemic lack of capacity in quantitative science among academics and practitioners within conservation. This is not the case within population ecology, as Nilson (Chapter 8) clearly demonstrates, but there is still little use of models in interdisciplinary, practical conservation science. If MSE is to become the powerful tool that it has the potential to be, this needs to change. More recognition of the value of conceptual modelling, which doesn't require quantitative skills, is also needed. Potentially, the development of new software packages to support SDM and adaptive management might help, although these would require good understanding of their conceptual foundations if they are not to be misused and misunderstood. Woodhouse et al. (2016) have produced a guide for practitioners, laying out in simple terms the different approaches to assessing the social impact of conservation interventions, and when each may be suitable, depending on budget, capacity and the questions being asked. Importantly, the guidance recognises the need for a spectrum of approaches, including both qualitative and quantitative tools, but is clear about the need for expertise and methodological rigour, even in the low-capacity, low-budget options. A similar type of product would be extremely useful to encourage the broad and varied uptake of the types of approaches we have presented here.

In tandem with better use of SDM approaches within adaptive management, there is also a need for a much stronger emphasis on learning about the system and its response to management, in order to inform these approaches. As both Moore et al. and Nicholson et al. suggest (Chapters 6 and 9), cycling between modelling, reflection, decision-making and informed data collection can be a powerful way to move forward towards a more sustainable social-ecological system. However, there is a need to be aware of the potential for unintended consequences of interventions in the context of fast-shifting social and ecological circumstances. For example, Woodhouse et al. (Chapter 5) highlight the case of the Northern Plains of Cambodia where the granting of vast economic land concessions and the subsequent deforestation and alienation of rural farmers from their lands has completely altered both the natural landscape and the social and political economy in the space of a few years (Beauchamp 2016). Conservation can struggle to keep up with changes of this speed and magnitude, and SDM can soon give way to rolling with the punches in circumstances like these.

Nonetheless, careful planning, monitoring and reevaluation are still fundamental to long-term conservation success; they just need to be in sync with the dynamics of the system, and planners need to think forward beyond the short term, however difficult that may be. However, strong calls for more and better monitoring and evaluation of the impact of conservation interventions were made ten years ago (Ferraro and Pattanyak 2006), but are still largely not being taken up into practice (Baylis et al. 2016). Similarly, adaptive management, so attractive and intuitive in concept, is still not being taken up into practice to any great degree, and academic discussion about it is mired in confusion and sloppy thinking (Rist et al. 2013).

So how can the approaches we have discussed, such as SDM and MSE, hope to be taken up into conservation, when they support adaptive management, and require monitoring and evaluation, neither of which are yet mainstream? A powerful answer to this is to look at the fisheries sector, where these approaches are now widely seen as standard, and have been demonstrated to improve management performance and reduce conflict (Chapter 2). Then we need to look clear-eyed at the structural issues in conservation; some can be addressed (such as the lack of expertise and motivation to implement these approaches), others are more fundamental (such as the messiness of the governance and institutional contexts within which much conservation happens; Chapter 7). A clear priority need, then, is to implement a programme such as set out in Figure 10.1, in a few challenging situations, and test empirically whether this approach can work in conservation.

10.4.2 Aiming for Optimality?

One often-quoted strength of the MSE approach is that it explicitly does not search for the optimal solution, but instead informs decision-makers about the performance of different strategies against pre-agreed metrics under different scenarios, hopefully enabling them to make better choices (Chapter 2). On the face of it, this is in contra-distinction to SDM, which is used to lead users through a structured process towards an agreed solution, often referred to as the optimal solution. All our authors subscribe to the philosophy that science works best when it is giving managers guidance on the consequences of their actions and lets them get on with implementing these actions. So how can these two different understandings be reconciled?

The key issue is what people mean when they use the term 'optimal'. It is a term that has very different connotations scientifically than in common usage. The common use of the term implies that an optimal solution is the best thing decision-makers can do in the circumstances.

This definition acknowledges trade-offs and messy multiple solutions. It implies that the decision-making process may be more concerned with producing a negotiated result that is robust to changing circumstances, than with producing the result that might give the most benefit on a given dimension. 'Optimal' in scientific language is specifically the solution that maximises the value of the variable for which the decision problem is being solved (Schoemaker 1991). Under this definition, it is not possible to optimise for more than one variable at a time, because trade-offs occur. Instead you can find the optimal set of solutions over a number of variables that describes the best available option for each variable that doesn't reduce the value of the others. This is called Pareto optimisation (Deb 2001). The decision-makers then choose amongst the Pareto set, depending on how they weigh the different objectives against which they are optimising, using approaches such as multi-criteria decision analysis (e.g. Mendoza and Martins 2006). Another interesting set of approaches involves 'robust optimisation', including info-gap decision theory (Ben-Haim 2006), which finds the solution that minimises the probability of unacceptable performance in the face of quantifiable uncertainty. For example, McDonald-Madden et al (2008) modelled the optimal allocation of financial resources to Sumatran tiger sub-populations in order to maximise the number of extant sub-populations after a certain time, on the basis of a relationship between funding for a population's conservation and probability of extirpation of that sub-population.

The message from the contributions in this book is that for some problems (for example, the invasive willow in Chapter 6), it is possible to get to the Pareto set in a quantitative way, or to optimise along a single dimension while taking uncertainty into account. Then managers can make an informed decision to act based on their needs and priorities. In many other cases, however, when the problems are more 'wicked', and particularly when the well-being and livelihoods of people are intimately connected to the decision problem, this may not be possible. In these cases, it is important not to talk about optimisation in the strict scientific sense, even when using quantitative models and structured frameworks, but to be very clear that the aim is to find robust or acceptable solutions that allow decisions to be made that improve management. The frameworks and modelling approaches described in this book are helpful in these circumstances, and our feeling is that this is how they are best used in most conservation and natural resource management situations.

10.5 NEW TECHNOLOGIES AND EXPANDING HORIZONS

One of the most exciting developments of the modern age is the huge expansion of mobile communication technology into all parts of the world. For example, in rural Northern Cambodia, in 2008, having a mobile phone was considered a basic necessity – that everyone should have and no one should be without – by 32 per cent of the households interviewed, and 12 per cent of households owned one. In 2014, 93 per cent of households considered it to be a basic necessity, and 75 per cent owned one (Beauchamp 2016). Concommitent with this increase in communication penetration is a huge increase in interest among researchers and conservationists in citizen science. In the developed world, this mostly involves the general public reporting observations to scientists, and is seen both as a way of massively expanding the scope and scale of data collection, and also sparking the public's interest in science or conservation (Silvertown 2009). More interestingly from our perspective, an equivalent revolution has occurred among conserva- tionists working with local rural people in developing countries, called 'participatory monitoring'. Generally, this is still relatively low-tech, but involves local people carrying out ecological monitoring towards bet- ter conservation and resource management. There is a continuum of degrees of participation but generally local people are engaged only in data collection, and not in framing the problem, designing or analysing the monitoring or implementing management (Danielsen et al. 2009). However, practitioners are seeing benefits in terms of improved feel- ings of ownership and engagement with the conservation programme, as well as in the collection of ecological data and in some cases participa- tion in management (Danielsen et al. 2005).

There is clear potential to harness the power of new technologies in order to support participatory monitoring in a way that integrates it into MSE or SDM, and brings new voices into the decision-making pro- cess (as suggested in Figure 10.1). If this were done, then the challenges highlighted by Woodhouse et al. (Chapter 5) could be addressed within an integrated decision-making framework. The best progress to date on this front has been made by the ExCiteS (Extreme Citizen Science) team at University College London, who are using open-source geographical information system (GIS) software on a smartphone to enable margin- alised groups to map the resources that are important to them (Stevens et al. 2014). Clever technological fixes have been needed in order to make this work in areas where there is infrequent access to power and phone signals, for example using a boiling pot to charge the phone's batteries. This group has enabled Mbendjele hunter-gathers in the Congo forests to report poaching in their areas directly to conservation authorities, bypassing corrupt or ineffective ecoguards (Vitos et al. 2013).

Democratisation of decision-making is also happening online, in areas where the internet is ubiquitous. However, at the moment this seems limited to information-provision, consultations, social media and news stories, rather than more direct participation in decision-making through citizen ballots or participatory deliberation (e.g. Conroy and Evans-Cowley 2006, Firmstone and Coleman 2015). Deliberative techniques like online Delphi processes could easily be integrated within SDM, enabling broader engagement than is possible with face-to-face meetings (Mukherjee et al. 2015), though at the cost of limiting the trust-building that is so vital to finding solutions in contested situations (Chapter 2). 'Gamification' of conservation is also a trend which may become more prevalent and could also feed into SDM (Sandbrook et al. 2015).

There is clearly much scope for using new technologies to improve decision-making at the local level. Even within more conventional management, Moore et al. (Chapter 6) show how the use of GPS units by invasive clearance contractors massively improved the scope for informed decision-making. But this can also go further in terms of transferring information and understanding between policy scales, from the very local to the global. This has the potential to support better participation and more representation, both from the local to the global level and in the other direction. For example, there has been a concerted effort to include women's groups into the process of formulating the UN's Sustainable Development Goals (Gabizon 2016), while a project in India enabled marginalised sex workers to have a platform at UN decision-making bodies (Narayanan et al. 2015). In the other direction, the global public is getting more engaged in supporting small-scale conservation projects through crowd-funding, which arguably is enabling a wide public to express their values for nature in a very direct and focussed way (e.g. through sites such as www.indiegogo.com). The question arises, however, of the degree to which the SDM or MSE approaches rely for their legitimacy and effectiveness on intensive, local engagement and long-term personal trust-building, and therefore how much they can be integrated into processes at the national, cross-sectoral or even international level. This will require careful thought about the best approach to ensuring fair representation at larger scales, and about how to translate priorities and world views between sectors and cultures. The humanities and social sciences will need to be heavily involved in research on this issue, because there is a danger that dominant voices will prevail at a given scale, precluding true equity of participation between scales.

10.6 A WAY OF THINKING, NOT A ONE-OFF EVENT

This book is not just about how to use models more effectively in conservation, it's about changing the way in which conservationists and managers think about problems, into the long term. The structured approach to decision-making laid out by our authors is not new; it is tried and tested within fisheries in particular and has been discussed in mostly theoretical terms within conservation. However, it needs to be embraced and brought into mainstream conservation, in order to produce a revolution in how researchers, managers, policymakers and resource users interact, closing the research–implementation gap.

This will require a commitment to engage, and an investment of resources and time which can seem hard to justify for a sector that is often in crisis mode, and where budget limitation is the norm. Hopefully, we have made the case that this needs to happen, so that those who have responsibility for natural resource management and conservation can make better decisions, informed by the best evidence (of all types), in a way that is seen as fair and legitimate by those affected, and therefore that are more likely to be implemented and complied with.

Wicked problems are called that for a reason; they don't have easy solutions, they are prone to conflict and people trying to address them can feel like they are standing on quicksand. However, they are not insoluble; although there are no easy prescriptions and generalisations are dangerous, there are ways of thinking and acting that can help us to make progress towards better outcomes. Rather than indulging in a counsel of despair, all sides need to commit to move forward together, inching towards a better, fairer and more sustainable world. The authors of this book have given us insights into how this can be done.

References

Aanes, S., Engen, S., Saether, B.E., Willebrand, T. and Marcstrom, V. (2002) Sustainable harvesting strategies of Willow Ptarmigan in a fluctuating environment. *Ecological Applications*, 12, 281–290.

Abdallah, S., Michaelson, J., Shah, S., Stoll, L. and Marks, N. (2012) *Happy Planet Index: 2012 Report. A Global Index of Sustainable Well-Being*. London: New Economics Foundation.

Abunge, C., Coulthard, S. and Daw, T.M. (2013) Connecting marine ecosystem services to human well-being: insights from participatory well-being assessment in Kenya. *Ambio*, 42, 1010–1021.

Adams, W.M. (2004) *Against Extinction: The Story of Conservation*. London: Earthscan.

Adams, W.M. and Sandbrook, C. (2013) Conservation, evidence and policy. *Oryx*, 47, 329–335.

Adato, M. (2008) *Integrating survey and ethnographic methods to evaluate conditional cash transfer programs. IFPRI Discussion Paper*. Washington, DC: International Food Policy Research Institute.

Addison, P.F.E., de Bie, K. and Rumpff, L. (2015) Setting conservation management thresholds using a novel participatory modelling approach. *Conservation Biology*, 29, 1411–1422.

Addison, P.F.E., Rumpff, L., Bau, S.S., et al. (2013) Practical solutions for making models indispensable in conservation decision-making. *Diversity and Distributions*, 19, 490–502.

Aguilera, P.A., Fernández, A., Fernández, R., Rumí, R. and Salmerón, A. (2011) Bayesian networks in environmental modelling. *Environmental Modelling & Software*, 26, 1376–1388.

Ajzen, I. (1991) The theory of planned behavior. *Organizational Behavior and Human Decision Processes*, 50, 179–211.

Alkemade, R., Oorschot, M., Miles, L., et al. (2009) GLOBIO3: a framework to investigate options for reducing global terrestrial biodiversity loss. *Ecosystems*, 12, 374–390.

Alkire, S., Boyden, J., Hammock, J., et al. (2012) *Understanding Poverty and Wellbeing. A Note with Implications for Research and Policy*. London: Overseas Development Institute [online]. Available at: www.odi.org/publications/6512-understanding-poverty-wellbeing-research-policy

Andersen, O., Kaltenborn, B.P., Vitterso, J. and Willebrand, T. (2014) Preferred harvest principles and regulations amongst willow ptarmigan hunters in Norway. *Wildlife Biology*, 20, 285–290.

Andrèn, H., Linnell, J.D.C., Liberg, O., et al. (2006) Survival rates and causes of mortality in Eurasian lynx (*Lynx lynx*) in multi-use landscapes. *Biological Conservation*, 131, 23–32.

Arcese, P., Hando, J. and Campbell, K. (1995) Historical and present-day anti-poaching efforts in Serengeti. In A.R.E. Sinclair and P. Arcese, eds. *Serengeti II: Dynamics, Management, and Conservation of an Ecosystem.* Chicago: Chicago University Press, pp. 506–533.

Arlettaz, R., Schaub, M., Fournier, J., et al. (2010) From publications to public actions: when conservation biologists bridge the gap between research and implementation. *BioScience*, 60, 835–842.

Arrow, K.J. (1974) *The Limits of Organization.* New York: W.W. Norton & Company.

Ascough II, J.C., Maier, H.R., Ravalico, J.K. and Strudley, M.W. (2008) Future research challenges for incorporation of uncertainty in environmental and ecological decision-making. *Ecological Modelling*, 219, 383–399.

Atickem, A., Loe, L.E., Langangen, O., et al. (2011) Estimating population size and habitat suitability for mountain nyala in areas with different protection status. *Animal Conservation*, 14, 409–418.

Australian Bureau of Statistics (2011) *Information Paper: Census of Population and Housing – Products and Services.* Australian Bureau of Statistics.

Australian Bureau of Statistics (2012) *State and Territory Statistical Indicators.* Technical Report 1367.0. Australian Bureau of Statistics.

Baillie, J.E.M., Collen, B., Amin, R., et al. (2008) Toward monitoring global biodiversity. *Conservation Letters*, 1, 18–26.

Bain, M.B. (1987) Structured decision making in fisheries management. *North American Journal of Fisheries Management*, 7, 475–481.

Baird, T.D., Leslie, P.W. and McCabe, J.T. (2009) The effect of wildlife conservation on local perceptions of risk and behavioral response. *Human Ecology*, 37, 463–474.

Balmford, A., Crane, P., Dobson, A., Green, R.E. and Mace, G.M. (2005) The 2010 challenge: data availability, information needs and extraterrestrial insights. *Philosophical Transactions of Royal Society B*, 360, 221–228.

Barnett, R. (2000) *Food for Thought: The Utilisation of Wild Meat in Eastern and Southern Africa.* Nairobi, Kenya: TRAFFIC/WWF/IUCN.

Barrett, C.B. and Arcese, P. (1998) Wildlife harvest in integrated conservation and development projects: linking harvest to household demand, agricultural production, and environmental shocks in the Serengeti. *Land Economics*, 74, 449–465.

Barton, D.N., Kuikka, S., Varis, O., et al. (2012) Bayesian networks in environmental and resource management. *Integrated Environmental Assessment and Management*, 8, 418–429.

Baylis, K., Honey-Rosés, J., Börner, J., et al. (2016) Mainstreaming impact evaluation in nature conservation. *Conservation Letters*, 9, 58–64.

Bayliss, P., Buckworth, R. and Dichmont, C.M. (2014) *Assessing the Water Needs of Fisheries and Ecological Values in the Gulf of Carpentaria.* Brisbane, Australia: Queensland Department of Natural Resources and Mines (DNRM).

Beauchamp, E. (2016) *Seeing the people for the trees: Impacts of conservation on human well-being in Northern Cambodia.* PhD thesis, Imperial College London. Available online at: www.iccs.org.uk

Beddington, J.R., Agnew, D.J. and Clark, C.W. (2007) Current problems in the management of marine fisheries. *Science,* 316, 1713–1716.

Ben-Haim, Y. (2006) *Info-Gap Decision Theory: Decisions under Severe Uncertainty.* Sydney: Academic Press.

Beratan, K.K. (2014) Summary: addressing the interactional challenges of moving collaborative adaptive management from theory to practice. *Ecology and Society,* 19(1), 46.

Beverton, R.J.H. and Holt, S.J. (1957) *On the Dynamics of Exploited Fish Populations.* London: Chapman and Hall.

Bhagwat, S.A. and Rutte, C. (2006) Sacred groves: potential for biodiversity management. *Frontiers in Ecology and the Environment,* 4, 519–524.

Biggs, D., Courchamp, F., Martin, R. and Possingham, H.P. (2013) Legal trade of Africa's rhino horns. *Science,* 339, 1038–1039.

Binder, C.R., Hinkel, J., Bots, P.W.G. and Pahl-Wostl, C. (2013) Comparison of frameworks for analyzing social-ecological systems. *Ecology and Society,* 18, 26.

Bischof, R., Nilsen, E.B., Brøseth, H., et al. (2012) Implementation uncertainty when using recreational hunting to manage carnivores. *Journal of Applied Ecology,* 49, 824–832.

Blomquist, S.M., Johnson, T.D., Smith, D.R., et al. (2010) Structured decision-making and rapid prototyping to plan a management response to an invasive species. *Journal of Fish and Wildlife Management,* 1, 19–32.

Bond, S.D., Carlson, K.A. and Keeney, R.L. (2008). Generating objectives: Can decision makers articulate what they want? *Management Science,* 54(1), 56–70.

Bradbury, R.B., Stoate, C. and Tallowin, J.R.B. (2010) FORUM: lowland farmland bird conservation in the context of wider ecosystem service delivery. *Journal of Applied Ecology,* 47, 986–993.

Branch, T.A., Jensen, O.P., Ricard, D., Ye, Y. and Hilborn, R. (2011) Contrasting global trends in marine fishery status obtained from catches and from stock assessments. *Conservation Biology,* 25, 777–786.

Branch, T.A., Watson, R., Fulton, E.A., et al. (2010) The trophic fingerprint of marine fisheries. *Nature,* 468, 431–435.

Britton, E. and Coulthard, S. (2013) Assessing the social wellbeing of Northern Ireland's fishing society using a three-dimensional approach. *Marine Policy,* 37, 28–36.

Bromley, J., Jackson, N.A., Clymer, O.J., Giacomello, A.M. and Jensen, F.V. (2005) The use of Hugin® to develop Bayesian networks as an aid to integrated water resource planning. *Environmental Modelling & Software,* 20, 231–242.

Brøseth, H. and Pedersen, H.C. (2000) Hunting effort and game vulnerability studies on a small scale: a new technique combining radio-telemetry, GPS and GIS. *Journal of Applied Ecology,* 37, 182–190.

Brosius, J.P. (2006) Common ground between anthropology and conservation biology. *Conservation Biology,* 20, 683–685.

Brosius, J.P. (2010) Conservation trade-offs and the politics of knowledge. In N. Leader-Williams, W.M. Adams and R.J. Smith, eds., *Trade-Offs in Conservation: Deciding What to Save*. Chichester: Wiley-Blackwell, pp. 311–328.

Buckland, S.T., Magurran, A.E., Green, R.E. and Fewster, R.M. (2005) Monitoring change in biodiversity through composite indices. *Philosophical Transactions of the Royal Society B: Biological Sciences*, 360, 243–254.

Buckland, S.T., Studeny, A.C., Magurran, A.E., Illian, J.B. and Newson, S.E. (2011) The geometric mean of relative abundance indices: a biodiversity measure with a difference. *Ecosphere*, 2, art100.

Buckworth, R., Venables, W.N., Lawrence, E., et al. (2014) *Incorporation of predictive models of banana prawn catch for MEY-based harvest strategy development for the Northern Prawn Fishery*. Fisheries Research and Development Corporation Report No. 2011/239. Brisbane, Australia: CSIRO.

Bull, J., Nilsen, E.B., Mysterud, A. and Milner-Gulland, E.J. (2009) Survival on the border: a population model to evaluate management options for Norway's wolves *Canis lupus*. *Wildlife Biology*, 15, 412–424.

Bunnefeld, N., Hoshino, E. and Milner-Gulland, E.J. (2011) Management strategy evaluation: a powerful tool for conservation? *Trends in Ecology & Evolution*, 26, 441–447.

Bunnefeld, N., Edwards, C., Atickem, A., Hailu, F. and Milner-Gulland, E.J. (2013) Incentivizing monitoring and compliance in trophy hunting. *Conservation Biology*, 27, 1344–1354.

Burgman, M., Carr, A., Godden, L., et al. (2011a) Redefining expertise and improving ecological judgment. *Conservation Letters*, 4, 81–87.

Burgman, M.A., McBride, M., Ashton, R., Speirs-Bridge, A., Flander, L., Wintle, B., Fidler, F., Rumpff, L. and Twardy, C. (2011b). Expert status and performance. *PLoS One*, 6(7), e22998.

Butchart, S.H.M., Stattersfield, A.J., Bennun, L.A., et al. (2004) Measuring global trends in the status of biodiversity: Red List Indices for birds. *PLoS Biology*, 2, e383.

Butchart, S.H.M., Akçakaya, H.R., Chanson, J., et al. (2007) Improvements to the Red List Index. *PLoS One*, 2, e140.

Butchart, S.H.M., Walpole, M., Collen, B., et al. (2010) Global biodiversity: indicators of recent declines. *Science*, 328, 1164–1168.

Butler, J.K. (1991) Toward understanding and measuring conditions of trust: evolution of a conditions of trust inventory. *Journal of Management*, 17, 643–663.

Cain, J. (2001) *Planning Improvements in Natural Resources Management*. Wallingford, UK: Centre for Ecology and Hydrology (CEH).

Camfield, L., Crivello, G. and Woodhead, M. (2009) Wellbeing research in developing countries: reviewing the role of qualitative methods. *Social Indicators Research*, 90, 5–31.

Carbone, C. and Gittleman, J.L. (2002) A common rule for the scaling of carnivore density. *Science*, 295, 2273–2276.

Carmona, G., Molina, J., Bromley, J., Varela-Ortega, C. and García-Aróstegui, J. (2011) Object-oriented Bayesian networks for participatory water management: two case studies in Spain. *Journal of Water Resources Planning and Management*, 137, 366–376.

Carr, G.W., Bedgood, S.E., Muir, A.M. and Peake, P. (1994) *Distribution and Management of Willows (Salix) in the Australian Alps National Parks*. Victoria, Australia: Ecology Australia Pty Limited.

Carwardine, J., O'Connor, T., Legge, S., et al. (2012) Prioritizing threat management for biodiversity conservation. *Conservation Letters*, 5, 196–204.

Caswell, H. (2001) *Matrix Population Models: Construction, Analysis, and Interpretation*, 2nd ed. Sunderland, MA: Sinauer Associates.

Catley, A., Burns, J., Abebe, D. and Suji, O. (2013) *Participatory impact assessment: A guide for practitioners*. Somerville: Feinstein International Centre, Tufts University.

Caughley, G. (1994) Directions in conservation biology. *Journal of Animal Ecology*, 63, 215–244.

Chapron, G., Kaczensky, P., Linnell, J.D.C., et al. (2014) Recovery of large carnivores in Europe's modern human-dominated landscapes. *Science*, 346, 1517–1519.

Chee, Y.E. and Wintle, B.A. (2010) Linking modelling, monitoring and management: an integrated approach to controlling overabundant wildlife. *Journal of Applied Ecology*, 47, 1169–1178.

Chu, C. (2009) Thirty years later: the global growth of ITQs and their influence on stock status in marine fisheries. *Fish and Fisheries*, 10, 217–230.

Cinner, J.E., Folke, C., Daw, T. and Hicks, C.C. (2011) Responding to change: using scenarios to understand how socioeconomic factors may influence amplifying or dampening exploitation feedbacks among Tanzanian fishers. *Global Environmental Change*, 21, 7–12.

Clark, C.W. (1990) *Mathematical Bioeconomics: The Optimal Management of Renewable Resources*, 2nd edn. New York: Wiley.

Clark, C.W. (2006) *The Worldwide Crisis in Fisheries: Economic Models and Human Behavior*. Cambridge: Cambridge University Press.

Clemen, R.T. (1991) *Making Hard Decisions: An Introduction to Decision Analysis*. Belmont, CA: Duxbury Press, p. 557.

Clements, T. (2010) Reduced expectations: the political and institutional challenges of REDD+. *Oryx*, 44, 309–310.

Clements, T., John, A., Nielsen, K., et al. (2010) Payments for biodiversity conservation in the context of weak institutions: comparison of three programs from Cambodia. *Ecological Economics*, 69, 1283–1291.

Clements, T. and Milner-Gulland, E.J. (2015) Impact of payments for environmental services and protected areas on local livelihoods and forest conservation in northern Cambodia. *Conservation Biology*, 29, 78–87.

Cockburn, J., Rouget, M., Slotow, R., et al. (2016) How to build science-action partnerships for local land-use planning and management: lessons from Durban, South Africa. *Ecology and Society*, 21(1), 28.

Collen, B. and Baillie, J.E.M. (2010) Barometer of life: sampling. *Science*, 329, 140.

Collen, B., Loh, J., Whitmee, S., et al. (2009a) Monitoring change in vertebrate abundance: the Living Planet Index. *Conservation Biology*, 23, 317–327.

Collen, B. and Nicholson, E. (2014) Taking the measure of change. *Science*, 346, 166–167.

Collen, B., Ram, M., Dewhurst, N., et al. (2009b) Broadening the coverage of biodiversity assessments. In J-C. Vie, C. Hilton-Taylor and S.N. Stuart, eds. *Wildlife in a Changing World – An Analysis of the 2008 IUCN Red List of Threatened Species*. Gland: IUCN, pp. 67–76.

Conroy, M.J. and Peterson, J.T. (2013) *Decision Making in Natural Resource Management. A Structured, Adaptive Approach*. Chichester: Wiley-Blackwell.

Conroy, M.M. and Evans-Cowley, J. (2006) E-participation in planning: an analysis of cities adopting on-line citizen participation tools. *Environment and Planning C: Government and Policy*, 24, 371–384.

Conservation Measures Partnership (2012) *Addressing social results and human wellbeing targets in conservation projects. Draft Guidance*. [online] Available at: http://cmp-openstandards.org/wp-content/uploads/2014/03/Guidance-on-HWT-and-Social-Results-in-Conservation-Projects-v2012

Convention on Biological Diversity (2011) *Strategic Plan for Biodiversity 2011–2020, including Aichi Biodiversity Targets*. Retrieved from www.cbd.int/sp/.

Converse, S.J., Shelley, K.J., Morey, S., et al. (2011) A decision-analytic approach to the optimal allocation of resources for endangered species consultation. *Biological Conservation*, 144, 319–329.

Converse, S.J., Moore, C.T. and Armstrong, D.P. (2013a) Demographics of reintroduced populations: estimation, modeling, and decision analysis. *Journal of Wildlife Management*, 77, 1081–1093.

Converse, S.J., Moore, C.T., Folk, M.J. and Runge, M.C. (2013b) A matter of tradeoffs: reintroduction as a multiple objective decision. *Journal of Wildlife Management*, 77, 1145–1156.

Converse, S.J., Royle, J.A., Adler, P.H., Urbanek, R.P. and Barzen, J.A. (2013c) A hierarchical nest survival model integrating incomplete temporally varying covariates. *Ecology and Evolution*, 3, 4439–47.

Copestake, J. and Camfield, L. (2009) Measuring subjective wellbeing in Bangladesh, Ethiopia, Peru and Thailand using a personal life goal satisfaction approach. *WeD Working Paper 09*. Bath: University of Bath.

Costello, C., Gaines, S.D. and Lynham, J. (2008) Can catch shares prevent fisheries collapse? *Science*, 321, 1678–1681.

Costelloe, B.T., Collen, B., Milner-Gulland, E.J., et al. (2016) Global biodiversity indicators reflect the modelled impacts of protected area policy change. *Conservation Letters*, 9, 14–20.

Costin, A., Gray, M., Totterdell, C. and Wimbush, D. (2000) *Kosciuszko alpine flora*. Collingwood, Victoria: CSIRO Publishing.

Coulthard, S., Johnson, D. and McGregor, J.A. (2011) Poverty, sustainability and human wellbeing: a social wellbeing approach to the global fisheries crisis. *Global Environmental Change*, 21, 453–463.

Craigie, I.D., Baillie, J.E.M., Balmford, A., et al. (2010) Large mammal population declines in Africa's protected areas. *Biological Conservation*, 143, 2221–2228.

Cremer, K. (2003) Introduced willows can become invasive pests in Australia. *Biodiversity and Conservation*, 4, 17–24.

Cremer, K., van Kraayenoord, C., Parker, N. and Streatfield, S. (1995) Willows spreading by seed. Implications for Australian River Management. *Australian Journal of Soil and Water Conservation*, 8, 18–27.

Cross, M.S., Zavaleta, E.S., Bachelet, D., et al. (2012) The adaptation for conservation targets (ACT) framework: a tool for incorporating climate change into natural resource management. *Environmental Management, 50*, 341–351.

Crowder, L. and Norse, E. (2008) Essential ecological insights for marine ecosystem-based management and marine spatial planning. *Marine Policy, 32*, 772–778.

DAFF (2007) *Commonwealth Fisheries Harvest Strategy: Policy and Guidelines*. Canberra, Australia: Department of Agriculture, Fisheries and Forestry.

Damania, R., Milner-Gulland, E.J. and Crookes, D.J. (2005) A bioeconomic analysis of bushmeat hunting. *Proceedings of the Royal Society B: Biological Sciences, 272*, 259–266.

Daniel, T.C., Muhar, A., Arnberger, A., et al. (2012) Contributions of cultural services to the ecosystem services agenda. *Proceedings of the National Academy of Sciences, 109*, 8812–8819.

Daniell, K.A., Coad, P., Ferrand, N., et al. (2008) Participatory values-based risk management for the water sector [online]. In M. Lambert, T.M. Daniell, and M. Leonard, eds. *Proceedings of Water Down Under 2008*. Modbury, SA: Engineers Australia; Causal Productions, pp. 969–981. Available at: http://search.informit.com.au/documentSummary;dn=573777437948042 ;res=IELENG ISBN: 0858257351.

Danielsen, F., Mendoza, M.M., Alviola, P.A., et al. (2003) Biodiversity monitoring in developing countries: what are we trying to achieve? *Oryx, 37*, 407–409.

Danielsen, F., Burgess, N.D. and Balmford, A. (2005) Monitoring matters: examining the potential of locally-based approaches. *Biodiversity & Conservation, 14*, 2507–2542.

Danielsen, F., Burgess, N.D., Balmford, A., et al. (2009) Local participation in natural resource monitoring: a characterization of approaches. *Conservation Biology, 23*, 31–42.

Davies, R. and Smith, W. (1998) *The Basic Necessities Survey: The Experience of ActionAid Vietnam*. Hanoi: ActionAid.

Daw, T., Brown, K., Rosendo, S. and Pomeroy, R. (2011) Applying the ecosystem services concept to poverty alleviation: the need to disaggregate human well-being. *Environmental Conservation, 38*, 370–379.

Daw, T.M., Coulthard, S., Cheung, W.W.L., et al. (2015) Evaluating taboo trade-offs in ecosystems services and human well-being. *Proceedings of the National Academy of Sciences, 112*, 6949–6954.

Daw, T.M., Hicks, C.C., Brown, K., et al. (2016) Elasticity in ecosystem services: exploring the variable relationship between ecosystems and human well-being. *Ecology and Society, 21*(2), 11

De Lange, E., Woodhouse, E. and Milner-Gulland, E.J. (2016) Approaches used to evaluate the social impacts of protected areas. *Conservation Letters*. doi: 10.1111/conl.12223

De Ornellas, P., Milner-Gulland, E.J. and Nicholson, E. (2011) The impact of data realities on conservation planning. *Biological Conservation*, 144, 1980–1988.

Deb, K. (2001) *Multi-Objective Optimisation Using Evolutionary Algorithms*. Chichester: John Wiley.

Deci, E.L. and Ryan, R.M. (2000) The 'what' and 'why' of goal pursuits: human needs and the self-determination of behavior. *Psychological Inquiry*, 11, 227–268.

Degteva, S.V., Ponomarev, V.I., Eisenman, S.W. and Dushenkov, V. (2015) Striking the balance: challenges and perspectives for the protected areas network in northeastern European Russia. *Ambio*, 44, 473–490.

Department of Sustainability, Environment, Water, Population and Communities (2013) *Approved Conservation Advice for the Alpine Sphagnum Bogs and Associated Fens ecological community*. Species Profile and Threats Database. Department of Sustainability, Environment, Water, Population and Communities, Canberra.

Di Marco, M., Boitani, L., Mallon, D., et al. (2014) A retrospective evaluation of the global decline of carnivores and ungulates. *Conservation Biology*, 28, 1109–1118.

Dichmont, C.M., Punt, A.E., Deng, A., Dell, Q. and Venables, W. (2003) Application of a weekly delay-difference model to commercial catch and effort data for tiger prawns in Australia's Northern Prawn Fishery. *Fisheries Research*, 65, 335–350.

Dichmont, C.M., Deng, A.R., Punt, A.E., Venables, W. and Haddon, M. (2006a) Management strategies for short lived species: the case of Australia's Northern Prawn Fishery 2. Choosing appropriate management strategies using input controls. *Fisheries Research*, 82, 221–234.

Dichmont, C.M., Deng, A.R., Punt, A.E., Venables, W. and Haddon, M. (2006b) Management strategies for short lived species: the case of Australia's Northern Prawn Fishery 3. Factors affecting management and estimation performance. *Fisheries Research*, 82, 235–245.

Dichmont, C.M., Deng, A.R., Punt, A.E., Venables, W. and Haddon, M. (2006c) Management strategies for short-lived species: the case of Australia's Northern Prawn Fishery 1. Accounting for multiple species, spatial structure and implementation uncertainty when evaluating risk. *Fisheries Research*, 82, 204–220.

Dichmont, C.M., Loneragan, N.R., Brewer, D.T. and Poiner, I.R. (2007) Partnerships towards sustainable use of Australia's Northern Prawn Fishery. In *Fisheries Management*. Oxford: Blackwell, pp. 205–230.

Dichmont, C.M., Deng, A., Punt, A. E., et al. (2008) Beyond biological performance measures in management strategy evaluation: bringing in economics and the effects of trawling on the benthos. *Fisheries Research*, 94, 238–250.

Dichmont, C.M. and Brown, I.W. (2010) A case study in successful management of a data-poor fishery using simple decision rules: the Queensland Spanner Crab Fishery. *Marine and Coastal Fisheries*, 2, 1–13.

Dichmont, C.M., Deng, R.A., Punt, A.E., Venables, W.N. and Hutton, T. (2012) From input to output controls in a short-lived species: the case of Australia's Northern Prawn Fishery. *Marine and Freshwater Research*, 63, 727.

Dichmont, C.M., Ellis, N., Bustamante, R.H., et al. (2013) Evaluating marine spatial closures with conflicting fisheries and conservation objectives. *Journal of Applied Ecology*, 50, 1060–1070.

Dietz, G. and Den Hartog, D.N. (2006) Measuring trust inside organizations. *Personnel Review*, 35, 557–588.

Dietz, T., Ostrom, E. and Stern, P.C. (2003) The struggle to govern the commons. *Science*, 302, 1907–1912.

Diez, E. and McIntosh, B. (2009) A review of the factors which influence the use and usefulness of information systems. *Environmental Modelling & Software*, 24, 588–602.

Dirzo, R., Young, H.S., Galetti, M., et al. (2014) Defaunation in the Anthropocene. *Science*, 345, 401–406.

Dowling, N.A., Smith, D.C., Knuckey, I., et al. (2008) Developing harvest strategies for low-value and data-poor fisheries: case studies from three Australian fisheries. *Fisheries Research*, 94, 380–390.

Dowling, N.A., Dichmont, C.M., Venables, W., et al. (2013) From low- to high-value fisheries: Is it possible to quantify the trade-off between management cost, risk and catch? *Marine Policy*, 40, 41–52.

Drury, R., Homewood, K. and Randall, S. (2010) Less is more: the potential of qualitative approaches in conservation research. *Animal Conservation*, 14, 18–24.

Dutra, L.X.C., Ellis, N., Perez, P., et al. (2014) Drivers influencing adaptive management: a retrospective evaluation of water quality decisions in South East Queensland (Australia). *Ambio*, 43, 1069–1081

Dutra, L.X.C., Thebaud, O., Boschetti, F., Smith, A.D.M. and Dichmont, C.M. (2015) Key issues and drivers affecting coastal and marine resource decisions: participatory management strategy evaluation to support adaptive management. *Ocean & Coastal Management*, 116, 382–395.

Edwards, C.T.T., Bunnefeld, N., Balme, G.A. and Milner-Gulland, E.J. (2014) Data-poor management of African lion hunting using a relative index of abundance. *Proceedings of the National Academy of Sciences*, 111, 539–543.

Edwards, W. (1977) How to use multiattribute utility measurement for social decision-making. *IEEE Transactions on Systems, Man and Cybernetics*, 7, 326–340.

Elston, D.A., Spezia, L., Baines, D. and Redpath, S.M. (2014) Working with stakeholders to reduce conflict – modelling the impact of varying hen harrier *Circus cyaneus* densities on red grouse *Lagopus lagopus* populations. *Journal of Applied Ecology*, 51, 1236–1245.

FAO (1995) *Code of Conduct for Responsible Fishing*. Rome: Food and Agriculture Organisation.

FAO (1996) *FAO Technical Guidelines for Responsible Fisheries: 2 Precautionary approach to capture fisheries and species introductions*. Lysekil, Sweden, 6–13 June 1995.

FAO (2003) *FAO Technical Guidelines for Responsible Fisheries: 4 Fisheries management (2) The ecosystem approach to fisheries*. Rome: Food and Agriculture Organisation.

Fay, G., Large, S.I., Link, J.S. and Gamble, R.J. (2013) Testing systemic fishing responses with ecosystem indicators. *Ecological Modelling*, 265, 45–55.

Ferraro, P.J. and Pattanayak, S.K. (2006) Money for nothing? A call for empirical evaluation of biodiversity conservation investments. *PLoS Biology*, 4, e105.

Ferraro, P.J., Hanauer, M.M. and Sims, K.R.E. (2011) Conditions associated with protected area success in conservation and poverty reduction. *Proceedings of the National Academy of Sciences*, 108, 13913–13918.

Firmstone, J. and Coleman, S., (2015) Public engagement in local government: the voice and influence of citizens in online communicative spaces. *Information, Communication & Society*, 18, 680–695.

Fischhoff, B., Slovic, P. and Lichtenstein, S. (1982) Lay foibles and expert fables in judgments about risk. *American Statistician*, 36, 240–255.

Fisher, R. (1993) Social desirability bias and the validity of indirect questioning. *Journal of Consumer Research*, 20, 303–315.

Fitzgibbon, C.D., Mogaka, H. and Fanshawe, J.H. (1995) Subsistence hunting in Arabuko-Sokoke Forest, Kenya, and its effects on mammal populations. *Conservation Biology*, 9, 1116–1126.

Foley, J., Clifford, D., Castle, K., Cryan, P. and Ostfeld, R.S. (2011). Investigating and managing the rapid emergence of White-Nose Syndrome, a novel, fatal, infectious disease of hibernating bats. *Conservation Biology*, 25(2), 223–231.

Friis-Hansen, E. and Duveskog, D. (2012) The empowerment route to well-being: an analysis of farmer field schools in East Africa. *World Development*, 40, 414–427.

Fryxell, J.M., Packer, C., McCann, K., Solberg, E.J. and Sæther, B.E. (2010) Resource management cycles and the sustainability of harvested wildlife populations. *Science*, 328, 903–906.

Fulton, E.A., Smith, A.D.M. and Punt, A.E. (2005) Which ecological indicators can robustly detect effects of fishing? *ICES Journal of Marine Science*, 62, 540–551.

Fulton, E.A., Gray, R., Sporcic, M., et al. (2011a) *Ningaloo Collaboration Cluster: Adaptive Futures for Ningaloo*. Ningaloo Collaboration Cluster Final Report. No. 5.3.

Fulton, E.A., Link, J.S., Kaplan, I. C., et al. (2011b) Lessons in modelling and management of marine ecosystems: the Atlantis experience. *Fish and Fisheries*, 12, 171–188.

Fulton, E.A., Smith, A.D.M., Smith, D.C. and van Putten, I.E. (2011c) Human behaviour: the key source of uncertainty in fisheries management. *Fish and Fisheries*, 12, 2–17.

Fulton, E.A. and Link, J.S. (2014) Approaches for marine ecosystem-based management. In M.J. Fogarty and J.J. McCarthy, eds. *The Sea: Marine Ecosystem-based Management*. Cambridge, MA: Harvard University Press.

Fulton, E.A., Smith, A.D.M., Smith, D.C. and Johnson, P. (2014) An integrated approach is needed for ecosystem based fisheries management: insights from ecosystem-level management strategy evaluation. *PLOS One*, 9, e84242.

Fulton, E.A., Bax, N.J., Bustamante, R.H., et al. (2015) Modelling marine protected areas: insights and hurdles. *Philosophical Transactions of the Royal Society of London B: Biological Sciences*, 370, 20140278.

Fyumagwa, R., Gereta, E., Hassan, S., et al. (2013) Roads as a Threat to the Serengeti Ecosystem. *Conservation Biology*, 27, 1122–1125.

Gabizon, S. (2016) Women's movements' engagement in the SDGs: lessons learned from the Women's Major Group. *Gender & Development*, 24, 99–110.

Gangaas, K.E., Kaltenborn, B.P. and Andreassen, H.P. (2013) Geo-spatial aspects of acceptance of illegal hunting of large carnivores in Scandinavia. *PLoS ONE*, 8, e68849.

Garcia, S.M., Kolding, J., Rice, J., et al. (2012) Reconsidering the consequences of selective fisheries. *Science*, 335, 1045–1047.

Gavin, M.C., Solomon, J.N. and Blank, S.G. (2010) Measuring and monitoring illegal use of natural resources. *Conservation Biology*, 24, 89–100.

Gee, G.F., Nicholich, J.M., Nesbitt, S.A., et al. (2001) Water conditioning and whooping crane survival after release in Florida. *Proceedings of the North American Crane Workshop*, 8, 160–165.

Gell, F.R. and Roberts, C.M. (2003) Benefits beyond boundaries: the fishery effects of marine reserves. *Trends in Ecology and Evolution*, 18, 448–455.

Gervasi, V., Brøseth, H., Nilsen, E.B., et al. (2015) Compensatory immigration counteracts contrasting conservation strategies of wolverines (*Gulo gulo*) within Scandinavia. *Biological Conservation*, 191, 632–639.

Gervasi, V., Nilsen, E.B., Sand, H., et al. (2012) Predicting the potential demographic impact of predators on their prey: a comparative analysis of two carnivore-ungulate systems in Scandinavia. *Journal of Animal Ecology*, 81, 443–454.

Gervasi, V., Nilsen, E. B., Odden, J., Bouyer, Y. and Linnell, J.D.C. (2014) The spatio-temporal distribution of wild and domestic ungulates modulates lynx kill rates in a multi-use landscape. *Journal of Zoology*, 292, 175–183.

Ghebremichael, L.T., Veith, T.L. and Hamlett, J.M. (2013) Integrated watershed- and farm-scale modeling framework for targeting critical source areas while maintaining farm economic viability. *Journal of Environmental Management*, 114, 381–394.

Gibbons, P., Zammit, C., Youngentob, K., et al. (2008) Some practical suggestions for improving engagement between researchers and policy-makers in natural resource management. *Ecological Management and Restoration*, 9, 182–186.

Giljohann, K.M. (2009) *Modelling the distribution of the invasive willow* Salix cinerea *on the Bogong High Plains of the Victorian Alpine National Park.* Honours thesis, University of Melbourne.

Giljohann, K.M. and Moore, J.L. (2011a) *Optimal allocation model update for the prioritisation of willow* Salix cinerea *control effort on the Bogong High Plains 2010–2011.* Report to Parks Victoria. University of Melbourne.

Giljohann, K.M. and Moore, J.L. (2011b) *Optimal allocation model update for the prioritisation of willow* Salix cinerea *control effort on the Bogong High Plains 2011–2012.* Report to Parks Victoria. University of Melbourne.

Giljohann, K.M., Hauser, C.E., Williams, N.S.G. and Moore, J.L. (2009) *Prioritising control of an invasive willow,* Salix cinerea, *across the Bogong High Plains of the Victorian National Park.* Report to Parks Victoria. University of Melbourne.

Giljohann, K.M., Hauser, C.E., Williams, N.S.G. and Moore, J.L. (2011) Optimizing invasive species control across space: willow invasion management in the Australian Alps. *Journal of Applied Ecology,* 48, 1286–1294.

Gillett, R. (2008) Global Study of Shrimp Fisheries. FAO Fisheries Technical Paper. No. 475. Rome: Food and Agricultural Organisation.

Gislason, H., Sinclair, M., Sainsbury, K. and O'Boyle, R. (2000) Symposium overview: incorporating ecosystem objectives within fisheries management. *ICES Journal of Marine Science,* 57, 468–475.

Gockel, C.K. and Gray, L.C. (2009) Integrating conservation and development in the Peruvian Amazon. *Ecology and Society,* 14, 11.

Goodwin, P. and Wright, G. (2004) *Decision Analysis for Management Judgment.* Chichester, UK: John Wiley & Sons.

Gordon, H.S. (1954) The economic theory of a common-property resource: the Fishery. *Journal of Political Economy,* 62, 124–142.

Gordon, A., Bastin, L., Langford, W.T., Lechner, A.M. and Bekessy, S.A. (2013) Simulating the value of collaboration in multi-actor conservation planning. *Ecological Modelling,* 249, 19–25.

Grafton, Q., Arnason, R., Bjørndal, T., et al. (2006) Incentive-based approaches to sustainable fisheries. *Canadian Journal of Fisheries and Aquatic Sciences,* 63, 699–710.

Grafton, R.Q., Kompas, T. and Hilborn, R. W. (2007) Economics of overexploitation revisited. *Science,* 318, 1601–1601.

Grafton, Q.R., Kompas, T., Che, T.N., Chu, L. and Hilborn, R. (2012) BMEY as a fisheries management target. *Fish and Fisheries,* 13, 303–312.

Grand, J., Cummings, M.P., Rebelo, T.G., Ricketts, T.H. and Neel, M.C. (2007) Biased data reduce efficiency and effectiveness of conservation reserve networks. *Ecology Letters,* 10, 364–374.

Gray, R., Fulton, E.A. and Little, L.R. (2013) Human–ecosystem interaction in large ensemble-model systems. In A. Smajgl, and O. Barreteau, eds. *Empirical Agent-Based Modeling: Challenges and Solutions.* Berlin: Springer, 249 pp.

Gregory, R. and Long, G. (2009) Using structured decision making to help implement a precautionary approach to endangered species management. *Risk Analysis,* 29, 518–532.

Gregory, R., Failing, L., Harstone, M., et al. (2012) *Structured Decision Making: A Practical Guide to Environmental Management Choices.* Chichester: John Wiley.

Gregory, R., Arvai, J. and Gerber, L.R. (2013) Structuring decisions for managing threatened and endangered species in a changing climate. *Conservation Biology,* 27, 1212–1221.

Greig, L.A., Marmorek, D.R., Murray, C. and Robinson, D.C.E. (2013) Insight into enabling adaptive management. *Ecology and Society,* 18(3).

Groves, R.M. (2006) Nonresponse rates and nonresponse bias in household surveys. *Public Opinion Quarterly,* 70, 646–675.

Gurney, G.G., Cinner, J., Ban, N.C., et al. (2014) Poverty and protected areas: an evaluation of a marine integrated conservation and development project in Indonesia. *Global Environmental Change,* 26, 98–107.

Gutrich, J., Donovan, D., Finucane, M., et al. (2005) Science in the public process of ecosystem management: lessons from Hawaii, Southeast Asia, Africa and the US Mainland. *Journal of Environmental Management,* 76, 197–209.

Haddon, M. (2012) *Reducing Uncertainty in Stock Status: Harvest Strategy Testing Evaluation and Development. General Discussion and Summary.* Hobart: CSIRO Marine and Atmospheric Research.

Hadorn, G.H., Hoffmann-Riem, H., Biber-Klemm, S., et al. (2008) *Handbook of Transdisciplinary Research.* Dordrecht: Springer.

Halpern, B.S., Klein, C.J., Brown, C.J., et al. (2013) Achieving the triple bottom line in the face of inherent trade-offs among social equity, economic return, and conservation. *Proceedings of the National Academy of Sciences,* 110, 6229–34.

Hammond, J.S., Keeney, R.L. and Raiffa, H. (1999). Smart choices: a practical guide to making better decisions. *Medical Decision Making,* 19(3), 364–365.

Hardin, G. (1968) The tragedy of the commons. *Science,* 162(3859), 1243–1248.

Harrison, M., Roe, D., Baker, J., et al. (2015) *Wildlife Crime: A Review of the Evidence on Drivers and Impacts in Uganda.* London: International Institute for Environment and Development.

Harwood, J. and Stokes, K. (2003) Coping with uncertainty in ecological advice: lessons from fisheries. *Trends in Ecology & Evolution,* 18, 617–622.

Hauser, C.E. and McCarthy, M.A. (2009) Streamlining 'search and destroy': cost-effective surveillance for invasive species management. *Ecology Letters,* 12, 683–692.

Haywood, M., Hill, B., Donovan, A., et al. (2005) Quantifying the Effects of Trawling on Seabed Fauna in the Northern Prawn Fishery. Final Report on FRDC Project 2002/102.

Head, B.W. (2008) Wicked problems in public policy. *Public Policy,* 3, 101–118.

Henriksen, H.J. and Barlebo, H.C. (2008) Reflections on the use of Bayesian belief networks for adaptive management. *Journal of Environmental Management,* 88, 1025–1036.

Henriksen, H.J., Zorrilla-Miras, P., de la Hera, A. and Brugnach, M. (2012) Use of Bayesian belief networks for dealing with ambiguity in integrated groundwater management. *Integrated Environmental Assessment and Management,* 8, 430–444.

Hilborn, R. (2007) Defining success in fisheries and conflicts in objectives. *Marine Policy,* 31, 153–158.

Hilborn, R., Arcese, P., Borner, M., et al. (2006) Effective enforcement in a conservation area. *Science,* 314, 1266.

Hilborn, R. and Sinclair, A.R.E. (2010) Summary of Wildebeest 2009 Count Evaluation. Technical report.

Hilborn, R., Walters, C.J. and Ludwig, D. (1995) Sustainable exploitation of renewable resources. *Annual Review of Ecology and Systematics,* 26, 45–67.

Hobday, A.J. and Pecl, G.T. (2013) Identification of global marine hotspots: sentinels for change and vanguards for adaptation action. *Reviews in Fish Biology and Fisheries*, 24, 415–425.

Hofer, H., Campbell, K., East, M.L. and Huish, S.A. (1996) The impact of game meat hunting on target and non-target species in the Serengeti. In V.J. Taylor and N. Dunstone, eds. *The Exploitation of Mammal Populations*. London: Chapman & Hall, pp. 117–146.

Holdo, R.M., Galvin, K.A., Knapp, E., et al. (2010) Responses to alternative rainfall regimes and antipoaching in a migratory system. *Ecological Applications*, 20, 381–397.

Holdo, R.M., Fryxell, J.M., Sinclair, A.R.E., Dobson, A.P. and Holt, R.D. (2011a) Predicted impact of barriers to migration on the Serengeti wildebeest population. *PloS One*, 6, e16370.

Holdo, R.M., Sinclair, A.R.E., Holt, R.D., Godley, B. and Thirgood, S. (2011b) Migration impacts on communities and ecosystems: empirical evidence and theoretical insights. In E.J. Milner-Gulland, J.M. Fryxell and A.R.E. Sinclair, eds. *Animal Migration: A Synthesis*.

Holland, D. and Herrera, G. (2009) Uncertainty in the management of fisheries: contradictory implications and a new approach. *Marine Resource Economics*, 24, 289–299.

Holland-Clift, S. and Davies, J. (2007) *Willows National Management Guide: Current Management and Control Options for Willows (Salix spp.) in Australia*. Victorian Department of Primary Industries.

Holling, C.S. (1978) *Adaptive Environmental Assessment and Management*. Chichester: John Wiley.

Holmern, T., Muya, J. and Røskaft, E. (2007) Local law enforcement and illegal bushmeat hunting outside the Serengeti National Park, Tanzania. *Environmental Conservation*, 34, 55–63.

Homewood, K., Brockington, D. and Sullivan, S. (2010) Alternative view of Serengeti road. *Nature*, 467, 788–789.

Homewood, K., Kristjanson, P. and Chenevix Trench, P. (2009) *Staying Maasai? Livelihoods, Conservation and Development in East African Rangelands*. Studies in Human Ecology and Adaptation Volume 5. Berlin: Springer.

Hopcraft, J.G.C., Mduma, S.A.R., Borner, M., et al. (2015) Conservation and economic benefits of a road around the Serengeti. *Conservation Biology*, 29, 932–936.

Hopley, T. and Young, A.G. (2015) Knowledge of the reproductive ecology of the invasive *Salix cinerea*, in its invaded range, assists in more targeted management strategies. *Australian Journal of Botany*, 63, 477–483.

Hörnberg, S. (2001) Changes in population density of moose (*Alces alces*) and damage to forests in Sweden. *Forest Ecology and Management*, 149, 141–151.

Hornborg, S., Belgrano, A., Bartolino, V., Valentinsson, D. and Ziegler, F. (2013) Trophic indicators in fisheries: a call for re-evaluation. *Biology Letters*, 9, 20121050.

Howe, C. and Milner-Gulland, E.J. (2012) Evaluating indices of conservation success: A comparative analysis of outcome- and output-based indices. *Animal Conservation*, 15, 217–226.

Hulme, P.E., Pysek, P., Pergl, J., et al. (2014) Greater focus needed on alien plant impacts in protected areas. *Conservation Letters*, 7, 459–466.

Ives, M.C., Scandol, J.P. and Greenville, J. (2013) A bio-economic management strategy evaluation for a multi-species, multi-fleet fishery facing a world of uncertainty. *Ecological Modelling*, 256, 69–84.

Jack, B.K., Kousky, C. and Sims, K.R.E. (2008) Designing payments for ecosystem services: Lessons from previous experience with incentive-based mechanisms. *Proceedings of the National Academy of Sciences of the United States of America*, 105, 9465–70.

Jenkins, C. N. and Joppa, L. (2009) Expansion of the global terrestrial protected area system. *Biological Conservation*, 142, 2166–2174.

Johannesen, A.B. (2005) Wildlife conservation policies and incentives to hunt: an empirical analysis of illegal hunting in western Serengeti, Tanzania. *Environment and Development Economics*, 10, 271–292.

Johnson, F.A., Breininger, D.R., Duncan, B.W., et al. (2011) A Markov decision process for managing habitat for Florida scrub-jays. *Journal of Fish and Wildlife Management*, 2, 234–246.

Jokinen, M., Mäkeläinen, S. and Ovaskainen, O. (2014) 'Strict', yet ineffective: legal protection of breeding sites and resting places fails with the Siberian flying squirrel. *Animal Conservation*, 18, 167–175.

Jones, J.P.G., Andriamarovololona, M.M. and Hockley, N. (2008) The importance of taboos and social norms to conservation in Madagascar. *Conservation Biology*, 22, 976–986.

Jones, J.P.G., Collen, B., Atkinson, G., et al. (2011) The why, what and how of global biodiversity indicators beyond the 2010 target. *Conservation Biology*, 25, 450–457.

Joseph, L.N., Maloney, R.F. and Possingham, H.P. (2009) Optimal allocation of resources among threatened species: a project prioritization protocol. *Conservation Biology*, 23, 328–338.

Juffe-Bignoli, D., Burgess, N.D., Bingham, H., et al. (2014) *Protected Planet Report 2014*. UNEP-WCMC, Cambridge, UK.

Kahneman, D. (2011) *Thinking, Fast and Slow*. New York: Farrar, Straus and Giroux.

Kålås, J.A., Husby, M., Nilsen, E.B. and Vang, R. (2014) *Bestandsvariasjoner for terrestriske fugler i Norge 1996–2014*. NOF Rapport 4-2014.

Kaltenborn, B.P., Nyahongo, J.W. and Tingstad, K.M. (2005) The nature of hunting around the Western Corridor of Serengeti National Park, Tanzania. *European Journal of Wildlife Research*, 51, 213–222.

Keane, A., Jones, J.P.G., Edwards-Jones, G. and Milner-Gulland, E.J. (2008) The sleeping policeman: understanding issues of enforcement and compliance in conservation. *Animal Conservation*, 11, 75–82.

Keane, A., Jones, J.P.G. and Milner-Gulland, E.J. (2011) Encounter data in ecology and resource management: pitfalls and possibilities. *Journal of Applied Ecology* 48, 1164–1173.

Keeney, R.L. (1994) Creativity in decision making with value-focused thinking. *Sloan Management Review*, Summer, 33–41.

Keeney, R.L. (2007) Developing objectives and attributes. In W. Edwards, R.F.J. Miles and D. Von Winterfeldt, eds. *Advances in Decision Analysis: From*

Foundations to Applications. Cambridge: Cambridge University Press, pp. 104–128.

Keith, D.A., McCarthy, M.A., Regan, H., eds. (2004) Protocols for listing threatened species can forecast extinction. *Ecology Letters*, 7, 1101–1108.

Keith, D.A., Martin, T.G., McDonald-Madden, E. and Walters, C. (2011) Uncertainty and adaptive management for biodiversity conservation. *Biological Conservation*, 144, 1175–1178.

Kell, L.T., Mosqueira, I., Grosjean, P., et al. (2007) FLR: an open-source framework for the evaluation and development of management strategies. *ICES Journal of Marine Science*, 64, 640–646.

Kideghesho, J.R. and Mtoni, P.E. (2008) The potentials for co-management approaches in western Serengeti, Tanzania. *Tropical Conservation Science*, 1, 334–358.

Knapp, E.J. (2007) Who poaches? Household economies of illegal hunters in western Serengeti, Tanzania. *Human Dimensions of Wildlife*, 12, 195–196.

Knapp, E.J. (2012) Why poaching pays: a summary of risks and benefits illegal hunters face in Western Serengeti, Tanzania. *Tropical Conservation Science*, 5, 434–445.

Knott, E.J., Bunnefeld, N., Huber, D., et al. (2014) The potential impacts of changes in bear hunting policy for hunting organisations in Croatia. *European Journal of Wildlife Research*, 60, 85–97.

Kompas, T., Dichmont, C.M., Punt, A.E., et al. (2010) Maximizing profits and conserving stocks in the Australian Northern Prawn Fishery. *Australian Journal of Agricultural and Resource Economics*, 54, 281–299.

Korb, K.B. and Nicholson, A.E. (2010) *Bayesian Artificial Intelligence*, 2nd edn, Boca Raton, FL: Chapman & Hall/CRC Press.

Kramer, R.M. (1999) Trust and distrust in organizations: emerging perspectives, enduring questions. *Annual Review of Psychology*, 50, 569–598.

Krebs, C.J. (2001) *Ecology: The Experimental Analysis of Distribution and Abundance*, 5th edn. San Francisco, CA: Benjamin-Cummings.

Kujala, H., Burgman, M.A. and Moilanen, A. (2013) Treatment of uncertainty in conservation under climate change. *Conservation Letters*, 6, 73–85.

Lande, R., Engen, S. and Saether, B. E. (1994) Optimal harvesting, economic discounting and extinction risk in fluctuating populations. *Nature*, 372, 88–90.

Lande, R., Engen, S. and Saether, B.E. (1995) Optimal harvesting of fluctuating populations with a risk of extinction. *American Naturalist*, 145, 728–745.

Lande, R., Engen, S. and Sæther, B. E. (2003) *Stochastic Population Dynamics in Ecology and Conservation*, Oxford Series in Ecology and Evolution, 1st ed., Oxford: Oxford University Press.

Larrosa, C., Carrasco, L.R. and Milner-Gulland, E.J. (2016) Unintended feedbacks: challenges and opportunities for improving conservation effectiveness. *Conservation Letters*, 9(5), 316–326.

Laurance, W.F., Useche, D.C., Rendeiro, J., et al. (2012) Averting biodiversity collapse in tropical forest protected areas. *Nature*, 489, 290–294.

Leadley, P., Pereira, H.M., Alkemade, R., et al. (2010) *Biodiversity Scenarios: Projections of 21st Century Change in Biodiversity and Associated Ecosystem*

Services. Technical Series no. 50. Secretariat of the Convention on Biological Diversity, Montreal.

Lee, J.D. and See, K.A. (2004) Trust in automation: designing for appropriate reliance. *Human Factors,* 46, 50–80.

Leeuw, F. and Vaessen, J. (2009) *Impact Evaluations and Development: NONIE Guidance on Impact Evaluation.* Washington, DC: NONIE – The Network of Networks on Impact Evaluation.

Lehikoinen, A., Green, M., Husby, M., Kålås, J.A. and Lindström, Å. (2014) Common montane birds are declining in northern Europe. *Journal of Avian Biology,* 45, 3–14.

Leisher, C., Hess, S., Boucher, T.M., et al. (2012) Measuring the impacts of community-based grasslands management in Mongolia's Gobi. *PloS One,* 7, e30991.

Lewis, J. and Nkuintchua, T. (2012) Accessible technologies and FPIC: independent monitoring with forest communities in Cameroon. *Participatory Learning and Action,* 65, 151–165.

Liberg, O., Chapron, G., Wabakken, P., et al. (2012) Shoot, shovel and shut up: cryptic poaching slows restoration of a large carnivore in Europe. *Proceedings of the Royal Society B-Biological Sciences,* 279, 910–915.

Link, J.S., Yemane, D., Shannon, L.J., et al. (2010) Relating marine ecosystem indicators to fishing and environmental drivers: an elucidation of contrasting responses. *ICES Journal of Marine Science: Journal du Conseil,* 67, 787–795.

Linnell, J.D.C. and Boitani, L. (2012) Building biological realism into wolf management policy: the development of the population approach in Europe. *Hystrix,* 23, 80–91.

Linnell, J.D.C., Broseth, H., Odden, J. and Nilsen, E.B. (2010) Sustainably harvesting a large carnivore? Development of Eurasian lynx populations in Norway during 160 years of shifting policy. *Environmental Management,* 45, 1142–1154.

Linnell, J.D.C., Nilsen, E.B., Lande, U.S., et al. (2005) Zoning as a means of mitigating conflicts with large carnivores: principles and reality. In R. Woodrof, S. Thirgood and A. Rabinowitz, eds. *People and Wildlife: Conflict or Coexistence?* Cambridge: Cambridge University Press. pp. 162–175.

Little, L.R., Wayte, S.E., Tuck, G.N., et al. (2011) Development and evaluation of a cpue-based harvest control rule for the southern and eastern scalefish and shark fishery of Australia. *ICES Journal of Marine Science,* 68, 1699–1705.

Liu, J., Dietz, T., Carpenter, S.R., et al. (2007) Complexity of coupled human and natural systems. *Science,* 317, 1513–1516.

Liu, S., Walshe, T., Long, G., and Cook, D. (2012) Evaluation of potential responses to invasive non-native species with structured decision making. *Conservation Biology,* 26, 539–546.

Loh, J., Green, R.E., Ricketts, T., et al. (2005) The Living Planet Index: using species population time series to track trends in biodiversity. *Philosophical Transactions of the Royal Society,* 360, 289–295.

Loibooki, M., Hofer, H., Campbell, K. and East, M.L. (2002) Bushmeat hunting by communities adjacent to the Serengeti National Park, Tanzania: the importance of livestock ownership and alternative sources of protein and income. *Environmental Conservation*, 29, 391–398.

Lötter, M.C. (2014) *Technical report for the Mpumalanga Biodiversity Sector Plan – MBSP*. Mpumalanga Tourism & Parks Agency, Nelspruit.

Ludwig, D. (2001) The era of management is over. *Ecosystems*, 4, 758–764.

Mace, G.M. (2014) Whose conservation? *Science*, 345, 1558–1560.

Mace, G.M. and Baillie, J.E.M. (2007) The 2010 biodiversity indicators: challenges for science and policy. *Conservation Biology*, 21, 1406–1413.

Mace, G.M. and Lande, R. (1991) Assessing extinction threats: toward a reevaluation of IUCN Threatened Species categories. *Conservation Biology*, 5, 148–157.

Mace, G.M., Collar, N.J., Gaston, K.J., et al. (2008) Quantification of extinction risk: IUCN's system for classifying threatened species. *Conservation Biology*, 22, 1424–1442.

Mace, G. M., Cramer, W., Diaz, S., et al. (2010) Biodiversity targets after 2010. *Current Opinion in Environmental Sustainability*, 2, 1–6.

Mace, G.M., Norris, K. and Fitter, A.H. (2012) Biodiversity and ecosystem services: a multilayered relationship. *Trends in Ecology & Evolution*, 27, 19–26.

Madsen, J., Bunnefeld, N., Nagy, S., et al. (2015) *Guidelines on Sustainable Harvest of Migratory Waterbirds*. AEWA Conservation Guidelines No. 5, AEWA Technical Series No. 62. Bonn, Germany.

Madsen, J. and Williams, J.H. (2012) International species management plan for the Svalbard population of the pink-footed goose *Anser brachyrhynchus*. AEWA Technical Series No. 48. Bonn, Germany.

Maguire, L.A. (2004) What can decision analysis do for invasive species management? *Risk Analysis*, 24, 859–68.

Maher, S.P., Kramer, A.M., Pulliam, J.T., Zokan, M.A., Bowden, S.E., Barton, H.D., Magori, K. and Drake, J.M. (2012). Spread of white-nose syndrome on a network regulated by geography and climate. *Nature Communications*, 3, 1306.

Malthus, T.R. (1798) *An Essay on the Principle of Population*. London: J. Johnson.

Mapstone, B., Little, L., Punt, A., et al. (2008) Management strategy evaluation for line fishing in the Great Barrier Reef: balancing conservation and multisector fishery objectives. *Fisheries Research*, 94, 315–329.

Marcot, B.G., Thompson, M.P., Runge, M.C., et al. (2012) Recent advances in applying decision science to managing national forests. *Forest Ecology and Management*, 285, 123–132.

Mardle, S. and Pascoe, S. (2002) Modelling the effects of trade-offs between long and short-term objectives in fisheries management. *Journal of Environmental Management*, 65, 49–62.

Martin, J., Fackler, P.L., Nichols, J.D., et al. (2011) An adaptive-management framework for optimal control of hiking near Golden Eagle nests in Denali National Park. *Conservation Biology*, 25, 316–323.

Martin, J., Runge, M.C., Nichols, J.D., Lubow, B.C. and Kendall, W.L. (2009) Structured decision making as a conceptual framework to identify thresholds for conservation and management. *Ecological Applications*, 19, 1079–1090.

Martin, T.G., Burgman, M.A., Fidler, F., et al. (2012) Eliciting expert knowledge in conservation science. *Conservation Biology*, 26, 29–38.

Matthews, R. (2007) Modelling the sustainability of rural systems: concepts, approaches and tools. *Journal of Agricultural Science*, 145, 636–641.

Mattisson, J., Odden, J., Nilsen, E.B., et al. (2011) Factors affecting Eurasian lynx kill rates on semi-domestic reindeer in northern Scandinavia: can ecological research contribute to the development of a fair compensation system? *Biological Conservation*, 144, 3009–3017.

Maxwell, S., Milner-Gulland, E.J., Jones, J.P.G., et al. (2015) Being smart about SMART environmental targets. *Science*, 347, 1075–1076.

Mayer, R.C., Davis, J.H. and Schoorman, F.D. (1995) An integrative model of organizational trust. *Academy of Management Review*, 20, 709–734.

McAllister, M., Starr, P.J., Restrepo, V.R. and Kirkwood, G. (1999) Formulating quantitative methods to evaluate fishery-management systems: what fishery processes should be modelled and what trade-offs should be made? *ICES Journal of Marine Science*, 56, 900–916.

McCarthy, M.A., Moore, A.L., Krauss, J., Morgan, J.W. and Clements, C.F. (2014) Linking indices for biodiversity monitoring to extinction risk theory. *Conservation Biology*, 28, 1575–1583.

McDonald-Madden, E., Baxter, P.W.J., Fuller, R.A., et al. (2010) Monitoring does not always count. *Trends in Ecology & Evolution*, 25, 547–550.

McDonald-Madden, E., Baxter, P.W.J. and Possingham, H.P. (2008) Making robust decisions for conservation with restricted money and knowledge. *Journal of Applied Ecology*, 45, 1630–1638.

McDonald-Madden, E., Chades, I., McCarthy, M.A., Linkie, M. and Possingham, H.P. (2011) Allocating conservation resources between areas where persistence of a species is uncertain. *Ecological Applications*, 21, 844–858.

McDougall, K.L. (1982) *Alpine vegetation of the Bogong High Plains in Victoria.* Victorian Ministry for Conservation, Melbourne.

McDougall, K.L. (2007) Grazing and fire in two subalpine peatlands. *Australian Journal of Botany*, 55, 42–47.

McDougall, K.L. and Walsh, N.G. (2007) Treeless vegetation of the Australian Alps. *Cunninghamia*, 10, 1–57.

McDougall, K.L., Morgan, J.W., Walsh, N.G. and Williams, R.J. (2005) Plant invasions in treeless vegetation of the Australian Alps. *Perspectives in Plant Ecology Evolution and Systematics*, 7, 159–171.

McFall, L. (1987) Integrity. *Ethics*, 98, 5–20.

McGraw, J.B. and Furedi, M.A. (2005) Deer browsing and population viability of a forest understory plant. *Science*, 307, 920–922.

McGregor, J.A. (2004) Researching well-being: communicating between the needs of policy makers and the needs of people. *Global Social Policy*, 4, 337–358.

McGregor, J.A. (2007) Researching wellbeing: from concepts to methodology. In I. Gough and J.A. McGregor, eds., *Wellbeing in Developing Countries: From Theory to Research*. Cambridge: Cambridge University Press, pp. 316–350.

McGregor, J.A., Camfield, L., Masae, A. and Promphaking, B. (2008) Wellbeing, development and social change in Thailand. *Thammasat Economic Journal*, 26, 1–27.

McGregor, J.A. and Sumner, A. (2010) Beyond business as usual: what might 3-D wellbeing contribute to MDG momentum? *IDS Bulletin*, 41, 104–112.

McIntosh, B. S., Giupponi, C., Smith, C., et al. (2008) Bridging the gaps between design and use: developing tools to support environmental management and policy. In A.J. Jakeman, A. Voinov, A.E. Rizzoli and S.H. Chen, eds. *Environmental Modelling and Software, Developments in Integrated Environmental Assessment*. Amsterdam: Elsevier. pp. 33–48.

McIntosh, B.S., Ascough, J.C., Twery, M., et al. (2011) Environmental decision support systems (EDSS) development – challenges and best practices. *Environmental Modelling & Software*, 26, 1389–1402.

McKinnon, M.C., Cheng, S.H., Dupre, S., et al. (2016) What are the effects of nature conservation on human well-being? A systematic map of empirical evidence from developing countries. *Environmental Evidence*, 5, 8.

McShane, T.O., Hirsch, P.D., Trung, T.C., et al. (2011) Hard choices: Making trade-offs between biodiversity conservation and human well-being. *Biological Conservation*, 144, 966–972.

Mduma, S., Sinclair, A.R.E. and Hilborn, R. (1999) Food regulates the Serengeti wildebeest: a 40-year record. *Journal of Animal Ecology*, 68, 1101–1122.

Mech, L.D. (1996) A new era for carnivore conservation. *Wildlife Society Bulletin*, 24, 397–401.

Mendoza, G.A. and Martins, H. (2006) Multi-criteria decision analysis in natural resource management: a critical review of methods and new modelling paradigms. *Forest Ecology and Management*, 230, 1–22.

Messer, N. and Townsley, P. (2003) *Local Institutions and Livelihoods: Guidelines for Analysis*. Rome: Food and Agricultural Organisation.

Millennium Ecosystem Assessment (2005) *Ecosystems and Human Wellbeing: Synthesis*. Washington, DC: Island Press.

Miller, B.W., Caplow, S.C. and Leslie, P.W. (2012) Feedbacks between conservation and social-ecological systems. *Conservation Biology*, 26, 218–227.

Mills, M., Nicol, S., Wells, J.A., et al. (2014) Minimizing the cost of keeping options open for conservation in a changing climate. *Conservation Biology*, 28, 646–653

Milner-Gulland, E.J. (1994) A population model for the management of the saiga antelope. *Journal of Applied Ecology*, 31, 25–39.

Milner-Gulland, E.J. (2011) Integrating fisheries approaches and household utility models for improved resource management. *Proceedings of the National Academy of Sciences*, 108, 1741–1746.

Milner-Gulland, E.J. (2012) Interactions between human behaviour and ecological systems. *Philosophical Transactions of the Royal Society of London. Series B, Biological Sciences*, 367, 270–278.

Milner-Gulland, E.J. and Rowcliffe, J.M. (2007) *Conservation and Sustainable Use: A Handbook of Techniques*. Oxford: Oxford University Press.

Milner-Gulland, E.J., Beddington, J.R. and Leader-Williams, N. (1992) Dehorning African rhinos: a model of optimal frequency and profitability. *Proceedings of the Royal Society B*, 249, 83–87.

Milner-Gulland, E.J., Arroyo, B., Bellard, C., et al. (2010) New directions in management strategy evaluation through cross-fertilization between fisheries science and terrestrial conservation. *Biology Letters*, 6, 719–722.

Milner-Gulland, E.J., McGregor, J.A., Agarwala, M., et al. (2014) Accounting for the impact of conservation on human well-being. *Conservation Biology*, 28, 1160–1166.

Ministerial Taskforce on Bushfire Recovery (2003) Final report from the Ministerial Taskforce on Bushfire Recovery The Victorian State Government, Melbourne

MNRT (1998) *The Wildlife Policy of Tanzania*. Ministry of Natural Resources and Tourism, united Republic of Tanzania, Dar es Salaam.

Moore, J.L. (2007) *Managing willow invasion in alpine bogs. 3 month report to Parks Victoria*. University of Melbourne.

Moore, J.L. (2008) *Managing willow invasion on the Bogong High Plains. 12 month report to Parks Victoria*. University of Melbourne.

Moore, J.L. (2009) *Managing willow invasion on the Bogong High Plains. 24 month report to Parks Victoria*. University of Melbourne.

Moore, J.L. (2013) *Estimating willow search effectiveness on the Bogong High Plains. Report to Parks Victoria*. Australian Research Centre for Urban Ecology, Royal Botanic Gardens Melbourne.

Moore, J.L. and Runge, M.C. (2010a) *Developing a long term strategy for managing willow invasion on the Bogong High Plains: Building the prototype model Technical Report. Report for Parks Victoria*. University of Melbourne.

Moore, J.L. and Runge, M.C. (2010b) *Developing a long term strategy for managing willow invasion on the Bogong High Plains: Prototype model results. Report for Parks Victoria*. University of Melbourne.

Moore, J.L. and Runge, M.C. (2012) Combining structured decision making and value-of-information analyses to identify robust management strategies. *Conservation Biology*, 26, 810–820.

Moore, J.L. and McAllister, A.J. (2013) *Willow Population Structure study 2011–12. Report to Parks Victoria*. Australian Research Centre for Urban Ecology, Royal Botanic Gardens Melbourne.

Moro, M., Fischer, A., Czajkowski, M., et al. (2013) An investigation using the choice experiment method into options for reducing illegal bushmeat hunting in western Serengeti. *Conservation Letters*, 6, 37–45.

Moro, M., Fischer, A., Milner-Gulland, E.J., et al. (2015) A stated preference investigation of household demand for illegally hunted bushmeat in the Serengeti, Tanzania. *Animal Conservation*, 18, 377–386.

Mueller, T., O'Hara, R.B., Converse, S.J., Urbanek, R.P. and Fagan, W.F. (2013) Social learning of migratory performance. *Science*, 341, 999–1002.

Mukherjee, N., Hugé, J., Sutherland, W.J., et al. (2015) The Delphi technique in ecology and biological conservation: applications and guidelines. *Methods in Ecology and Evolution*, 6, 1097–1109.

Muradian, R., Corbera, E., Pascual, U., Kosoy, N. and May, P.H. (2010) Reconciling theory and practice: an alternative conceptual framework for understanding payments for environmental services. *Ecological Economics*, 69, 1202–1208.

Myers, N., Mittermeier, R.A., Mittermeier, C.G., da Fonseca, G.A. and Kent, J. (2000) Biodiversity hotspots for conservation priorities. *Nature*, 403, 853–858.

Mysterud, A. (2004) Temporal variation in the number of car-killed red deer *Cervus elaphus* in Norway. *Wildlife Biology*, 10, 203–211.

Naidoo, R., Balmford, A., Ferraro, P.J., et al. (2006) Integrating economic costs into conservation planning. *Trends in Ecology and Evolution*, 21, 681–687.

Narayan, D., Chambers, R., Shah, M.K. and Petesch, P. (2000) *Voices of the Poor: Crying Out for Change*. New York: Oxford University Press for the World Bank.

Narayanan, P., Vineetha, S., Sarangan, G. and Bharadwaj, S. (2015) Charting new territory: community participation at the centre of global policy making. *Community Development Journal*, 50, 608–623.

Narloch, U., Pascual, U. and Drucker, A.G. (2013) How to achieve fairness in payments for ecosystem services? Insights from agrobiodiversity conservation auctions. *Land Use Policy*, 35, 107–118.

Naumann, J.D. and Jenkins, A.M. (1982) Prototyping: the new paradigm for systems development. *MIS Q*, 6, 29–44.

Neckles, H.A., Lyons, J.E., Guntenspergen, G.R., Shriver, W.G. and Adamowicz, S.C. (2014) Use of structured decision making to identify monitoring variables and management priorities for salt marsh ecosystems. *Estuaries and Coasts*, 1–18.

Nichols, J.D., Runge, M.C., Johnson, F.A. and Williams, B.K. (2007) Adaptive harvest management of North American waterfowl populations: a brief history and future prospects. *Journal of Ornithology*, 148, S343–S349.

Nichols, J.D. and Williams, B.K. (2006) Monitoring for conservation. *Trends in Ecology & Evolution*, 21, 668–673.

Nicholson, E. and Possingham, H.P. (2007) Making conservation decisions under uncertainty for the persistence of multiple species. *Ecological Applications*, 17, 251–265.

Nicolson, C.R., Starfield, A.M., Kofinas, G.P. and Kruse, J.A. (2002) Ten heuristics for interdisciplinary modeling projects. *Ecosystems*, 5, 376–384.

Nicholson, E., Westphal, M.I., Frank, K., et al. (2006) A new method for conservation planning for the persistence of multiple species. *Ecology Letters*, 9, 1049–1060.

Nicholson, E., Collen, B., Barausse, A., et al. (2012) Making robust policy decisions using global biodiversity indicators. *PLoS One*, 7, e41128.

Nilsen, E.B., Pettersen, T., Gundersen, H., et al. (2005) Moose harvesting strategies in the presence of wolves. *Journal of Applied Ecology*, 42, 389–399.

Nilsen, E.B., Gaillard, J.M., Andersen, R., et al. (2009a) A slow life in hell or a fast life in heaven: demographic analyses of contrasting roe deer populations. *Journal of Animal Ecology*, 78, 585–594.

Nilsen, E.B., Skonhoft, A., Mysterud, A., et al. (2009b) The role of ecological and economic factors in the management of a spatially structured moose Alces alces population. *Wildlife Biology*, 15, 10–23.

Nilsen, E.B., Brøseth, H., Odden, J., Andrén, H. and Linnell, J.D.C. (2011) *Prognosemodell for bestanden av gaupe i Norge*. NINA Rapport 774: NINA.

Nilsen, E.B., Broseth, H., Odden, J. and Linnell, J.D.C. (2012a) Quota hunting of Eurasian lynx in Norway: patterns of hunter selection, hunter efficiency and monitoring accuracy. *European Journal of Wildlife Research*, 58, 325–333.

Nilsen, E.B., Linnell, J.D.C., Odden, J., Samelius, G. and Andren, H. (2012b) Patterns of variation in reproductive parameters in Eurasian lynx (*Lynx lynx*). *Acta Theriologica*, 57, 217–223.

Nielsen, M.R., Pouliot, M. and Bakkegaard, R. (2012) Combining income and assets measures to include the transitory nature of poverty in assessments of forest dependence: evidence from the Democratic Republic of Congo. *Ecological Economics*, 78, 37–46.

Norton-Griffiths, M. (1978) *Counting Animals*. Nairobi, Kenya: African Wildlife Leadership Foundation.

Norton-Griffiths, M. (2007) How many wildebeest do you need? *World Economics*, 8, 41–64.

Nuno, A. (2013) Managing social-ecological systems under uncertainty: implications for conservation. PhD thesis, Imperial College London, UK.

Nuno, A., Bunnefeld, N. and Milner-Gulland, E.J. (2013) Matching observations and reality: using simulation models to improve monitoring under uncertainty in the Serengeti. *Journal of Applied Ecology*, 50, 488–498.

Nuno, A., Bunnefeld, N., Naiman, L.C. and Milner-Gulland, E.J. (2013) A novel approach to assessing the prevalence and drivers of illegal bushmeat hunting in the Serengeti. *Conservation Biology*, 27, 1355–1365.

Nuno, A., Bunnefeld, N. and Milner-Gulland, E.J. (2014) Managing social-ecological systems under uncertainty: implementation in the real world. *Ecology and Society*, 19, 52.

Nuno, A., Milner-Gulland, E.J. and Bunnefeld, N. (2015) Detecting abundance trends under uncertainty: the influence of budget, observation error and environmental change. *Animal Conservation*, 18, 331–340.

Nuno, A. and St John, F.A.V. (2015) How to ask sensitive questions in conservation: a review of specialised questioning techniques. *Biological Conservation*, 189, 5–15.

Nystrom, J., Dalen, L., Hellstrom, P., et al. (2006) Effect of local prey availability on gyrfalcon diet: DNA analysis on ptarmigan remains at nest sites. *Journal of Zoology*, 269, 57–64.

Nystrom, J., Ekenstedt, J., Engstrom, J. and Angerbjorn, A. (2005) Gyr Falcons, ptarmigan and microtine rodents in northern Sweden. *Ibis*, 147, 587–597.

Odden, J., Linnell, J.D.C. and Andersen, R. (2006) Diet of Eurasian lynx, *Lynx lynx*, in the boreal forest of southeastern Norway: the relative importance of livestock and hares at low roe deer density. *European Journal of Wildlife Research*, 52, 237–244.

Odden, J., Nilsen, E.B. and Linnell, J.D.C. (2013) Density of wild prey modulates lynx kill rates on free-ranging domestic sheep. *PLoS One*, 8, e79261.

Ostrom, E. (1990) *Governing the Commons: The Evolution of Institutions for Collective Action*. Cambridge: Cambridge University Press.

Ostrom, E. (2009) A general framework for analyzing sustainability of social-ecological systems. *Science*, 325, 419–422.

Pagiola, S., Arcenas, A. and Platais, G. (2005) Can payments for environmental services help reduce poverty? An exploration of the issues and the evidence to date from Latin America. *World Development*, 33, 237–253.

Palmer Fry, B., Agarwala, M., Atkinson, G., et al. (2015) Monitoring local wellbeing in environmental interventions: A consideration of practical trade-offs. *Oryx*. [online] doi:10.1017/S003060531500112X.

Parks Victoria (2014) *Bogong High plains and Mount Buffalo Seeding Willow Strategy*. Prepared for Parks Victoria, North East, by Sarah Nicholas.

Pauly, D., Christensen, V., Dalsgaard, J., Froese, R. and Torres, F. (1998) Fishing down marine food webs. *Science*, 279, 860–863.

Pauly, D., Christensen, V. and Walters, C. (2000) Ecopath, Ecosim, and Ecospace as tools for evaluating ecosystem impact of fisheries. *ICES Journal of Marine Science*, 57, 697–706.

Pauly, D. and Watson, R. (2005) Background and interpretation of the 'Marine Trophic Index' as a measure of biodiversity. *Philosophical Transactions of the Royal Society B*, 360, 415–423.

Pauly, D., Hilborn, R. and Branch, T.A. (2013) Fisheries: does catch reflect abundance? *Nature*, 494, 303–306.

Pearl, J. (1991) *Probabilistic Reasoning in Intelligent Systems: Networks of Plausible Inference*, Revised second printing. ed., San Mateo, CA: Morgan Kaufmann Publishers.

Pedersen, H.C., Steen, H., Kastdalen, L., et al. (2004) Weak compensation of harvest despite strong density-dependent growth in willow ptarmigan. *Proceedings of the Royal Society of London Series B – Biological Sciences*, 271, 381–385.

Pereira, H.M., Leadley, P.W., Proença, V., et al. (2010) Scenarios for global biodiversity in the 21st century. *Science*, 330, 1496–1501.

Pereira, H.M., Navarro, L.M. and Martins, I.S. (2012) Global biodiversity change: the bad, the good, and the unknown. *Annual Review of Environment and Resources*, 37, 25.

Pereira, H.M., Ferrier, S., Walters, M., et al. (2013) Essential biodiversity variables. *Science*, 339, 277–278.

Perrings, C., Naeem, S., Ahrestani, F., et al. (2010) Ecosystem services for 2020. *Science*, 330, 323–324.

Perrings, C., Duraiappah, A., Larigauderie, A. and Mooney, H. (2011) The biodiversity and ecosystem services science–policy interface. *Science*, 331, 1139–1140.

Phillips, S.J. and Dudik, M. (2008) Modeling of species distributions with Maxent: new extensions and a comprehensive evaluation. *Ecography*, 31, 161–175.

Pikitch, E.K., Santora, C., Babcock, E.A., et al. (2004) Ecosystem-based fishery management. *Science*, 305, 346–347.

Pitcher, C.R., Burridge, C.Y., Wassenberg, T.J., Hill, B.J. and Poiner, I.R. (2009) A large scale BACI experiment to test the effects of prawn trawling on seabed biota in a closed area of the Great Barrier Reef Marine Park, Australia. *Fisheries Research*, 99, 168–183.

Plaganyi, E.E., Rademeyer, R.A., Butterworth, D.S., Cunningham, C.L. and Johnston, S.J. (2007) Making management procedures operational – innovations implemented in South Africa. *ICES Journal of Marine Science*, 64, 626–632.

Polasky, S. (2008) Why conservation planning needs socioeconomic data. *Proceedings of the National Academy of Sciences*, 105, 6505–6506.

Pollnac, R.B. and Poggie, J.J. (2008) Happiness, well-being and psychocultural adaptation to the stresses associated with marine fishing. *Human Ecology Review*, 15, 194–200.

Pomeroya, R.S., Katonb, B.M. and Harkes, I. (2001) Conditions affecting the success of fisheries co-management: lessons from Asia. *Marine Policy*, 25, 197–208.

Pooley, S. (2013) Historians are from Venus, ecologists are from Mars. *Conservation Biology*, 27, 1481–1483.

Pooley, S.P., Mendelsohn, J.A. and Milner-Gulland, E.J. (2014) Hunting down the chimera of multiple disciplinarity in conservation science. *Conservation Biology*, 28, 22–32.

Possingham, H.P., Andelman, S.J., Noon, B.R., Trombulak, S. and Pulliam, H.R. (2001) Making smart conservation decisions. In M. Soule and G. Orians, eds. *Conservation Biology: Research Priorities for the Next Decade*. Washington DC: Island Press, pp. 225–244.

Possingham, H.P., Ball, I. and Andelman, S.J. (2000) Mathematical methods for identifying representative reserve networks. In S. Ferson and M.A. Burgman, eds. *Quantitative Methods for Conservation Biology*. New York: Springer, pp. 291–306.

Potts, S.G., Biesmeijer, J.C., Kremen, C., et al. (2010) Global pollinator declines: trends, impacts and drivers. *Trends in Ecology & Evolution*, 25, 345–353.

Prell, C., Hubacek, K., Reed, M., et al. (2007) If you have a hammer everything looks like a nail: traditional versus participatory model building. *Interdisciplinary Science Reviews*, 32, 263–282.

Pressey, R.L., Humphries, C.J., Margules, C.R., Vanewright, R.I. and Williams, P.H. (1993) Beyond opportunism – key principles for systematic reserve selection. *Trends in Ecology & Evolution*, 8, 124–128.

Pressey, R.L. and Nicholls, A.O. (1989) Application of a numerical algorithm to the selection of reserves in semi-arid New-South-Wales. *Biological Conservation*, 50, 263–278.

Pullin, A.S., Bangpan, M., Dalrymple, S., et al. (2013) Human well-being impacts of terrestrial protected areas. *Environmental Evidence*, 2, 1–41.

Pullin, A.S. and Knight, T.T.M. (2003) Support for decision making in conservation practice: an evidence-based approach. *Journal for Nature Conservation*, 11, 83–90.

Punt, A.E., A'Mar, T., Bond, N.A., et al. (2013) Fisheries management under climate and environmental uncertainty: control rules and performance simulation. *ICES Journal of Marine Science*, doi:10.1093/icesjms/fst057

Punt, A.E. and Butterworth, D.S. (1995) The effects of future consumption by the Cape fur seal on catches and catch rates of the cape hakes .4. Modelling the biological interaction between Cape fur seals *Arctocephalus pusillus pusillus* and the cape hakes *Merluccius capensis* and *M-paradoxus*. *South African Journal of Marine Science*, 16, 255–285.

Punt, A.E., Butterworth, D.S., de Moor, C.L., De Oliveira, J.A.A. and Haddon, M. (2016) Management strategy evaluation: best practices. *Fish and Fisheries*, 17, 303–334.

Punt, A.E., Deng, R.A., Dichmont, C.M., et al. (2010) Integrating size-structured assessment and bioeconomic management advice in Australia's northern prawn fishery. *ICES Journal of Marine Science*, 67, 1785–1801.

Punt, A.E., Deng, R., Pascoe, S., et al. (2011) Calculating optimal effort and catch trajectories for multiple species modelled using a mix of size-structured, delay-difference and biomass dynamics models. *Fisheries Research*, 109, 201–211.

Punt, A.E. and Donovan, G.P. (2007) Developing management procedures that are robust to uncertainty: lessons from the International Whaling Commission. *ICES Journal of Marine Science*, 64, 603–612.

Putman, R.J. (1986) Foraging by roe deer in agricultural areas and impact on arable crops. *Journal of Applied Ecology*, 23, 91–99.

Putman, R.J. (2003) Deer-related traffic accidents. *Veterinary Record*, 153, 64.

Putman, R.J. and Moore, N.P. (1998) Impact of deer in lowland Britain on agriculture, forestry and conservation habitats. *Mammal Review*, 28, 141–163.

Ravallion, M. (2003) The debate on globalization, poverty and inequality: why measurement matters. *International Affairs*, 79, 739–753.

Reckhow, K.H. (1999) Water quality prediction and probability network models. *Canadian Journal of Fisheries and Aquatic Sciences*, 56, 1150–1158.

Redpath, S.M., Arroyo, B.E., Leckie, F.M., et al. (2004) Using decision modeling with stakeholders to reduce human–wildlife conflict: a Raptor–Grouse case study. *Conservation Biology*, 18, 350–359.

Redpath, S.M., Gutiérrez, R.J., Wood, K.A. and Young, J.C., eds. (2015) *Conflicts in Conservation: Navigating Towards Solutions*. Cambridge: Cambridge University Press.

Redpath, S.M., Young, J., Evely, A., et al. (2013) Understanding and managing conservation conflicts. *Trends in Ecology and Evolution*, 28, 100–109.

Reed, M.S. (2008) Stakeholder participation for environmental management: a literature review. *Biological Conservation*, 141, 2417–2431.

Regan, H.M., Ben-Haim, Y., Langford, B., et al. (2005) Robust decision-making under severe uncertainty for conservation management. *Ecological Applications*, 15, 1471–1477.

Regan, H.M., Colyvan, M. and Burgman, M. (2002) A taxonomy and treatment of uncertainty for ecology and conservation biology. *Ecological Applications*, 12, 618–628.

Rentsch, D. (2011) *The nature of bushmeat hunting in the Serengeti Ecosystem, Tanzania : socio-economic drivers of consumption of migratory wildlife*. PhD thesis, University of Minnesota, USA.

Rentsch, D. and Damon, A. (2013) Prices, poaching, and protein alternatives: an analysis of bushmeat consumption around Serengeti National Park, Tanzania. *Ecological Economics*, 91, 1–9.

Rice, J. (2014) Evolution of international commitments for fisheries sustainability. *ICES Journal of Marine Science*, 71, 157–165.

Rice, J.C. and Rochet, M.-J. (2005) A framework for selecting a suite of indicators for fisheries management. *ICES Journal of Marine Science*, 62, 516–527.

Ripple, W.J. and Beschta, R.L. (2003) Wolf reintroduction, predation risk, and cottonwood recovery in Yellowstone National Park. *Forest Ecology and Management*, 184, 299–313.

Rist, L., Campbell, B.M. and Frost, P. (2013) Adaptive management: where are we now? *Environmental Conservation*, 40, 5–18.

Rittel, H.W.J. and Webber, M.M. (1973) Dilemmas in a general theory of planning. *Policy Sciences*, 4, 155–169.

Rochet, M.-J. and Rice, J.C. (2009) Simulation-based management strategy evaluation: ignorance disguised as mathematics? *ICES Journal of Marine Sciences*, 66, 754–762.

Rout, T.M., Hauser, C.E. and Possingham, H.P. (2009) Optimal adaptive management for the translocation of a threatened species. *Ecological Applications*, 19, 515–526.

Rout, T., Kirkwood, R., Sutherland, D., Murphy, S. and McCarthy, M.A. (2014) When to declare successful eradication of an invasive predator? *Animal Conservation*, 17, 125–132.

Rowe, G. and Frewer, L.J. (2000) Public participation methods: a framework for evaluation. *Science, Technology & Human Values*, 25, 3–29.

Runge, M.C. (2011) An introduction to adaptive management for threatened and endangered species. *Journal of Fish and Wildlife Management*, 2, 220–233.

Runge, M.C., Bean, E., Smith, D.R. and Kokos, S. (2011a) *Non-native fish control below Glen Canyon Dam*. Report from a structured decision-making project.

Runge, M.C., Converse, S.J. and Lyons, J.E. (2011b) Which uncertainty? Using expert elicitation and expected value of information to design an adaptive program. *Biological Conservation*, 144, 1214–1223.

Sæther, B.E., Engen, S. and Solberg, E.J. (2001) Optimal harvest of age-structured populations of moose *Alces alces* in a fluctuating environment. *Wildlife Biology*, 7, 171–179.

Sæther, B.E., Engen, S., Solberg, E.J. and Heim, M. (2007) Estimating the growth of a newly established moose population using reproductive value. *Ecography*, 30, 417–421.

Sæther, B.E., Engen, S., Odden, J., et al. (2010) Sustainable harvest strategies for age-structured Eurasian lynx populations: the use of reproductive value. *Biological Conservation*, 143, 1970–1979.

Sainsbury, K.J., Punt, A.E. and Smith, A.D.M. (2000) Design of operational management strategies for achieving fishery ecosystem objectives. *ICES Journal of Marine Science*, 57, 731–741.

Sainsbury, K., Burgess, N.D., Sabuni, F., et al. (2015) Exploring stakeholder perceptions of conservation outcomes from alternative income generating activities in Tanzanian villages adjacent to Eastern Arc Mountain forests. *Biological Conservation*, 191, 20–28.

Sandbrook, C., Adams, W.M. and Monteferri, B. (2015) Digital games and biodiversity conservation. *Conservation Letters*, 8, 118–124.

Sandercock, B.K., Nilsen, E.B., Broseth, H. and Pedersen, H.C. (2011) Is hunting mortality additive or compensatory to natural mortality? Effects of experimental harvest on the survival and cause-specific mortality of willow ptarmigan. *Journal of Animal Ecology*, 80, 244–258.

Schley, L. and Roper, T.J. (2003) Diet of wild boar Sus scrofa in Western Europe, with particular reference to consumption of agricultural crops. *Mammal Review*, 33, 43–56.

Schlüter, M., McAllister, R.R.J., Arlinghaus, R., et al. (2012) New horizons for managing the environment: a review of coupled social-ecological systems modeling. *Natural Resource Modeling*, 25, 219–272.

Schoemaker, P.J.H. (1991) The quest for optimality: a positive heuristic of science? *Behavioral and Brain Sciences*, 14, 205–215.

Scholes, R.J., Mace, G.M., Turner, W., et al. (2008) Toward a global biodiversity observing system. *Science*, 321, 1044–1045.

Secretariat of the CBD (2010) *Global Biodiversity Outlook 3*. Secretariat of the Convention on Biological Diversity, Montreal.

Seiler, A., Helldin, J.O. and Seiler, C. (2004) Road mortality in Swedish mammals: results of a drivers' questionnaire. *Wildlife Biology*, 10, 225–233.

SEMP (2006) *Report of a study of stakeholders of the Serengeti ecosystem. Serengeti Ecosystem Management Project.*

Sen, A. (1999) *Development as Freedom*. New York: Knopf Press.

Sen, S. and Neilsen, J.R. (1996) Fisheries co-management a comparative analysis. *Marine Policy*, 20, 405–418.

Servanty, S., Converse, S.J. and Bailey, L.L. (2014) Demography of a reintroduced population: moving toward management models for an endangered species, the whooping crane. *Ecological Applications*, 24, 927–937.

Shannon, L., Coll, M., Bundy, A., et al. (2014) Trophic level-based indicators to track fishing impacts across marine ecosystems. *Marine Ecology Progress Series*, 512, 115–140.

Shea, K. and The NCEAS Working Group on Population Management (1998) Management of populations in conservation, harvesting and control. *Trends in Ecology & Evolution*, 13, 371–374.

Shetler, J.B. (2007) *Imagining Serengeti: A History of Landscape Memory in Tanzania from Earliest Times to the Present*. Athens, OH: Ohio University Press.

Silvertown, J. (2009) A new dawn for citizen science. *Trends in Ecology & Evolution*, 24, 467–471.

Sinclair, A.R.E. (2003) Mammal population regulation, keystone processes and ecosystem dynamics. *Philosophical transactions of the Royal Society of London. Series B, Biological Sciences*, 358, 1729–1740.

Sinclair, A.R.E. (2012) *Serengeti Story: Life and Science in the World's Greatest Wildlife Region*. Oxford: Oxford University Press.

Sinclair, A.R.E., Mduma, S., Hopcraft, J.G.C., et al. (2007) Long-term ecosystem dynamics in the Serengeti: lessons for conservation. *Conservation Biology*, 21, 580–590.

Skogen, K. and Thrane, C. (2008) Wolves in context: using survey data to situate attitudes within a wider cultural framework. *Society & Natural Resources*, 21, 17–33.

Skonhoft, A. (2005) The costs and benefits of a migratory species under different management schemes. *Journal of Environmental Management*, 76, 167–175.

Skonhoft, A. and Olaussen, J.O. (2005) Managing a migratory species that is both a value and a pest. *Land Economics*, 81, 34–50.

Smith, A.D.M. (1994) Management strategy evaluation – the light on the hill. In D. Hancock, ed. *Population Dynamics for Fisheries Management*. Perth: Australian Society for Fish Biology, pp. 249–253.

Smith, D.W., Peterson, R.O. and Houston, D.B. (2003) Yellowstone after wolves. *Bioscience*, 53, 330–340.

Smith, A.D.M., Sachse, M., Smith, D.C., et al. (2004) *Alternative management strategies for the Southern and Eastern Scalefish and Shark Fishery. Qualitative Assessment, Stage 1.* Report to Australian Fisheries Management Authority. Canberra, CSIRO.

Smith, A.D.M., Fulton, E.J., Hobday, A.J., Smith, D.C. and Shoulder, P. (2007a) Scientific tools to support the practical implementation of ecosystem-based fisheries management. *ICES Journal of Marine Science*, 64, 633–639.

Smith, A.D.M., Sachse, M., Fulton, E.A., et al. (2007b) *Evaluation of Alternative Strategies for Management of Commonwealth Fisheries in Southeastern Australia – Report on the Qualitative Evaluation of Additional Scenarios.* Canberra: Australian Fisheries Management Authority.

Smith, A.D.M., Smith, D.C., Tuck, G.N., et al. (2008) Experience in implementing harvest strategies in Australia's south-eastern fisheries. *Fisheries Research*, 94, 373–379.

Smith, A.D.M., Brown, C.J., Bulman, C.M., et al. (2011a) Impacts of fishing low-trophic level species on marine ecosystems. *Science*, 333, 1147–1150.

Smith, D.C., Fulton, E.A., Johnson, P., et al. (2011b) *Developing Integrated Performance Measures for Spatial Management of Marine Systems.* Final Report FRDC Project No: 2004/005.

Smith, A.D.M., Smith, D.C., Haddon, M., et al. (2013) Implementing harvest strategies in Australia: 5 years on. *ICES Journal of Marine Science*, 71, 195–203.

Solberg, E.J. and Saether, B.E. (1999) Hunter observations of moose Alces alces as a management tool. *Wildlife Biology*, 5, 107–117.

Solberg, E.J., Sæther, B.-E., Strand, O. and Loison, A. (1999) Dynamics of a harvested moose population in a variable environment. *Journal of Animal Ecology*, 68, 186–204.

Somers, I. and Wang, Y. (1997) A simulation model for evaluating seasonal closures in Australia's multispecies Northern Prawn Fishery. *North American Journal of Fisheries Management*, 17, 114–130.

Somers, I.F. (1994) Species composition and distribution of commercial peneaid prawn catches in the Gulf of Carpentaria, Australia, in relation to depth and sediment type. *Australian Journal of Marine and Freshwater Research*, 45, 317–335.

Sommerville, M., Jones, J.P.G., Rahajaharison, M. and Milner-Gulland, E.J. (2010) The role of fairness and benefit distribution in community-based payment for environmental services interventions: a case study from Menabe, Madagascar. *Ecological Economics*, 69, 1262–1271.

St John, F.A.V., Edwards-Jones, G. and Jones, J.P.G. (2010) Conservation and human behaviour: lessons from social psychology. *Wildlife Research*, 37, 658–667.

Stankey, G.H., Clark, R.N. and Borman, B.T. (2005) *Adaptive Management of Natural Resources: Theory, Concepts and Management Institutions.* Portland, OR: U.S. Department of Agriculture, Forest service, Pacific Northwest Research Station.

Stanton, J.C. (2014) Present-day risk assessment would have predicted the extinction of the passenger pigeon (*Ectopistes migratorius*). *Biological Conservation,* 180, 11–20.

Stephanson, S.L. and Mascia, M.B. (2014) Putting people on the map through an approach that integrates social data in conservation planning. *Conservation Biology,* 28, 1236–1248.

Stevens, M., Vitos, M., Altenbuchner, J., et al. (2014) Taking participatory citizen science to extremes. *IEEE Pervasive Computing,* 13, 20–29.

Stiglitz, J., Sen, A. and Fitoussi, J. (2009) *Final Report of the Commission on the Measurement of Economic Performance and Social Progress.* Paris, France.

Storaas, T., Gundersen, H., Henriksen, H. and Andreassen, H.P. (2001) The economic value of moose in Norway – a review. *Alces,* 37, 97–107.

Summers, J.K., Smith, L.M., Case, J.L. and Linthurst, R.A. (2012) A review of the elements of human well-being with an emphasis on the contribution of ecosystem services. *Ambio,* 41, 327–340.

Sunderland, T., Sunderland-Groves, J., Shanley, P. and Campbell, B. (2009), Bridging the gap: how can information access and exchange between conservation biologists and field practitioners be improved for better conservation outcomes? *Biotropica,* 41, 549–554.

Sutherland, W.J., Pullin, A.S., Dolman, P.M. and Knight, T.M. (2004) The need for evidence-based conservation. *Trends in Ecology & Evolution,* 19, 305–308.

Swenson, J.E., Sandegren, F., Bjarvall, A., et al. (1994) Size, trend, distribution and conservation of the brown bear Ursus-Arctos population in Sweden. *Biological Conservation,* 70, 9–17.

Sylvèn, S. (1995) Moose harvest strategy to maximize yield value for multiple goal management – a simulation study. *Agricultural Systems,* 49, 277–298.

Szabo, J.K., Briggs, S.V., Lonie, R., et al. (2009) The feasibility of applying a cost-effective approach for assigning priorities for threatened species recovery with a case study from New South Wales, Australia. *Pacific Conservation Biology,* 15, 238–245.

Szymanski, J.A., Runge, M.C., Parkin, M.J. and Armstrong, M. (2009). White-nose syndrome management: report on structured decision making initiative. Department of Interior, US Fish and Wildlife Service, Fort Snelling, Minn.

Teh, L.S.L., Teh, L.C.L. and Rashid Sumaila, U. (2014) Time preference of small-scale fishers in open access and traditionally managed reef fisheries. *Marine Policy,* 44, 222–231.

Terama, E., Milligan, B., Jiménez-Aybar, R., Mace, G.M. and Ekins, P. (2015) Accounting for the environment as an economic asset: global progress and realizing the 2030 Agenda for Sustainable Development. *Sustainability Science,* 1–6.

Tetlock, P.E. (2003) Thinking the unthinkable: sacred values and taboo cognitions. *Trends in Cognitive Sciences,* 7, 320–324.

Vitos, M. Stevens, M., Lewis, J. and Haklay, M. (2013) Making local knowledge matter: supporting non-literate people to monitor poaching in Congo. DEV '13, 11–12 January 2013, Bangalore, India.

Thebaud, O., Little, L.R. and Fulton, E.A. (2014) Evaluation of management strategies in Ningaloo Marine Park, Western Australia. *International Journal of Sustainable Society*, 6, 102–119.

Thogmartin, W.E., Sanders-Reed, C.A., Szymanski, J.A., McKann, P.C., Pruitt, L., King, R.A., Runge, M.C. and Russell, R.E. (2013). White-nose syndrome is likely to extirpate the endangered Indiana bat over large parts of its range. *Biological Conservation*, 160, 162–172.

Tittensor, D.P., Walpole, M., Hill, S.L., et al. (2014) A mid-term analysis of progress toward international biodiversity targets. *Science*, 346, 241–244.

Tolsma, A., and Shannon, J. (2007) *Evaluating the rehabilitation needs of mossbeds in the Alpine and Mt Buffalo National Parks after the 2006/07 fires*. Arthur Rylah Institute for Environmental Research, Department of Sustainability and Environment

Toscas, P.J., Vance, D.J., Burridge, C.Y., et al. (2009) Spatio-temporal modelling of prawns in Albatross Bay, Karumba and Mornington Island. *Fisheries Research*, 96, 173–187.

Travers, H., Clements, T., Keane, A. and Milner-Gulland, E.J. (2011) Incentives for cooperation: the effects of institutional controls on common pool resource extraction in Cambodia. *Ecological Economics*, 71, 151–161.

Trimble, M. and Johnson, D. (2013) Artisanal fishing as an undesirable way of life? The implications for governance of fishers' wellbeing aspirations in coastal Uruguay and southeastern Brazil. *Marine Policy*, 37, 37–44.

Tyre, A.J., Peterson, J.T., Converse, S.J., et al. (2011) Adaptive management of bull trout populations in the Lemhi Basin. *Journal of Fish and Wildlife Management*, 2, 262–281.

UNDP (2012) Protected areas In *International Guidebook of Environmental Finance Tools – A Sectoral Approach: Protected Areas, Sustainable Forests, Sustainable Agriculture and Pro-Poor Energy*. pp. 1–54.

University of Bath (2002) *Wellbeing in Developing Countries (WeD)*. ESRC Research Group. [online]. Available at: www.welldev.org.uk/research/research.htm.

University of Bath (2011) *Wellbeing & Poverty Pathways* [online]. Available at: www.wellbeingpathways.org/

Urbanek, R.P., Fondow, L.E.A., Satyshur, C.D., et al. (2005) First cohort of migratory whooping cranes reintroduced to eastern North America: the first year after release. *Proceedings of the North American Crane Workshop*, 9, 213–223.

Usoro, A., Sharratt, M.W., Tsui, E. and Shekhar, S. (2007) Trust as an antecedent to knowledge sharing in virtual communities of practice. *Knowledge Management, Research & Practice*, 5, 199–212.

Vačkář, D., ten Brink, B., Loh, J., Baillie, J.E.M. and Reyers, B. (2012) Review of multispecies indices for monitoring human impacts on biodiversity. *Ecological Indicators*, 17, 58–67.

van Strien, A.J., Soldaat, L.L. and Gregory, R.D. (2012) Desirable mathematical properties of indicators for biodiversity change. *Ecological Indicators*, 14, 202–208.

Van Vugt, M. (2009) Averting the tragedy of the commons: using social psychological science to protect the environment. *Current Directions in Psychological Science*, 18, 169–173.

Venables, W.N. and Dichmont, C.M. (2004) A generalised linear model for catch allocation: an example from Australia's Northern Prawn Fishery. *Fisheries Research*, 70, 409–426.

Venter, O., Sanderson, E.W., Magrach, A., et al. (2016) Sixteen years of change in the global terrestrial human footprint and implications for biodiversity conservation. *Nature Communications*, 7, 12558.

Victorian Department of Sustainability and Parks Victoria (2008) *Great Divide Fire Recovery Plan*. Victorian Department of Sustainability and Parks Victoria.

Visconti, P., Bakkenes, M., Baisero, D., et al. (2016) Projecting global biodiversity indicators under future development scenarios. *Conservation Letters*, 9, 5–13.

Voinov, A. and Bousquet, F. (2010) Modelling with stakeholders. *Environmental Modelling & Software*, 25, 1268–1281.

Wabakken, P., Sand, H., Liberg, O. and Bjarvall, A. (2001) The recovery, distribution, and population dynamics of wolves on the Scandinavian peninsula, 1978–1998. *Canadian Journal of Zoology*, 79, 710–725.

Waldron, A., Mooers, A.O., Miller, D.C., et al. (2013) Targeting global conservation funding to limit immediate biodiversity declines. *Proceedings of the National Academy of Sciences*, 110, 12144–12148.

Walker, W.E., Harremoës, P., Rotmans, J., et al. (2003) Defining uncertainty: a conceptual basis for uncertainty management in model-based decision support. *Integrated Assessment*, 4, 5–17.

Walpole, M., Almond, R.E.A., Besançon, C., et al. (2009) Tracking progress toward the 2010 biodiversity target and beyond. *Science*, 325, 1503–1504.

Walters, C.J. (1986) *Adaptive Management of Renewable Resources*. New York: Macmillan.

Walters, C.J. (2007) Is adaptive management helping to solve fisheries problems? *Ambio*, 36, 304–307.

Walters, C.J. and Hilborn, R. (1978) Ecological optimization and adaptive management. *Annual Review of Ecology and Systematics*, 9, 157–188.

Wam, H.K., Pedersen, H.C. and Hjeljord, O. (2012) Balancing hunting regulations and hunter satisfaction: an integrated biosocioeconomic model to aid in sustainable management. *Ecological Economics*, 79, 89–96.

Wam, H.K., Andersen, O. and Pedersen, H.C. (2013) Grouse hunting regulations and hunter typologies in Norway. *Human Dimensions of Wildlife*, 18, 45–57.

Wang, Y.G. and Die, D. (1996) Stock-recruitment relationships of the tiger prawns (*Penaeus esculentus* and *Penaeus semisulcatus*) in the Australian northern prawn fishery. *Marine and Freshwater Research*, 47, 87–95.

Wassen, M.J., Runhaar, H., Barendregt, A. and Okruszko, T. (2011) Evaluating the role of participation in modeling studies for environmental planning. *Environment & Planning B: Planning and Design*, 38, 338–358.

Watling, L. and Norse, E.A. (1998) Disturbance of the seabed by mobile fishing gear: a comparison to forest clearcutting. *Conservation Biology*, 12, 1180–1197.

Watson, R.M. (1965) Game utilization in the Serengeti: preliminary investigations. I. *The British Veterinary Journal*, 121, 540–546.

Webb, J.A., Stewardson, M.J., Chee, Y.E., et al. (2010) Negotiating the turbulent boundary: the challenges of building a science-management collaboration for landscape-scale monitoring of environmental flows. *Marine and Freshwater Research*, 61, 798–807.

West, P., Igoe, J. and Brockington, D. (2006) Parks and peoples: the social impact of protected areas. *Annual Review of Anthropology*, 35, 251–277.

Westgate, M.J., Likens, G.E. and Lindenmayer, D.B. (2013) Adaptive management of biological systems: a review. *Biological Conservation*, 158, 128–139.

White, P.C.L. and Ward, A.I. (2010) Interdisciplinary approaches for the management of existing and emerging human–wildlife conflicts. *Wildlife Research*, 37, 623–629.

White, S.C. (2010) Analysing wellbeing: a framework for development practice. *Development in Practice*, 20, 158–172.

White, S.C. and Jha, S. (2013) *The Politics of Wellbeing, Conservation and Development in Chiawa, Zambia*. Wellbeing & Poverty Pathways Briefing No. 2. Bath: University of Bath.

Whitehead, A.L., Kujala, H., Ives, C.D., et al. (2014) Integrating biological and social values when prioritizing places for biodiversity conservation. *Conservation Biology*, 28, 992–1003.

Williams, B.K. (2001) Uncertainty, learning, and the optimal management of wildlife. *Environmental and Ecological Statistics*, 8, 269–288.

Williams, B.K., Nichols, J.D. and Conroy, M.J. (2002) *Analysis and Management of Animal Populations*. San Diego, CA: Academic Press.

Williams, B.K., Szaro, R.C. and Shapiro, C.D. (2007). Adaptive management: the U.S. Department of the Interior technical guide. Washington, D.C.: U.S. Department of the Interior, Adaptive Management Working Group. Available at: http://www.doi.gov/initiatives/AdaptiveManagement/TechGuide.pdf (Accessed November 2011).

Williams, B.K., Szaro, R.C. and Shapiro, C.D. (2009) *Adaptive Management. The U.S. Department of the Interior Technical Guide*. Department of the Interior, Washington, DC.

Williams, R.J. and Costin, A.B. (1994) Alpine and subalpine vegetation. In R.H. Groves, ed. *Australian Vegetation*, 2nd edn. Melbourne: Cambridge University Press, pp. 467–500.

Williams, R.J., Wahren, C.H., Tolsma, A.D., et al. (2008) Large fires in Australian alpine landscapes: their part in the historical fire regime and their impacts on alpine biodiversity. *International Journal of Wildland Fire*, 17, 793–808.

Wilson, K.A., Carwardine, J. and Possingham, H.P. (2009) Setting conservation priorities. *Annals of the New York Academy of Sciences*, 1162, 237–264.

Winkler, R. (2011) Why do ICDPs fail? The relationship between agriculture, hunting and ecotourism in wildlife conservation. *Resource and Energy Economics*, 33, 55–78.

Woodhouse, E., Mills, M.A., McGowan, P.J.K. and Milner-Gulland, E.J. (2015a) Religious relationships with the environment in a Tibetan rural community: interactions and contrasts with popular notions of indigenous environmentalism. *Human Ecology*, 43, 295–307.

Woodhouse, E., Homewood, K.M., Beauchamp, E., et al. (2015b) Guiding principles for evaluating the impacts of conservation interventions on human well-being. *Philosophical Transactions of the Royal Society of London. Series B, Biological Sciences,* 370, 20150103.

Woodhouse, E., de Lange, E. and Milner-Gulland, E.J. and contributors (2016) *Evaluating the Impact of Conservation Interventions on Human Wellbeing: Guidance for Practitioners.* International Institute for Environment and Development, London.

Wright, J.H., Hill, N.A.O., Roe, D., et al. (2016) Reframing the concept of alternative livelihoods. *Conservation Biology,* 30, 7–13.

Wynne, B. (1992) Misunderstood misunderstanding: social identities and public uptake of science. *Public Understanding of Science,* 1, 281–304.

Ye, Y. (2000) Is recruitment related to spawning stock in penaeid shrimp fisheries? *ICES Journal of Marine Science,* 57, 1103–1109.

Zhou, S.J., Vance, D.J., Dichmont, C.M., Burridge, C.Y. and Toscas, P.J. (2008) Estimating prawn abundance and catchability from catch-effort data: comparison of fixed and random effects models using maximum likelihood and hierarchical Bayesian methods. *Marine and Freshwater Research,* 59, 1–9.

Zurell, D., Berger, U., Cabral, J.S., Jeltsch, F., Meynard, C.N., Münkemüller, T., Nehrbass, N., Pagel, J., Reineking, B., Schröder, B. and Grimm, V. (2010) The virtual ecologist approach: simulating data and observers. *Oikos,* 119(4), 622–635.

Index